eDirectory Field Guide

Rick Killpack

Apress®

eDirectory Field Guide

ISBN-13 (paperback): 978-1-59059-553-4
ISBN-13 (electronic): 978-1-4302-0085-7

Printed and bound in the United States of America (POD)

Lead Editor: Jim Sumser
Technical Reviewer: Kevin Fenn
Editorial Board: Steve Anglin, Dan Appleman, Ewan Buckingham, Gary Cornell, Tony Davis, Jason Gilmore, Jonathan Hassell, Chris Mills, Dominic Shakeshaft, Jim Sumser
Associate Publisher: Grace Wong
Project Manager: Sofia Marchant
Copy Edit Manager: Nicole LeClerc
Copy Editor: Bill McManus
Assistant Production Director: Kari Brooks-Copony
Compositor: Dina Quan
Proofreader: Dan Shaw
Indexer: Valerie Perry
Artist: Kari Brooks-Copony
Cover Designer: Kurt Krames
Manufacturing Director: Tom Debolski

Distributed to the book trade worldwide by Springer-Verlag New York, Inc., 233 Spring Street, 6th Floor, New York, NY 10013. Phone 1-800-SPRINGER, fax 201-348-4505, e-mail `orders-ny@springer-sbm.com`, or visit `http://www.springeronline.com`.

For information on translations, please contact Apress directly at 2855 Telegraph Avenue, Suite 600, Berkeley, CA 94705. Phone 510-549-5930, fax 510-549-5939, e-mail `info@apress.com`, or visit `http://www.apress.com`.

Contents at a Glance

Contents

About the Author

Rick Killpack is currently the eDirectory product manager for Novell, Inc. He started at Novell in 1991 and has been involved in the technology business ever since that time. He spent seven years as a third-tier eDirectory technical support engineer for Novell. Rick contributes once a month to Novell's eDirectory LogicSource, which is a document that describes at a pseudo-code level all processes within eDirectory. With his in-depth knowledge of how eDirectory works from reviewing the code, supporting the product, and helping customers implement the product, Rick is considered one of the world's authorities on Novell eDirectory.

About the Technical Reviewer

Kevin Fenn, a native of the San Diego, California area, has worked in the support industry since September 1997 and has been with Novell since May of 2000. He is currently a World Wide Support Escalation Engineer at Novell supporting NMAS, eDirectory, Security Components (PKI, NICI, etc.), and iManager. He is a member of the iManager Core Team representing Novell Technical Services (NTS) and works tightly with iManager product developers and product managers. He graduated with a master's degree in Information Systems Management from Brigham Young University in December 2000. Kevin is considered one of the lead support engineers for iManager. His hobbies include rock climbing, camping, and geocaching. He currently resides in Spanish Fork, Utah with his wife and two children.

Author's Note

Toward the goal of making this guide as easy as possible to use in the field, where relevant, I have provided the same material in more than one chapter, so you don't have to flip back and forth between chapters to get the full picture on a topic.

PART 1

Installation and Migration

Part 1 of the *eDirectory Field Guide* emphasizes things you need to know while installing or upgrading eDirectory. It is comprehensive insofar as it deals with the nuances of all the eDirectory-supported platforms, but it does not give step-by-step instructions on how to install or upgrade eDirectory. The purpose of Part 1 is to complement the *Novell eDirectory Administration Guide* to ensure that you have a successful experience while installing or migrating to eDirectory. However, it does include tips and tricks that are not contained in the *Novell eDirectory Administration Guide.*

CHAPTER 1

Installation

The following topics are covered in this chapter:

- Prerequisites
  - Supported operating systems
  - Applying patches
  - Hardware considerations
- Server-to-server communication
  - NetWare
  - Microsoft Windows
  - Linux, Solaris, HPUX, and AIX
  - General recommendations
- Time-synchronization considerations
- Troubleshooting installation failures
  - NetWare
  - Microsoft Windows
  - *nix
  - Capturing a DSTRACE log

Prerequisites

This chapter does not go into detailed eDirectory installation procedures, but rather discusses tips on how you can prevent failed installations and how you can troubleshoot various issues that may arise during the installation and configuration of eDirectory. For general information about installing Novell eDirectory, please see the *Novell eDirectory Administration Guide* for your version of eDirectory at `http://www.novell.com/documentation`.

It is beyond the scope of this chapter to discuss in detail all prerequisites for the installation of eDirectory, but I will discuss in this section the specific issues for you to pay special attention to before you install eDirectory.

Supported Operating Systems

As new releases of eDirectory are shipped, it is important to read the new README files and current documentation. Most releases of eDirectory, including Interim Releases (IRs), often drop certain operating systems and architectures and consistently add others. A good example of this can be seen with eDirectory 8.7.3 IR3. eDirectory 8.7.3 IR2 supported Red Hat Linux Advanced Server (AS) 2.1. eDirectory 8.7.3 IR3 added support for Red Hat AS 3.0.

Decisions made by Novell to drop support for a particular operating system (OS) or platform are often driven by the OS vendor's support position. As the OS vendor drops support for a particular OS version, eDirectory often drops support for that OS version as well.

Applying Patches

Another point of consideration is to keep your current eDirectory environment updated with the latest patches. As eDirectory IRs or support packs are released, recommendations of associated security component versions (NICI, NMAS, PKI, and NTLS) are listed in the IR patch README files. In the latest eDirectory IRs (IR4 or greater), the recommended security component patches are bundled with the eDirectory patch. To ensure quality and reliability, it is important to apply all patches together. Novell tests the security components and eDirectory patches together as a suite.

Hardware Considerations

Novell's documentation for eDirectory (`http://www.novell.com/documentation`) lists the minimum versions of the supported operating system as well as the minimum support packs that need to be in place to install eDirectory. These requirements change often. Make sure that you review the prerequisites listed in the eDirectory documentation before you install eDirectory.

An important note to keep in mind is that the prerequisites listed in the eDirectory documentation are *minimum* prerequisites. Most of the minimums are based on an average system, which is somewhere around 500 users. It is critical that you determine how eDirectory will be used in your environment. Determining what operating system or what platform should be used for each business solution is out of the scope of this book. However, Novell has published good documents on how to determine what resources are needed for each business solution. (See eDirectory LogicSource ➤ eDirectory Best Practices at Novell's subscription page, `http://support.novell.com/subscriptions/`, for more information on selecting operating systems and platforms that are right for your environment.)

If the hardware and operating system that you have selected do not have the resources required for how you want to implement eDirectory, failure and dissatisfaction will certainly follow. When determining what hardware to use, you first need to identify the biggest potential bottlenecks. Next, make that bottleneck large enough to handle the maximum amount of information that you need out of eDirectory. The major bottlenecks for eDirectory are described in the following sections.

Memory

Large numbers of objects and a lot of search requests will require more memory than other operations. According to Novell testing, allocating more than 1 GB of memory toward eDirectory database cache may actually decrease performance.

Number of Processors (CPUs)

If a large number of concurrent users are on the eDirectory servers, more CPUs will show performance increases.

Speed of Processors (CPUs)

The faster the processor, the more transactions per second that will be achieved. Remember that this statement is true only if the processor is maxed out (seeing high utilization). If the processor is not maxed out, there is another bottleneck and increasing processor speed will not help.

I/O Channel

If the database is too large to fit all objects into memory, the I/O channels will be a factor for all types of transactions. Typically, with large databases, the I/O channel is the biggest bottleneck. The following are some general recommendations:

- Increasing disk cache usually improves search performance. The I/O channel to memory is much faster than the I/O channel to the physical disk.
- Increasing the maximum dirty cache can improve systems that have a large number of writes.
- Increasing free disk space may help reduce high utilization, which can occur if there is not enough available local disk space.

■ **Note** The preceding recommendations may vary depending on your system and how the database is utilized.

Server-to-Server Communication

When an eDirectory server is added into an existing tree, the eDirectory Directory Agent (DA) needs a way to locate the server address of a server that holds a copy of the root partition of the tree. The DA on the new server must contact a copy of root for the following reasons:

- The DA needs to request the schema from the server holding a copy of root.
- The DA needs to make a request to add a new NCP server object into the existing eDirectory tree.

For all of this to occur, a connection must be established between the new server's DA and the DA on the server that holds a copy of the root partition. The root server's address must be obtained in order for a connection to be made. The methodology used to obtain the root server's address depends on the operating system that resides on the server that is being added to the eDirectory tree. Each address discovery method for each operating system is briefly discussed in the following sections.

NetWare

NetWare uses a proprietary version of Windows Sockets (Winsock) to perform the tree name resolution. NetWare's registry lists the namespaces that are available for service resolution. By default, Winsock is configured on NetWare 6.5 to try the following namespaces in the listed order:

- Domain Name Service (DNS)
- SYS:\ETC\HOSTS
- Service Location Protocol (SLP) (used by the TCP protocol)
- Service Advertising Protocol (SAP) (used by the IPX protocol)

Because SLP and SAP are the only namespace providers that store eDirectory tree names, DNS and the static HOSTS file cannot be used during the installation.

If the tree is not registered in SLP or SAP, or the name lookup fails for some other reason, eDirectory will allow you to manually specify the IP address at installation time.

Microsoft Windows

With eDirectory 8.7.1 and greater running on Microsoft Windows, eDirectory has three ways of discovering the tree name:

- *SLP provided by Novell Client32*: Novell Client32 ships with an SLP User Agent (UA). The UA communicates with a DA to query for service information. In order for this to work properly, Client32 needs to be configured to query the DA and the scope in which the server holding a copy of the root partition is registered.

Note For more information on how to configure SLP for Novell Client32, see the Novell Client32 documentation at `http://www.novell.com/documentation`.

- *SLP provided through OpenSLP*: When installing eDirectory 8.7.3 or greater onto Microsoft Windows, the installation checks to see if Novell Client32 is installed on the Windows server. If it is installed, eDirectory uses the UA from Client32. If Client32 is not installed, eDirectory installs and uses OpenSLP for tree name resolution.

  By default, the eDirectory installation configures OpenSLP to run as a UA and Server Agent (SA) only. OpenSLP is also set to auto-discover the DA. If multicasting and broadcasting are not allowed in the environment, configure OpenSLP to point to the specific DA and the specific scope in which the server that holds a copy of the root partition is registered.
- *Manual specification*: If, for whatever reason, the tree name lookup fails through SLP, the eDirectory installation prompts you to manually specify the IP address of the server that holds a copy of the root partition. If you are unsure of the SLP configuration in the tree, this option is recommended.

Linux, Solaris, HPUX, and AIX

The Linux, Solaris, HPUX, and AIX (all UNIX and Linux platforms collectively hereafter are referred to as *nix) operating systems function slightly differently from the other platforms. There are two distinct steps involved in installing eDirectory and adding the server into an existing tree:

1. Install the binaries onto the server.
2. Configure an instance of eDirectory on the server.

The address of the server that holds a copy of the root partition of the existing tree is required during the configuration stage. Like Microsoft Windows, the *nix operating systems use SLP for tree name discovery. There are four methods of finding the tree name, described in the following sections.

/etc/hosts.nds

The DA first looks for the presence of a static text file called /etc/hosts.nds. The tree name can be specified in the hosts.nds file along with an IP address of the server that holds a copy of the root partition.

If this file exists, it must have correct information about the tree name. If the address specified in the hosts.nds file is incorrect, or the tree name is specified incorrectly, the installation will not try to use other discovery methodologies. It will simply fail, with an error stating that the tree could not found.

By default, with the exception of a Novell Open Enterprise Server (OES), an /etc/hosts.nds file is not created. To create one, simply create a text file called hosts.nds in the /etc/ directory. Add to the text file the tree name with the following syntax:

```
Treename.     <server address>
e.g. MyEdirTree.     192.68.1.4
```

For more information about the /etc/hosts.nds file, see the man pages for hosts.nds on a *nix server where eDirectory is installed.

slpuasa

Starting with eDirectory 8.5 (and ending with eDirectory 8.7.3 IR5, as discussed in the next section), a Novell proprietary module called slpuasa was included with the default eDirectory installation. By default, this module is used while adding a server to an existing tree if the /etc/hosts.nds file is not present. This module acted as a UA as well as an SA. It could not act as a DA. This module performed a DA discovery and looked for the tree name. If the DA could not be discovered or the server that held a copy of the root partition of the existing tree was not registered to the DA that was found, the installation would fail.

Note There is a not a specific call to the slpuasa binary. The slpuasa binary loads in the ndsd process space by default. If it is loaded, any SLP request will be handled by the slpuasa daemon.

OpenSLP

Starting with eDirectory 8.7.3 IR5 (included with OES), Novell discontinued shipping or supporting the proprietary slpuasa on Linux. Also, the slpuasa daemon will not run on HP-UX. In both stated cases, Novell's supported SLP solution is OpenSLP.

Novell also recommends that OpenSLP be used instead of the slpuasa daemon on all *nix platforms, because the slpuasa module was based off of SLP version 1 specifications and has many limitations.

To disable the slpuasa daemon and enable the OpenSLP daemon, perform Task 1-1.

Task 1-1. Disabling slpuasa and Enabling OpenSLP

1. If the slpuasa daemon is running, stop the slpuasa daemon (/etc/init.d/slpuasa stop).
2. Remove the slpuasa script from the run levels:
    a. By default, the slpuasa script is configured to run in runlevel 3 and runlevel 5.
    b. Check the local operating system documentation on how to remove a script from a run level.
3. Make sure that the OpenSLP package has been installed.
4. Modify the /etc/slp.conf file and add applicable information to enable SLP to discover a DA.
5. Start the OpenSLP daemon (/etc/init.d/slpd start).
6. Modify runlevel 3 and runlevel 5 startup scripts and add the slpd script to the list of modules that load on startup.

Note For more information on how to configure run levels, see the specific operating system's documentation.

Manual Specification

If all other tree name discovery methodologies fail, configure the instance of eDirectory with the command-line tool `ndsconfig`, using the `-p` *<server address>* parameter. Specify the server IP address of a server that holds a replica of the root partition of the tree in the *<server address>* field; for example:

```
ndsconfig -p 192.65.1.2
```

assuming that 192.65.1.2 is a server that holds a replica of the root partition.

General Recommendations

Although each operating system allows you to manually specify a server address to establish communication when adding a server into an existing tree, it is highly recommended that SLP be configured correctly.

There are certain tools and features within eDirectory that require a tree name lookup and will always use SLP (or the static hosts.nds file on the *.nix platforms) to find the tree name. If SLP is not configured correctly, these tools will fail. The following are several examples of tools and features that may fail:

- `ndsconfig add`: This option allows you to add to eDirectory other eDirectory components on the *nix operating systems such as SAS, SNMP, LDAP, and HTTP.
- `ndsstat -s`: This option allows you to see all servers known to the database on the *nix operating system.
- *DSRepair ➤ Repair server addresses*: This is a cross-platform option that discovers the server address of any server in the tree and updates the information on the corresponding NCP server object in the tree as well as any replica ring of the replicas that the NCP server holds.

On the *nix platforms, the hosts.nds file or SLP is exclusively used. On NetWare, DNS or the SYS:\ETC\HOSTS file can also be used for this feature.

Time-Synchronization Considerations

NDS and eDirectory use time stamps extensively. Time stamps are used to verify the version of a specific object within the database. If an object has a time stamp newer than the time since the last synchronization cycle to a specific server, the object is sent to the remote server. For all of this to work properly, the local server and the remote server must have synchronized time.

NetWare ships a time-synchronization tool called TIMESYNC.NLM. This tool uses the Novell proprietary NCP protocol. It can communicate with other servers over IPX as well as IP. TIMESYNC.NLM has a built-in algorithm that ensures that the time is synchronized for all the servers within the defined time-synchronization environment.

As eDirectory added support for non-NetWare platforms, alternative time-synchronization methods became a necessity. Time-synchronization modules themselves are independent of eDirectory. As long as all servers within a tree have their time set the same, the method used to get time synchronized is irrelevant to eDirectory.

To make TIMESYNC.NLM compatible with other time-synchronization applications residing on non-NetWare platforms, it was enhanced to be able to send and receive NTP (an open-source time standard protocol) formatted packets. This is not to say that TIMESYNC.NLM follows the NTP-defined algorithm for keeping servers synchronized. TIMESYNC.NLM is simply able to send and receive NTP packets. TIMESYNC.NLM processes the NTP packet as if it came from another NetWare server running TIMESYNC.NLM and negotiates time with the proprietary TIMESYNC algorithm. To enable this functionality, you must perform the steps in Task 1-2 on the NetWare server that is running TIMESYNC.NLM if you wish to point the server to an NTP time source.

Note You can configure a server that is a SECONDARY, PRIMARY, or REFERENCE time-sync type to send packets in the NTP format.

Task 1-2. Enabling TIMESYNC

1. Type **monitor** at the NetWare console prompt.
2. Choose Server Parameters ➤ Time.
3. Make sure that the TIMESYNC ➤ Configured Sources is set to On.
4. Modify the TIMESYNC Time Sources by pressing Enter.
5. Add the server address of the NTP server by adding **:123** to the end of the address; for example (don't forget the semicolon at the end of the line):

```
192.68.2.34:123;
```

The server address specified in Task 1-2 may be one of the following:

- An external NTP time source
- A local server running the xntp daemon
- A local server running TIMESYNC.NLM also configured to communicate via NTP

If *all* servers within your time-synchronization environment are configured to communicate via IP and are configured to send time-synchronization packets with the NTP packet structure, it is advised that you disable NCP on TIMESYNC.NLM to reduce redundant traffic. This can be accomplished by performing Task 1-3.

Task 1-3. Disabling NCP on TIMESYNC.NLM

1. Edit the SYS:\SYSTEM\TIMESERV.NCF file.
2. Find the line that reads LOAD TIMESYNC.
3. Add **-T noncp** to the end of the line; for example:

```
LOAD TIMESYNC -T noncp
```

4. Reboot the server. (You can also just unload TIMESYNC.NLM and manually load it with the switch specified in Step 3).

To make time synchronization even more seamless, NetWare 6.5 implemented the open-source NTP daemon. This daemon is identical to the NTP daemon that ships on SLES 8 and 9 as well as on Red Hat 2.1 and 3.0 (identical because it came from the same open-source project, not because the versions are all exactly the same).

It is recommended, whenever possible, to use the NTP daemon on NetWare instead of TIMESYNC.NLM when introducing eDirectory into a mixed-platform environment. This ensures that all platforms use the same synchronization model, thus increasing the probability that all servers stay synchronized. If NTP is used as the time-synchronization method, it will also be easier to administer. Remember that on NetWare 6.5, you must use either TIMESYNC.NLM or the NTP daemon. They cannot run simultaneously.

If the eDirectory servers in the environment are running versions of NetWare other than NetWare 6.5, you still need to use TIMESYNC.NLM on the older NetWare versions. The NTP daemon is supported only on NetWare 6.5. In these scenarios, there are several ways to integrate time-synchronization methods across disparate platforms. Figure 1-1 shows one example of how this could be accomplished.

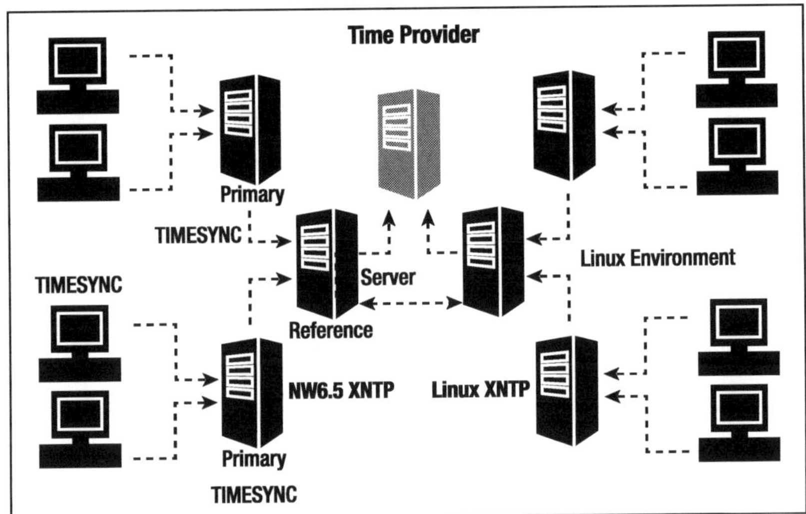

Figure 1-1. *Mixed Timesync environment*

The bottom line is that eDirectory requires all servers within the tree to be synchronized to within a few seconds of each other. It is really up to you to choose the time-synchronization method that makes the most sense for your specific environment.

Troubleshooting Installation Failures

eDirectory environments can be very complex. Adding to that complexity, many eDirectory trees have been around for a long time and carry a lot of baggage or old data that is no longer relevant. Because of these variables, there are many areas that could potentially cause you to fail to install a new server into an existing environment.

The purpose of this section is to discuss some of the most likely scenarios that you may encounter while installing eDirectory. Hopefully, this section will help you to avoid known pitfalls. However, if you run into an issue, this section should be an invaluable tool for you.

The eDirectory installation can be broken down into two basic parts: file copy and configuration.

During the configuration stage, the server is introduced into the eDirectory tree. A local database is created on the local server. All associated services are configured and started. All required objects for the services are also created. These services and objects are as follows:

- Security components
    - Tree key configuration
    - SAS object
    - KMO objects (server certificates)
    - Trusted root certificates
    - A file located in the SYS:\PUBLIC directory (NetWare only)
- LDAP
- SNMP
- HTTPSTK
    - NDS iMonitor
    - eMBox
- Volume objects
    - NetWare volume objects
    - SLES 9 SP1 running OES volume objects (volume objects on SLES 9 are created only if the NCP server or NSS is installed during the OES installation)

Troubleshooting methods for both the binary copy procedure and the configuration procedure during an eDirectory installation will vary from operating system to operating system. Therefore, troubleshooting on each eDirectory-supported operating system is discussed separately in the following sections.

NetWare

NetWare combines the file copy portion and the configuration portion into one process. However, for purposes of explaining what occurs, it is beneficial to break the troubleshooting procedures into two separate processes.

File Copy

All files required for eDirectory are copied to the SYS volume. The file locations are hard coded and cannot be altered. Most of the programs are written to the SYS:\SYSTEM directory. The eDirectory database files are created in the SYS:_NETWARE directory. The installation log files are created in the SYS:\NI\DATA directory.

eDirectory can be installed onto NetWare's legacy file system as well as onto NetWare's NSS file system. The only issue typically encountered with the eDirectory file copy stage is insufficient disk space. Make sure there is sufficient disk space before you start the installation (see `http://www.novell.com/documentation` for more information on the prerequisites).

If you are installing eDirectory 8.7.x on NetWare 5.1 (or Netware 6.0 where the SYS volume is the legacy file system), sometimes, the file copy portion of the installation can be a little bit slow. This can usually be remedied with two file system configuration changes:

- Set the Dirty Disk Cache Delay Time to 0.1 second. This can be set in MONITOR.NLM ➤ Server Parameters ➤ File Caching (the default is 3.3 seconds). This setting allows the file system to be more aggressive about allocating disk cache for data that needs to be written to disk.
- Set Directory Cache Allocation Wait Time to 0.1 second in MONITOR.NLM ➤ Server Parameters ➤ Directory Caching (the default is 2.2 seconds).

Other possible issues that may slow down the file copy process are the following:

- *Compression*: File compression decreases the file copy performance.
- *Antivirus software*: It is recommended that you disable antivirus software if performance during the file copy portion is unacceptable. With most antivirus software programs, each file must be scanned as it is copied to disk.

Configuration

During the configuration phase, a database is created and objects for the server are created. The following is the process of configuring an eDirectory server. References to where to find troubleshooting tips for each step of the process are provided in the next section in case a step does not complete successfully.

- An NCP server object is created in the tree.
- An instance of the DIB is created in the SYS:\NETWARE directory (a hidden directory) on the local file system of the server being installed.
- The schema is extended.
    - The schema necessary to bring the current DIB to the latest version of eDirectory is installed.
    - A reboot must occur.
    - The rest of the schema is installed.
- Any applicable replicas of the tree are synchronized to the local database.
- The SAS object and KMO object are created for the server being installed.

- If this is the first server installed into the tree, the Security container and all components underneath are created.
- The SNMP object is created for the server being installed.
- The NMAS objects are created.
- The LDAP objects are created for the server being installed.

Troubleshooting Tips

There are five basic areas that you can refer to if something goes wrong during the installation or configuration phase of eDirectory on NetWare:

- *NetWare server console*: This screen shows errors.
- *NetWare Logger screen*: Only on NetWare 6.x.
- *SYS:\SYSTEM\NI\DATA*.LOG*: Has information about the file copy as well as the configuration stages.
- *SYS:\SYSTEM\DSMISC.LOG*: Captures information about the schema extension process.
- *SYS:\SYSTEM\DSTRACE.DBG*: See the section "Capturing a DSTRACE Log" at the end of this chapter to get detailed steps.

Disaster Recovery

If an unrecoverable error occurs during installation, perform Task 1-4.

Note Some of these steps may not apply, depending on where the installation failed.

Task 1-4. Removing eDirectory After a Failed Installation

1. Run **nwconfig –dsremove**. Choose Directory Options ➤ Remove Directory Services from this server to remove the database from the local server.
2. Through iManager or ConsoleOne, delete the NCP server object of the failed server and all associated objects (e.g., LDAP server and group objects, SNMP object, Volume Objects, etc.).
3. At a console prompt of the failed server, type **uinstall edir**. This removes the entry in the products.dat file so that you can reinstall eDirectory.
4. Reinstall eDirectory.

Note If the first steps of adding the DIB were successful and the failure was with one or all of the components, you can skip removing the DIB and deleting the objects. Simply remove edir from the products.dat file and reinstall eDirectory. The installation will leave the DIB intact and just configure the missing components.

Microsoft Windows

As with NetWare, the eDirectory installation on Microsoft Windows performs the file copy and configuration in one integrated step. However, they are discussed separately here for clarity.

File Copy

All files required for eDirectory are copied to the drive that Windows is installed on (usually C:\). Most of the binaries are copied to \Novell\NDS (e.g., C:\Novell\NDS). The file locations are hard coded and cannot be altered.

The eDirectory database files are created in the \Novell\NDS\DIBFiles directory (e.g., c:\novell\nds\DIBFiles).

The installation log files are created in the %SystemDrive%:\Program Files\Common Files\Novell\ni\data directory. The files are ni.log, nierrors.log, and nioutput.log.

The file copy section is mostly handled by the Microsoft Windows operating system. Use the default Windows operating system logs as well as the NI logs just listed for any file copy errors.

Configuration

During the configuration phase, a DIB is created and objects for the server are created. The following is the process of configuring an eDirectory server. References to where you can find troubleshooting tips for each step of the process are provided in the next section in case a step does not complete successfully.

- An NCP server object is created in the tree.
- An instance of the DIB is created in the %systemrootdrive:\Novell\NDS\DIBFiles directory on the local file system of the server being installed.
- The schema is extended.
    - The schema necessary to bring the current DIB to the latest version of eDirectory is installed.

  - A reboot must occur.
  - The rest of the schema is installed.
- Any applicable replicas of the tree are synchronized to the local database.
- The SAS object and KMO object are created for the server being installed.
- If this is the first server installed into the tree, the Security container and all components underneath are created.
- The SNMP object is created for the server being installed.
- The HTTP server object is created; this is used for NDS iMonitor.
- The NMAS objects are created.
- The LDAP objects are created for the server being installed.

Troubleshooting Tips

The Microsoft event viewer and the %SystemDrive%:\Program Files\Common Files\Novell\ni\data log files are the primary troubleshooting tools for eDirectory installation issues on the Microsoft Windows operating system.

DSTRACE logs can also be evaluated to capture errors. For information on how to capture DSTRACE logs, see the "Capturing a DSTRACE Log" section at the end of the chapter.

Disaster Recovery

If an unrecoverable error occurs during installation, perform Task 1-5.

Note Some of these steps may not apply, depending on where the installation failed.

Task 1-5. Removing eDirectory on Windows After a Failed Installation

1. Run Add/Remove Programs from Control Panel. Select eDirectory and remove the product.

Note If Add/Remove Programs fails, stop the dhost service in the Windows services program and then manually delete the files in the following directories: %SystemDrive%:\Novell\NDS and SystemDrive%:\Program Files\Common Files\Novell\ni. Other applications use the latter directory, so if you do delete it, the uninstall procedure through Add/Remove Programs will be broken for those other applications.

---

2. Reinstall eDirectory.
3. Through iManager or ConsoleOne, delete the NCP server object of the failed server and all associated objects (e.g., LDAP server and group objects, SNMP object, Volume Objects, etc.).

---

*nix

The eDirectory installation on Linux, Solaris, HPUX, and AIX (*.nix) has two completely separate processes. The file copy and configuration are completely separated.

File Copy

To verify that the packages are installed, run the native operating system package database query commands. Most of the packages for eDirectory start with either NDS or NOVL. The following are the commands to query the installed packages:

- Linux
    - rpm –qa | grep NDS*
    - rpm –qa | grep NOVL*
- Solaris
    - pkginfo | grep NDS*
    - pkginfo | grep NOVL*
- AIX
    - lslpp –l | grep NDS*
    - lslpp –l | grep NOVL*
- HPUX
    - swlist –v | grep NDS*
    - swlist –v | grep NOVL*

Configuration

To configure an instance of eDirectory, launch the `ndsconfig` utility. For more information on `ndsconfig`, see the *Novell eDirectory Administration Guide* at `http://www.novell.com/documentation`.

During the configuration phase, a DIB is created and objects for the server are created. The following is the process of configuring an eDirectory server. References to where you can find troubleshooting tips for each step of the process are provided in the next section in case a step does not complete successfully.

- An /etc/nds.conf file is created.
- An NCP server object is created in the tree.
- An instance of the DIB is created in the /var/nds/data directory on the local file system of the server being installed.
- The schema is extended.
    - The schema necessary to bring the current DIB to the latest version of eDirectory is installed.
    - A reboot must occur.
    - The rest of the schema is installed.
- Any applicable replicas of the tree are synchronized to the local database.
- The SAS object and KMO object are created for the server being installed.
- If this is the first server installed into the tree, the Security container and all components underneath are created.
- The SNMP object is created for the server being installed.
- The HTTP object is created for the server being installed; the HTTP object is used for the NDS iMonitor.
- The NMAS objects are created.
- The LDAP objects are created for the server being installed.

Troubleshooting Tips

The primary log file for eDirectory issues is the /etc/ndsd.log file.

NDSTRACE can also be used to monitor issues during the configuration phase. For information on how to capture DSTRACE logs, see the "Capturing a DSTRACE Log" section at the end of the chapter.

Disaster Recovery

If an unrecoverable error occurs during installation, perform Task 1-6.

■ **Note** Some of these steps may not apply, depending on where the installation failed.

Task 1-6. Removing eDirectory on *nix After a Failed Installation

1. Run **ndsconfig rm** at the server terminal.
2. Through iManager or ConsoleOne, delete the NCP server object of the failed server and all associated objects (e.g., LDAP server and group objects, SNMP object, Volume Objects, etc.).
3. Reconfigure eDirectory by typing **ndsconfig add**, or **ndsconfig new** if it is a new tree.

Note If the first steps of adding the DIB were successful and the failure was with one or all of the components, you can skip removing the DIB and deleting the objects. At a terminal window, type **ndsconfig add –m [*module*]** to reconfigure the separate modules. The available modules are SAS, HTTP, NMAS, and LDAP.

Capturing a DSTRACE Log

To obtain replication, name resolution, schema information, and eDirectory agent activity through the eDirectory DSTRACE utility, you need to turn on and configure DSTRACE.

The steps vary depending on the operating system of the eDirectory server that holds the master of the partition that will hold the new server object. The following sections describe the different methods of obtaining a DSTRACE log.

Cross-Platform Solution

NDS iMonitor ships on all platforms. The look and feel is the same regardless of the platform. For this reason, it is recommended that you capture DSTRACE messages from NDS iMonitor. To access NDS iMonitor, follow these steps:

1. Type the following in the URL line of your browser:

   `http://<serveraddress>:<port where http stack is listening>/nds`

   For example, `http://eDirServer1.novell.com:8008/nds`.
2. Click the Trace Configuration icon or add **/trace** to the URL as follows:

   `http://eDirServer1.novell.com:8008/nds/trace`

3. Select the following from the configuration screen:
   - Schema
   - Inbound Synchronization
   - Outbound Synchronization
   - Resolve Name
   - LDAP
   - Lost Entry
   - DS Agent
   - NMAS
   - PKI

For more information about NDS iMonitor, see the *Novell eDirectory Administration Guide* at `http://www.novell.com/documentation`.

NetWare

If you suspect that a problem occurred while installing eDirectory, before installing an eDirectory server into the tree, type the following commands at the NetWare server console of the server that holds the master replica of the partition in which the new server is being added:

```
set dstrace = on
set ttf = on
set dstrace = *r
set dstrace = +schema +s +in +rn +lost +part +dsa +misc +nmas +pki
```

Start the installation on the new server. When the errors occur, stop DSTRACE on the master replica by typing **set dstrace=off** and **set ttf=off**. The output will be written to the sys:\system\dstrace.dbg file.

Microsoft Windows

If you suspect an issue, before installing into the tree, execute the following at the eDirectory server console of the server that holds the master replica of the partition in which the new server is being added:

1. Launch the NDSCons application from within Control Panel.
2. Select the dstrace.dlm service and click Start.
3. Select Edit ➤ Options.

4. Select the following events:
    - Schema
    - Inbound Synchronization
    - Outbound Synchronization
    - ResolveName
    - LDAP
    - Lost Entry
    - DS Agent
    - NMAS
    - PKI
5. Click OK.

There is not a log file. To save to disk, highlight the information and copy and paste it into a text editor.

*nix

If you suspect an issue, before installing into the tree, execute the following at the eDirectory server console of the server that holds the master replica of the partition in which the new server is being added:

1. At a terminal on the server, type the following:

```
ndstrace
set ndstrace file=on
set ndstrace screen=on
ndstrace +ldap +areq +lost +misc +part +scma +sklk +pkii +nmas
```

2. After the errors occur, type the following:

```
set ndstrace file=off
exit
```

The log file is in /var/nds/ndstrace.log.

CHAPTER 2

Installing into an Existing Tree

The following topics are covered in this chapter:

- Protocol considerations
- Security considerations
    - eDirectory security infrastructure
    - Existing tree considerations for the security components
- NDS and eDirectory patch levels
    - Loss of trustee assignments
    - Unknown objects

The eDirectory installation and configuration becomes much more complex when you are installing a new server into an existing tree. The issues to watch out for can increase depending on the age of the tree, the size of the tree, and the version of NDS or eDirectory that was used to create the tree.

This chapter discusses how you can prevent failed installations and how you can troubleshoot various issues that may arise during the installation and configuration of eDirectory.

Protocol Considerations

Novell developed a proprietary protocol called Internetwork Packet Exchange (IPX). This protocol was very popular in the 1980s and 1990s. As technology developed, it became critical for organizations to be able to communicate between different applications and network operating systems (NOSs). The best way to handle this was for the networking industry to develop and adopt a nonproprietary standard protocol that could be adopted by all applications that required interoperation with other vendors/applications.

TCP/IP became the standard protocol used by Novell in its products. In the 1980s and 1990s, the Internet came into full strength. The Internet also based its primary protocol on TCP/IP for data transfer, authentication, and so forth. For these reasons, Novell started to write NOSs and applications that run on and support the TCP/IP protocol. At the same time, Novell has aggressively attempted to phase out all IPX dependencies.

Both NetWare 3.x and NetWare 4.x were completely IPX-based. NetWare 5.x shipped with both IPX and TCP/IP support. At the time of NetWare 5.x, Novell developed NetWare IP. NetWare IP would take an IPX packet and "wrap" it into an IP header and send it back out on the wire. This enabled IPX-only NOSs to communicate with environments based on TCP/IP only.

Novell also developed a technology called Server Compatibility Mode Driver (SCMD). SCMD required a server such as NetWare 5.x that had both IPX and TCP/IP bound to the box. SCMD would route IPX traffic to IPX-only systems and TCP/IP traffic to TCP/IP-only systems.

With NetWare 6.x, more and more NetWare shops have migrated their NetWare 3.x and 4.x servers to NetWare 6.x and have created a pure TCP/IP environment.

The IPX/TCP communication issues came to the forefront of consideration with the introduction of Open Enterprise Server (OES) on SuSe Linux Enterprise Server 9 (SLES) systems. Linux does not support the IPX protocol. Linux is based exclusively off of the TCP/IP protocol. If eDirectory is being installed into an existing environment that is running IPX-only servers, special considerations are necessary.

Linux servers running eDirectory should not be put into replica rings that contain IPX-only servers. Doing so would cause partition operations to fail, because the Linux eDirectory servers would not be able to communicate with the IPX-only servers.

Time synchronization is another factor. Linux supports only NTP over TCP/IP. NetWare 3.x and 4.x must use the proprietary TIMESYNC.NLM, which can communicate on these platforms through IPX. Neither NetWare IP nor SCMD will run on Linux.

It is wise to get all IPX-dependent systems upgraded to a NOS that supports TCP/IP before implementing eDirectory on Linux into the system. If this is not possible, make sure that you handle the communication issues by not creating mixed replica rings where Linux servers and nonTCP/IP servers hold replicas of the same partition.

Security Considerations

In today's market, lots of people are trying to hack into private networks and steal information. Because of this, the entire industry has become very security conscious. As Novell products have evolved, Novell too has become more and more security conscious. You need to understand how Novell products can secure your environment.

With eDirectory version 8.6.2 and greater and with supporting products, such as iManager 2.x, iFolder, NetStorage, etc., configuring the existing security infrastructure correctly is critical.

eDirectory Security Infrastructure

Beginning with NDS 7 on NetWare 5.x, eDirectory introduced a method to generate, sign, and distribute certificates. These certificates can be used for Secure Sockets Layer (SSL) communication as well as user verification during a mutual authentication request. The user certificates can also be used to sign messages, such as GroupWise e-mail messages, to ensure the validity of the content. Although certificate functionality is present, Novell products do not configure and enforce secure connections on NetWare 5.x. Because of this, very few organizations paid much attention to the Novell security infrastructure with NetWare 5.x.

With the introduction of NetWare 6 and eDirectory 8.6.2, Lightweight Directory Access Protocol (LDAP) and the HTTP stack (httpstk.nlm) are configured by default to accept SSL connections, using certificates that were auto-generated and signed by eDirectory's certificate authority (CA).

NetWare 6.5, with eDirectory 8.7, introduces iManager 2.0.x and Virtual Office. The iManager 2.0.x installation requires Apache and Tomcat to be configured securely. iManager 2.0.x also requires a secure connection to LDAP. Because iManager 2.0.x rapidly has become Novell's management solution (replacing ConsoleOne), the Novell Security Domain has become more and more relevant.

The security dependencies are compounded further with the introduction of Native File Access Protocol (NFAP) in NetWare 6.5 and Universal Password support with eDirectory 8.7.1 on NetWare 6.5 SP1. These products store their secrets within eDirectory. The secrets are encrypted using a key called a tree key. The tree key is distributed and maintained by the Security Domain Infrastructure (SDI), which uses Novell's NICI technology.

With the introduction of NetWare 6—and exponentially compounded with the introduction of NetWare 6.5—inadequate security infrastructures have proven to be the cause of many upgrade and installation failures. Therefore, it is important to understand all the components of the Novell Security Infrastructure (SDI) as well as security infrastructure health check methods.

Table 2-1 lists the different components of the Novell Security Infrastructure as well as a brief description of their purpose.

Table 2-1. *The Security Infrastructure Components*

Component	Object Distinguished Name	Binaries	Usage
Server keys (NICI keys)	Not applicable. They are independent of eDirectory. They reside on the file system.	*NetWare* sys:\system\nici *Windows* %system32%\novell\nici **nix* /var/novell/nici/0	All other encryption in eDirectory is based off of the server keys. The CA and the tree keys are encrypted using the server keys. If the server keys are lost or changed, all eDirectory security must be set up again.
Certificate Server	[Tree Root].Security The default object name is <*tree name*> Organizational CA.	*NetWare* sys:\system\pki.nlm *Windows* *%RootDrive%*:\novell\nds\pki.dll **nix* /usr/sbin/npki	The CA is responsible for issuing and signing user certificates and server certificates. The certificates are used to sign data and to create SSL connections from the requester to the server.
Tree key	Key [Tree Root].Security.KAP.W0	*NetWare* sys:\system\nici\sdi.xlm *Windows* *%RootDrive%*:\novell\nds\nicisdi.xlm	The /usr/lib/nds-modules/ndsmodules.conf file lists the nicisdi as niciext. The W0 object contains the attribute "NDSPKI:SD Key Server DN."

Component	Object Distinguished Name	Binaries	Usage
Tree key *(continued)*		**nix* /user/lib/nds-modules/libniciext.so	This attribute contains the DN of a server or a set of servers that are the "Security Domain Servers." These servers maintain and distribute the tree key. Every time an eDirectory server reboots, nicisdi does a lookup on the W0 object. If the W0 object points to the local server object, then nicisdi verifies that there is a nicisdi.key file in the NICI directory on the local file system. If there is not a file, nicisdi creates one. If nicisdi finds that the local server object is not specified in the W0 object, then the local server creates a connection to one of the servers listed in the W0 object and verifies that it has the same tree keys that the W0 domain server holds. If it does not have all of the keys, the local server requests that the domain server send the tree keys to the local server.

Continued

Table 2-1. *Continued*

Component	Object Distinguished Name	Binaries	Usage
SAS objects	Objects placed in the same container as the NCP server object that corresponds to the SAS object. The default name of the object is SAS Service - *<server name>*.	*NetWare* sys:\system\pki.nlm *Windows* *%RootDrive%*:\novell\nds\pki.dll **nix* /usr/sbn/npki	The PKI modules (there are several binaries, with PKI being the key module) have two functions. If the server running PKI is specified as the CA, it issues certificates and signs them. Regardless of whether it is the CA, it also is responsible to accept SSL login requests and send certificates that are associated with the server to the requester for identity verification. The SAS object is used to keep track of all the server certificates that are associated with a specified server.
KMO objects	The same container in which the NCP server object resides. Four default KMO objects are created during an eDirectory installation: - SSL CertificateDNS - *<server name>* - SSL CertificateIP - *<server name>* - IP AG *<server IP address>* - *<server name>* (only in newer versions of eDirectory) - DNS AG *<server DNS address>* - *<server name>* (only in newer versions of eDirectory)	*NetWare* - sys:\system\sas.nlm - sys:\system\nile.nlm - sys:\system\ntls.nlm *Windows* -*%RootDrive%*c:\novell\nds\sas.dll - *%RootDrive%*:\novell\nds\ntls.dll **nix* /usr/lib/libntls.so	The KMO objects contain server-specific certificate information as well as a copy of the trusted root certificate. The server-specific information defines how long the certificate is valid for as well as the name of the server, commonly referred to as the "subject name." The subject name, along with other information, is passed to the client during an SSL connection request. The client verifies the information in the

Component	Object Distinguished Name	Binaries	Usage
KMO objects *(continued)*			certificate with information in its own database (this varies by client). If the information from both sources matches, the client allows the connection. Some clients allow the connection even if the information does not match. For example, if the client is Internet Explorer and the certificate information cannot be verified, the user is asked if the connection should be allowed anyway. If the user responds in the affirmative, the SSL connection is established even though the certificate names may not match.
Trusted root certificate	Anywhere in the tree or file system.	*NetWare* - sys:\system\sas.nlm - sys:\system\nile.nlm - sys:\system\ntls.nlm *Windows* - *%RootDrive%*:\novell\nds\sas.dll - *%RootDrive%*:\novell\nds\ntls.dll **nix* /usr/lib/libntls.so	The trusted root certificate contains information about the CA. During an SSL login request or identity verification, the client may only care about the information from the CA, not necessarily about the specific server. In this case, the trusted root certificate is used to verify the identity.

Continued

Table 2-1. *Continued*

Component	Object Distinguished Name	Binaries	Usage
Trusted root certificate *(continued)*			A trusted root certificate can be exported to a file. A trusted root container can be created in eDirectory. A trusted root object is created in this container and the client is pointed to the object for identity verification.
User Certificates	Contained on the user object.	*NetWare* sys:\system\pki.nlm *Windows* *%RootDrive%*:\novell\nds\pki.dll **nix* /usr/sbin/npki	User certificates are used to sign documents, like e-mail messages. This verifies to the recipient that the user is who it says it is. In order for this to be verified, the recipient must have the sender's certificate.
NMAS method object	<NMAS ,method>[Tree Root].Security - Authorized Login Methods - Authorized Post Login Methods - Login Policy - Security Policy - Password Policy	*NetWare* sys:\system\nmas.nlm *Windows* *%RootDrive%*:\novell\nds\nmas.dll **nix* /usr/lib/nds-modules/libnmas.so	Novell Modular Authentication Service (NMAS) is an engine that will accept various types of login requests and post login policies. The types of logins could be biometric, strong password policies, SmartCards, etc.

Existing Tree Considerations for the Security Components

The only two real security component issues to keep in mind have to do with the version of NICI in the tree and the version of PKI on the server that is acting as the CA.

NICI Versions

It is important to ensure that NICI is upgraded to version 2.4.2 or greater on each server in the tree that is running NDS version 8.x or eDirectory 8.5 or greater. The reason for this is that NICI 2.4.2 was the first version of NICI that supported multiple tree keys. There are many scenarios in which there can be more than one tree key within the SDI. If more than one key is present and an eDirectory server does not have NICI 2.4.2 or greater, it is possible that data such as NMAS passwords may not be able to be read, which would cause a denial of service for the user that is using the NMAS password.

Keep in mind that the tree key is used to encrypt the following information:

- User secrets that are used with NMAS methods
- Universal passwords
- User certificates
- Secret Store secrets

PKI Versions

With the introduction of NDS 7.x, a module called PKI was introduced. PKI has many functions. One of its main functions is to act as the CA. With NDS 7.x, PKI version 1.x was introduced.

With NDS 8, PKI version 2.x was introduced. There were significant changes in the module and how, when acting as the CA, it issued new certificates to requesting servers.

With new changes introduced in PKI version 2.x, when installing a new server running eDirectory 8.5 or greater, it is important to make sure that the server acting as the CA is running version 2.x of the PKI module.

If the PKI version on the server acting as the CA is version 1.x, this server should be migrated to eDirectory 7.x, which will upgrade PKI to a 2.x version before introducing a new eDirectory 8.7.x server into the tree.

If you are not sure which server is acting as the CA, perform Task 2-1 using iManager or ConsoleOne (with the PKI snap-ins installed).

Task 2-1. Finding the Certificate Authority Server

1. Modify the [Tree Name].Security.Organizational CA object; for example:

   ```
   NW6sp3edir87_Tree.Organizational CA.Security
   ```

   The default Organizational CA object name is [Tree Name] Organizational CA.

2. Under the General ➤ Identification tab, view the Host Server field to identify the DN of the server that is acting as the Organizational CA.

The process used to determine the version of PKI that is running on the host server varies depending on the operating system that resides on the host server. Tasks 2-2 through 2-4 show the different procedures for finding the version of PKI on NetWare, Windows, and UNIX systems, respectively.

Task 2-2. Finding the Version of PKI on NetWare

1. At a server console, type the following:

   ```
   modules PKI.NLM
   ```

2. You should see a version on the screen. The screen looks similar to this:

   ```
   Novell Certificate Server
   Version 2.52.01 July 1. 2003
   ```

3. As long as the Version is 2.x, you are okay. If the version is 1.x, you need to upgrade this server to a newer version of eDirectory and PKI before introducing new servers into the tree.

Task 2-3. Finding the Version of PKI on Windows

1. Go to *%RootDrive%*:\novellnds\pki.dlm.
2. Right-click the file.
3. Look in the File Version field for the version.

Task 2-4. Finding the Version of PKI on *nix

1. At a terminal prompt, type the following:

```
rpm -qa | grep pki
```

2. Look in the File Version field for the version.

NDS and eDirectory Patch Levels

The general rule of thumb when installing eDirectory 8.7.x into an existing tree is to make sure that all servers in the tree have the latest NDS or eDirectory public patch applied. The latest available patch for each version of NDS and eDirectory can be found at `http://support.novell.com`.

The NetWare 6.5 Deployment Manager (starting with SP1) has a feature that will check to make sure the tree contains the minimum versions of NDS 6.x and NDS 7.x. It is recommended that you execute the Deployment Manager before you add the first eDirectory 8.7.x into the tree or before you install NetWare 6.5 or OES for Linux for the first time.

Besides the obvious reasons for obtaining the latest bug fixes, there are a few important reasons to upgrade to the latest patches:

- Loss of trustee assignments
- Unknown objects

Loss of Trustee Assignments

With legacy file systems, the local EntryID of an eDirectory object is written to a file or directory in the file system when a file system trustee assignment is made. This poses a problem with the NetWare clustering products. When a clustered server goes down, a "failover" occurs and a different server in the cluster takes on the identity of the original server. All servers within the cluster share the same file system, so the trustee assignments that are written to the file system remain. eDirectory is not cluster enabled. This means that the eDirectory database does not reside on the shared file system. The eDirectory database must reside on the local file system of the server that is running the eDirectory process. The end result is that when the failover occurs, a different instance of the replica is enabled on the new server with new EntryIDs for the objects in the replica.

For each given object, a separate EntryID is assigned for each replica of the object. Keep in mind that it is the EntryID that is written to the file system. When a failover occurs and a new replica of a partition is used for the new online server, all trustee assignments on the shared file system are not recognized because of the change in EntryIDs. To deal with this issue, NetWare 6 clustering provided a trustee migration utility that was executed on every failover. Depending on the number of trustee assignments, this could significantly impact the length of time it takes to bring a new server online after a failover is triggered.

The introduction of NetWare 6.5 solved this issue. With NSS 3.0 in NetWare 6.5, the object's Globally Unique Identifier (GUID) is written to the file system for the trustee assignment rather than the EntryID. The advantage to this approach is that the object's GUID is a unique number that is the same for a particular object regardless of the replica in which that object resides.

The problem with this new approach is that older versions of NDS 6.x that are installed on NetWare 4.x servers do not recognize or support GUIDs. To ensure that objects that reside on an NDS 6.x server maintain their trustee assignments when NetWare 6.5 or greater is introduced into the tree, all NDS 6.x servers must be upgraded to a version that supports GUIDs. NDS 6.21 or greater supports GUIDs. It is recommended, however, that you apply the latest public patches for NDS 6.x to all servers in the tree to take advantage of all defect fixes included in the latest patches.

Unknown Objects

With NDS 8, a new schema type called auxiliary classes was introduced. Auxiliary classes are not actually added to an effective schema class. Auxiliary classes are "extended" on an object or on a set of objects. When this occurs, all attributes that are defined on that auxiliary class are now available for the specific object or set of objects that have been extended with the auxiliary class.

Auxiliary class support was not added to NDS versions 6.x and 7.x. This poses a problem in that objects on NDS 8 or eDirectory 8.5 or greater that are extended with an auxiliary class are not able to synchronize with replicas of the same objects on NDS 6.x or NDS 7.x servers. To get around this problem, Novell built functionality into NDS 8 and eDirectory in which they check whether the object that is extended with an auxiliary class is being sent to an NDS 6.x or NDS 7.x server. If it is, then the NDS 8 or eDirectory agent removes the auxiliary class definition and places it into an auxiliary class compatibility attribute on the object. The agent then marks the object as "unknown" and sends it to the NDS 6.x or NDS 7.x server. If the NDS 8 or eDirectory server receives an "unknown" object from an NDS 6.x or NDS 7.x server, the local agent checks for the auxiliary class compatibility attribute.

If the attribute is present, it extracts the auxiliary class information and places it back onto the object and removes the "unknown" type. This functionality allows an NDS 6.x and NDS 7.x server to reside in the same replica ring with an NDS 8 or eDirectory server without breaking synchronization.

This solution, however, does not come without problems. If the object that is extended with an auxiliary class is read through iManager, ConsoleOne, or any other directory management tool, the object will be read as an "unknown" object. As such, the management tools will not know what type of object it is displaying, so it will not be able to apply the applicable plug-in to that object. The end result is that the object cannot be managed when reading the object from NDS 6.x or NDS 7.x servers.

To get around this issue, NDS 6.x and NDS 7.x were updated. With the current releases of NDS 6.x and NDS 7.x, when any external utility requests that an object be read from these servers, the NDS agent checks for the auxiliary class compatibility attribute. If it finds the attribute, it converts the object back to its true form in memory and returns the valid "known" object to the requester. The end effect is that even though the object is still unknown in the database, the utilities that request to read the object see the object as a fully functional, known object.

CHAPTER 3

Migration Methodologies

The following topics are covered in this chapter:

- Updating the program files
    - NetWare
    - Microsoft Windows
    - Solaris and Linux
- Migrating the eDirectory Database (DIB) to eDirectory 8.7.3.x
    - Migrating the DIB from NDS 6.x or NDS 7.x to eDirectory 8.5
    - Migrating the DIB from NDS 8, eDirectory 8.5, eDirectory 8.6, or eDirectory 8.7 to eDirectory 8.7.3
- Mixed-environment considerations
    - Loss of trustee assignments
    - Unknown objects
- Administration options
    - NWAdmin
    - ConsoleOne
    - iManager
- Protocol considerations when introducing multiple platforms

An eDirectory migration consists of two key functions. First, the binaries are upgraded. Second, the database is migrated. These processes can get complex when performing migrations in an existing environment that is running older versions of NDS and eDirectory. With some insight about known issues that could arise during the migration phase, you can cleanly upgrade your eDirectory environment with little if any down time or data loss. The following are a few items that are considered in this chapter:

- *Migration methods*: Novell has provided methods to migrate older versions of NDS and/or eDirectory to eDirectory 8.7.x. Regardless of the platform or the migration method used, the following basic processes always are performed during an eDirectory migration (this chapter discusses these processes for each supported platform and each migration method):
    - *Product upgrade*: Old NDS or eDirectory program files need to be replaced with the new ones. This process is handled differently depending on the method you choose and the platform from which you are migrating eDirectory.
    - *Schema extension*: If the server being migrated is the first eDirectory 8.7.x server in the tree, you need to update the schema for the tree before you migrate the eDirectory database.
    - *Database upgrade*: The NDS or eDirectory database (FLAIM) is upgraded. With each new version of NDS and eDirectory, Novell has enhanced FLAIM to be more secure, more scalable, more fault tolerant, and faster.
- *Mixed-environment issues*: There are precautions that you need to be aware of when introducing eDirectory 8.7.x into an environment with older versions of NDS and/or eDirectory.
- *Administration changes*: With eDirectory 8.7.x, Novell has introduced new ways of administration. Also, some old ways of administering your NDS or eDirectory environment no longer work.
- *Protocol considerations*: Because Linux, AIX, HP-UX, Solaris, Windows, and NetWare 6.x are all supported with eDirectory 8.7.x, the proprietary IPX protocol is becoming more and more obsolete. This can cause issues during a migration to eDirectory 8.7.x. This chapter points out most of the pitfalls involved with protocol issues.

Note Hereafter in this chapter, the Linux, AIX, HP-UX, and Solaris platforms are referred to as *nix when speaking of the group collectively.

There are different methods used to update the program files and the eDirectory database. Although some components are similar on each platform, there are enough differences that each platform warrants its own separate discussion. The following section discusses two main topics, broken down by platform:

- Updating the eDirectory program files
- Migrating the eDirectory database

■ **Note** Although some of the methods discussed next support the migration from non-eDirectory databases to an eDirectory database, the scope of this book only deals with current NDS and eDirectory systems. For further information about migrating or converting non-eDirectory systems to eDirectory, see the *Novell eDirectory Administration Guide* at `http://www.novell.com/documentation`.

Updating the Program Files

Each platform that supports eDirectory has different methods to migrate to eDirectory 8.7.3. The NetWare methods will also upgrade the NetWare operating system and the file system.

However, the scope of this book is to address only eDirectory. For this reason, if you need more information on how to migrate the NetWare operating system and/or the file system, please refer to Novell's documentation at `http://www.novell.com/documentation`.

NetWare

NetWare has three main methods that are used to upgrade eDirectory to eDirectory 8.7.x:

- Server Consolidation Utility (SCU)
- Migration Wizard
- In-place upgrade

■ **Note** It is *highly* advisable that you use the latest NetWare overlay CDs (found at `http://support.novell.com` by clicking Download – Patches ➤ NetWare). These images will install both NetWare 6.5 and the current support pack simultaneously.

Server Consolidation Utility

The main purpose of SCU is to consolidate several servers into one. SCU is designed to consolidate the data on the file system of several servers to one server. This includes all trustee assignments and home directories that are stored in the file system and are associated to users within the eDirectory database. Currently, with the emergence of Novell Open Enterprise Server (OES), SCU has been updated to consolidate the following:

- NDS (NetWare) to eDirectory 8.7.3.x (NetWare or Linux)
- eDirectory 8.6.x or 8.7.x (NetWare) to eDirectory 8.7.x (NetWare or Linux)
- eDirectory 8.7.x (NetWare or Linux) to eDirectory 8.7.x (NetWare or Linux)

SCU copies all selected files from the server being migrated to a new target server (in a different tree) via the Storage Management Services (SMS) backup/restore technology.

SCU can either move all the file systems of several servers to a server in a new eDirectory tree or to a server within the same tree. If SCU is used to consolidate a server's file system onto a server in a new tree, it creates an eDirectory user that has a file system trustee on the original source server to the target server in the new eDirectory tree. The home directories and the file system trustee assignments are reestablished.

SCU allows you to move the data from as many source servers you want into one target server, thus consolidating servers. After all data is transferred from the source server(s) to the target server, the source server(s) can be decommissioned, leaving the new server with consolidated information from the other servers.

Pros

- Older hardware can be easily upgraded at the same time eDirectory is updated.
- Gives you an easy method to redesign your existing tree while building a new one.
- eDirectory users and groups are transferred to the new target server.
- The existing tree will not be affected by the new tree. All network activities should continue even though one of the servers has been removed from the tree.
- File system trustees and home directories are kept intact.

Cons

- Additional hardware is required (the old information is copied to a new server).
- Not all users are transferred. Only users that have file system trustee assignments are moved to the new server.
- Applications are not migrated. Any application, such as eDirectory, GroupWise, ZenWorks, etc., has to be reinstalled and reconfigured on the new target server.

Troubleshooting Tips

The original source server is not decommissioned until you manually remove it. It is wise to remove it fairly quickly or else the data on the old source server will be out of sync with the data on the new target server. However, this gives you a great backout plan. If the migration fails, you can restart it at the beginning or by re-executing the SCU utility.

The only danger of data loss with this utility is that, for some reason, the trustee assignments may not get transferred over. To prevent this, you can download a utility like TRUSTBAR.NLM or TRUSTEE.NLM and use it to manually back up your volume trustees before executing SCU.

■ **Note** You can download TRUSTBAR.NLM and TRUSTEE.NLM from `http://support.novell.com`. Other tools can be used to back up file system trustee assignments, but TRUSTBAR.NLM and TRUSTEE.NLM are the most commonly used.

You can use TRUSTBAR.NLM or TRUSTEE.NLM to back up file system trustees on the original server. Both utilities store the user's distinguished name as well as the filenames or directory names and the associated rights to those files and directories. If the trustee assignments do not successfully copy from the source server to the target server during the SCU process, you can restore the file system trustees on the users on the target server with the TRUSTBAR or TRUSTEE backup file. Pay attention to the documentation for these utilities, because some of them do not back up inherited rights filters that may exist on directories in the file system.

Migration Wizard

The Novell NetWare Migration Wizard was designed as a hardware replacement mechanism. The assumption is that if you are still running NetWare 4.x or NetWare 5.x, you probably have outdated server hardware. Often, customers choose to upgrade to the latest versions of NetWare at the same time that they are budgeted to replace their server hardware.

With the Migration Wizard, you install the new version of NetWare onto a new set of server hardware. You then move or migrate all the information from the old hardware. During the move or migration process, the old information on the old server is "migrated" to and updated on the new server.

It is beyond the scope of this book to go into extensive details about the Migration Wizard. This section focuses on the eDirectory migration process using the Migration Wizard.

When the new version of NetWare (NetWare 6.5.x) is installed onto the new server, an updated version of eDirectory (eDirectory 8.7.x) is installed and an instance of the eDirectory database is created. While preparing the new server to accept the old data, eDirectory is installed and a new, temporary tree is created with a temporary server name.

One of the steps during the migration is that the old eDirectory DIB from the old server that is being migrated is backed up and restored onto the new server. The Migration Wizard uses the NetWare SMS technology and the hardware upgrade technology to back up the DIB on the original server and restore it to the new server.

After the DIB is copied to the new server, different methods are used during the migration of the DIB. The method used depends on the DIB version. The different migration methods are discussed later in this chapter.

Pros

- Easy backout or disaster recovery. Because the original server is not destroyed, if an error occurs, you could unlock the original database and start over.
- Upgrades the hardware used by eDirectory efficiently. By transferring all the old file system information, trustee assignments, and the eDirectory database to the new hardware, the Migration Wizard provides a seamless way to upgrade the hardware.

Cons

- The migration requires additional hardware. Specifically, you need a Microsoft Windows workstation to run the Migration Wizard as well as a new server to which the old information will be copied.
- There are more processes involved than are involved in an in-place upgrade. With more processes, there are potentially more things that could go wrong.

Troubleshooting Tips

The troubleshooting tips provided in this section for the Migration Wizard address two issues: how you can undo a failed migration, and how you can address volume errors in DSREPAIR after the migration.

How to Undo a Failed Migration

If the migration got to the point where the new target server has already taken on the name and identity of the source tree, you should try to proceed by manually configuring whatever failed. By reversing the migration at this stage, you will potentially have two servers with the same name in the tree, which could cause various issues.

If the server has not taken on the old name or identity and the migration fails, you can safely turn off the new server and recover the originator by unlocking the eDirectory database.

To unlock the database, perform Task 3-1.

Task 3-1. Unlocking the eDirectory Database

1. Turn off the target server that has the failed migration.
2. Go to the source server.
3. Type **nwconfig**.
4. Go to Directory Options.
5. Go to Directory Backup and Restore Options.
6. Select Restore Local NDS Information After Hardware Upgrade.
7. Press F3 and type in the path and name of the NDS backup file made by the Migration Wizard.

Note The Migration Wizard creates a file called SYS:SYSTEM\NUW30\NDSBU.

The Migration Wizard backs up all the file system trustee assignments. If the trustee assignments fail for whatever reason, you can always rerun the file system trustee steps of the Migration Wizard.

If the file system trustee assignments still cannot be restored, you can restore the trustee assignments from a previous backup of file system trustees.

You can use TRUSTBAR.NLM or TRUSTEE.NLM to back up file system trustees on the original server. Both utilities store the user's distinguished name as well as the file or directory and the associated rights to those files and directories. If the trustee assignments do not successfully copy from the source server to the target server during the SCU process, you can restore the file system trustees on the users on the target server with the TRUSTBAR or TRUSTEE backup file.

■ **Note** TRUSTBAR.NLM and TRUSTEE.NLM can be downloaded from `http://support.novell.com`. Other tools can be used to back up file system trustee assignments, but TRUSTBAR.NLM and TRUSTEE.NLM are the most common tools used.

How to Address Volume Errors in DSREPAIR After the Migration

You may encounter a situation in which volume objects are not created correctly. When you use the Migration Wizard, the first step is to install a base version of NetWare 6.5 onto the target server. You add that server into a temporary tree. This process creates volume objects within the temporary tree and writes the eDirectory EntryIDs of the volume objects into the file system.

The second step involved in the Migration Wizard involves backing up the eDirectory database from the target server and restoring the backup onto the source server, replacing the source server's temporary tree with the real production tree. When this occurs, there is a small chance that some of the EntryIDs in the target server will be the same as EntryIDs that resided in the temporary server. If the EntryID that is duplicated happens to be the EntryID that used to be the volume object in the target server's temporary tree, a conflict occurs.

Most likely, the EntryID on the source server is not a volume object. It could be a user, group, or any other object within eDirectory. Because the file system on the source server is not removed during the migration process, the file system still has recorded the EntryID of the volume object in the temporary tree. Therefore, after the migration, if a utility such as DSREPAIR tries to read the volume object by looking up the EntryID from the file system, it may locate that object within eDirectory. If the EntryIDs are duplicated, you will get an error that the volume object could not be read. The error occurs in eDirectory because the duplicate EntryID may point to a user, group, or any other type of nonvolume object.

The quickest way to fix this issue is to simply delete the object within eDirectory that is using the EntryID and then run DSREPAIR and select Advanced Options Menu ➤ Check Volume Objects and Trustees.

This option creates a new volume and writes that volume object back to the file system.

In-place Upgrade

The in-place upgrade is probably the simplest of the three NetWare methods to upgrade eDirectory to eDirectory 8.7.x. You can perform this upgrade in two different ways:

- *Online mode*: You simply go into the NetWare GUI environment by typing **startx** at a NetWare console prompt and run the installation from the NetWare 6.5 CD-ROMs.
- *Offline or manual mode*: With offline mode, you bring the server down and boot off of the NetWare 6.5 CD-ROMs. During the boot process, you should select to go into manual mode. For more information about how to run manual mode, see the NetWare documentation at `http://www.novell.com/documentation`.

Note It is recommended that, when at all possible, you choose offline mode. This eliminates several variables that could cause an installation failure.

Pros

- Much simpler process. The across-the-wire file copy and migration is eliminated. The information is written to the local file system.
- Less hardware is required. You only need the original server to migrate.
- Typically faster, because the files are not copied from one server to another.

Cons

- Single point of failure. If something goes wrong with the installation, the information on the server has already been overwritten with the new updates. To back out of the installation, you have to use a complete restore from a tape backup or image taken before the upgrade.
- The in-place upgrade does not provide a mechanism to upgrade the hardware. The newer technology that is provided with eDirectory 8.7.3.x requires more hardware resources. If the servers that are running the older versions of the software do not meet the recommended hardware levels, the in-place upgrade method may not be the best choice for migration.

Troubleshooting Tips

Undoing a failed in-place upgrade can be tricky. It is important to understand the different stages of the in-place upgrade. Depending on the stage you are in, you may be better off moving forward, rather than back. The following are the different stages of an in-place upgrade on NetWare:

1. The DOS partition is backed up on the local server.
2. The new files are copied to the DOS partition.
3. If NDS 6.x or NDS 7.x is on the server, the DIBMIG process runs, which upgrades the database to eDirectory.
4. The new DSI.NLM and DSLOADER.NLM are copied to the SYS:\SYSTEM directory and are loaded into memory.
4. The schema for eDirectory 8.7.3.x is extended.
5. The server is rebooted. (During the reboot, DSLOADER.NLM for eDirectory 8.7.3.x is loaded into memory. When DSLOADER is loaded, it automatically updates the existing database to eDirectory 8.7.3.x.)
6. The rest of the schema is extended.
7. The main files are copied into SYS:\SYSTEM.
8. The eDirectory objects are updated for the server. The objects, such as the volume objects, SAS objects, KMO objects, LDAP objects, license objects, and others, are all updated (or created if they don't exist) for the server that is being upgraded.

Note If the installation fails any time after Step 2, you need to either restore the entire server from backup or manually proceed forward.

You can restore from a previous tape backup or from a server image that you took before you started the migration. Restoring an image is the easiest method because you don't have to worry about restoring eDirectory from tape, which can be time consuming. When eDirectory is stored on tape, partition boundaries are not recorded. Also, when restoring, it actually creates a new object (it does not restore the old object). With this in mind, all other replicas of the objects being restored must be restored before the tape backup can be restored. If you image your server, you will not have to do this.

If the eDirectory database was successfully migrated and opens after the server reboot, you can manually copy the new files to SYS:\SYSTEM and to SYS:\PUBLIC from the distribution CDs or from another server that has been migrated. You then have to use iManager or ConsoleOne to manually add all the eDirectory objects, such as LDAP, NMAS, SAS, KMOs, licensing, etc.

With all installation and upgrade methods on NetWare, the installation logs are stored in the SYS:\NI\DATA directory. It is wise to look in these files if errors occur during the migration and/or upgrade. The one exception to this rule is the schema extensions. When schema is being extended, the results are written to the SYS:\SYSTEM\DSMISC.LOG file.

Microsoft Windows

NDS 8 Corporate Edition and eDirectory versions 8.5.x, 8.6.x, and 8.7.x can run on Microsoft Windows. To upgrade these existing installations to eDirectory 8.7.3.x, you can simply install eDirectory 8.7.3 on the same server. The installation will detect that the DIB exists and will update the database to eDirectory 8.7.3.

The eDirectory upgrade performs the following:

- Looks for a file called Program Files\Common Files\novell\ni\data\ip.db.
- If the file exists, an upgrade procedure is called by the installation program.
- eDirectory removes all of the binaries (not the database) that are listed in the ip.db file.
- eDirectory then copies in the new libraries and loads them into memory.
- When the new libraries are loaded into memory, the eDirectory agent automatically upgrades the database to eDirectory 8.7.3.

All errors are written to the log files located in the Program Files\Common Files\novell\ni\data directory. If the upgrade process fails, check the logs for errors and find solutions at `http://support.novell.com`.

I have encountered a few situations in which the ip.db file was corrupt. The result is a failed installation. You will probably see Java errors in the Program Files\Common Files\novell\ni\data\ni.log file. In these cases, you can rename the ip.db file. The repercussion of doing this is that only binaries in 8.7.3 with the same name as files in the older versions of eDirectory will be updated. The residual files will remain. This should not cause any issues, but it leaves the directory cluttered with unused binaries.

You should also consider the fact that other products that also use Novell Installation Services (NIS) will store their binaries in the same ip.db file. By removing the ip.db file, you will no longer be able to uninstall these applications with the typical uninstall processes in Windows through Add/Remove Programs in the Control Panel.

Solaris and Linux

NDS 8 Corporate Edition and eDirectory versions 8.5.x, 8.6.x, and 8.7.x shipped on Solaris and Linux platforms. The only migration method supported for these versions of eDirectory is an in-place upgrade. However, depending on the version of eDirectory that exists on the box before the upgrade, different processes to migrate to eDirectory 8.7.3.x are required.

For eDirectory 8.5 as well as NDS 8 Corporate Edition, the NICI keys must be updated to a 2.x version before performing the upgrade. For eDirectory 8.6.x and 8.7.x, the NICI keys are adequate and do not need to be updated prior to the eDirectory upgrade.

To upgrade the NICI keys, you can use the NICI Migration Utility. This utility was made available in an upgrade package called f1s862up.tgz. To upgrade NICI, perform the steps in Task 3-2.

■ **Note** Make sure that you read the *eDirectory Administration Guide* at `http://www.novell.com/documentation` and complete all the prerequisites before installing eDirectory 8.7.3.

Task 3-2. Upgrading the NICI Keys

1. Download the installation files for eDirectory 8.7.3 and install them into a temporary directory.
2. Download the f1s862up.tgz file from `http://support.novell.com`.
3. Uncompress and untar the file to a temporary directory by typing the following:

```
gzip -dc f1s862up.tgz | tar xvf -
```

4. Change to the f1s862up directory.
5. On Linux, copy the nici-2.4/Linux files to your [*temporary directory*]/Linux/setup directory.

   On Solaris, copy the nici-2.4/Solaris files to your [*temporary directory*]/Solaris/setup directory.
6. Stop ndsd and back up the /var/nds/dib directory.
7. Back up the /etc/nds.conf file.
8. Change to the f1s862up/nicimig directory.
9. Type **./nici-upgrade** as the root user.

10. Install eDirectory 8.7.3.

11. Type **ndsconfig upgrade** to upgrade the DIB.

If you are updating eDirectory from eDirectory 8.6.2 or eDirectory 8.7.x to eDirectory 8.7.3, you simply need to install the eDirectory 8.7.3 binaries and then run `nwconfig upgrade` to upgrade the DIB.

eDirectory 8.7.1 was the first version of eDirectory that shipped on HP-UX or AIX. Migration from eDirectory 8.7.1 to 8.7.3 is straightforward. Simply install the 8.7.3 binaries and then run `nwconfig upgrade` to upgrade the DIB.

Migrating the eDirectory Database to eDirectory 8.7.3.x

There is not a supported method to migrate the eDirectory DIB from NDS 6.x or NDS 7.x to eDirectory 8.7.x. There is, however, a method provided to upgrade NDS 6.x or NDS 7.x to eDirectory 8.5. There is also a method of upgrading NDS 8, eDirectory 8.5.x, eDirectory 8.6.x, and eDirectory 8.7.x to eDirectory 8.7.3.x. So the migration from NDS 6.x or NDS 7.x to eDirectory 8.7.3 entails a two-step process.

Migrating the DIB from NDS 6.x or NDS 7.x to eDirectory 8.5

To migrate from NDS 6.x or NDS 7.x to eDirectory 8.5, you must execute a utility called DIBMIG.NLM. This utility has several phases, which are discussed in detail in the following sections.

Note All results of the DIBMIG process are recorded to SYS:SYSTEM\DSMISC.LOG.

Phase 1: Evaluation of the DIB

Phase 1 calculates the number of entries in the eDirectory database. The eDirectory database is initialized and the DIB is locked.

Failure Recovery During Phase 1

To recover from a phase 1 failure, simply reboot the server to unlock the database.

Phase 2: Memory Allocation

Memory is allocated for all objects within eDirectory. All objects are then added into memory. Depending on the number of objects and the amount of available memory, some objects may be swapped to disk. The object IDs (EntryIDs) are saved to a file called SYS:_NETWARE\IDS.FIL.

Failure Recovery During Phase 2

To recover from a phase 2 failure, reboot the server to unlock the database.

Phase 3: Database Conversion

Phase 3 is the phase that actually converts the eDirectory database from a RECMAN database to a FLAIM database. All objects in the directory are extracted from the RECMAN database and added into the FLAIM database files.

Failure Recovery During Phase 3

If this stage fails, you may end up having to restore the DIB from a backup. Because of this, it is very important that you ensure that your database is archived before you start the migration. The quickest way to perform a backup of the entire database is to simply type **dsrepair –rc** at the server console (NetWare).

Phase 4: Migration File System Trustees

Phase 4 is the file system trustee migration phase. To prevent changes occurring during the migration, logins are disabled. All volumes that are to be migrated must be mounted and available. The process that occurs is that the file system is scanned for trustee assignments. The old object IDs that are in memory (or stored in the ids.fil file) are searched for the correlating ID on the file system. If one is located, the new ID for the object is resolved and written to the file system.

Failure Recovery During Phase 4

By the time you have reached phase 4, the database has already been updated to eDirectory 8.5. The only remaining step is to convert the file system trustee assignments. If this phase fails, you can simply restore the file system trustees from backup.

Be sure to back up the file system trustees before you start the migration. TRUSTBAR.NLM and TRUSTEE.NLM are the most popular tools used to back up file system trustee assignments. Both of these tools are available on the `http://support.novell.com` web site.

Phase 4.5: All Current Connections Are Cleared

Before the volumes can be remounted in phase 5, you must clear all current connections.

Failure Recovery During Phase 4.5

To recover from a failure, reboot the server. The migration should have already occurred.

Phase 5: Dismount and Remount Volumes

The volumes are remounted so that the new entries can be loaded into memory and the old entries are flushed.

Failure Recovery During Phase 5

Reboot the server to recover from a failure.

Migrating the DIB from NDS 8, eDirectory 8.5, eDirectory 8.6, or eDirectory 8.7 to eDirectory 8.7.3

eDirectory 8.7.3 (as well as all versions of eDirectory) has a built-in feature with DSLOADER.NLM. When DSLOADER loads (DSLOADER always loads first before DS), it checks the version of the DIB. If the version is older than the version stamped in DSLOADER (in our case, this would be eDirectory 8.7.3), DSLOADER automatically executes an upgrade routine. The upgrade routine does the following:

- Removes old attributes off of the Pseudo Server object.
- Adds new attributes to the Pseudo Server object.
- Updates the version.
- Makes several structural changes to the database.

The upgrade of the DIB is transparent to the end user. DSLOADER makes the changes on the fly and loads the database as the new eDirectory 8.7.3 version.

Note For the first eDirectory 8.7.3.x server added to the tree, through migration or as a new server installation, schema that supports eDirectory 8.7.3.x must first be added to the tree. During the installation program (either through a NetWare upgrade or through an eDirectory install/upgrade), schema is extended before DSLOADER can perform the migration.

Mixed-Environment Considerations

When you perform an NDS migration to eDirectory 8.7.3.x, you need to consider a few issues when dealing with environments that have older versions of NDS.

The NetWare 6.5 Deployment Manager (starting with SP1) has a feature that will check to make sure the tree contains the minimum versions of NDS 6.x and NDS 7.x. It is advisable that you execute the Deployment Manager before you add the first eDirectory 8.7.x into the tree or before you install NetWare 6.5 or OES for Linux for the first time.

Besides the obvious reason of obtaining the latest bug fixes, there are a couple of important reasons to upgrade to the latest patches:

- Loss of trustee assignments
- Unknown objects

Loss of Trustee Assignments

With legacy file systems, the local EntryID of an eDirectory object is written to a file or directory in the file system when a file system trustee assignment is made. This poses a problem with the NetWare clustering products. When a clustered server goes down, a failover occurs and a different server in the cluster takes on the identity of the original server. All servers within the cluster share the same file system, so the trustee assignments that are written to the file system remain. eDirectory is not cluster enabled. This means that the eDirectory database does not reside on the shared file system. The eDirectory database must reside on the local file system of the server that is running the eDirectory process. The end result is that when the failover occurs, a different instance of the replica is enabled on the new server with new EntryIDs for the objects in the replica.

For each given object, a separate EntryID is assigned for each replica of the object. Keep in mind that it is the EntryID that is written to the file system. When a failover occurs and a new replica of a partition is used for the new online server, all trustee assignments on the shared file system are not recognized because of the change in EntryIDs. To deal with this issue, NetWare 6 clustering provided a trustee migration utility that had to run on every failover. Depending on the number of trustee assignments, this could significantly impact the length of time it takes to bring a new server online after a failover is triggered.

Novell solved this issue in NetWare 6.5 with the introduction of NSS 3.0. With NSS 3.0, the object's GUID is written to the file system for the trustee assignment rather than the EntryID. The advantage to this approach is that the object's GUID is a unique number that is the same for a particular object regardless of the replica in which that object resides.

The problem with this new approach is that older versions of NDS 6.x that are installed on NetWare 4.x servers do not recognize or support GUIDs. To ensure that objects that reside on an NDS 6.x server maintain their trustee assignments when NetWare 6.5 or greater is introduced into the tree, all NDS 6.x servers must be upgraded to a version that supports GUIDs. NDS 6.21 or greater supports GUIDs. It is recommended, however, that you apply the latest public patches for NDS 6.x to all servers in the tree to take advantage of all defect fixes included in the latest patches.

Unknown Objects

With NDS 8, a new schema type called auxiliary classes was introduced. Auxiliary classes are not actually added to an effective schema class. Auxiliary classes are "extended" on an object or on a set of objects. When this occurs, all attributes that are defined on that auxiliary class is now available for the specific object or set of objects that have been extended with the auxiliary class.

Auxiliary class support was not added to NDS versions 6.x and 7.x. This poses a problem in that objects on NDS 8 or eDirectory 8.5 or greater that are extended with an auxiliary class are not able to synchronize with replicas of the same objects on NDS 6.x or NDS 7.x servers. To get around this problem, Novell built functionality into NDS 8 and eDirectory in which they check whether the object that is extended with an auxiliary class is being sent to an NDS 6.x or NDS 7.x server. If it is, then the NDS 8 or eDirectory agent removes the auxiliary class definition and places it into an auxiliary class compatibility attribute on the object. The agent then marks the object as "unknown" and sends it to the NDS 6.x or NDS 7.x server. If the NDS 8 or eDirectory server receives an "unknown" object from an NDS 6.x or NDS 7.x server, the local agent checks for the auxiliary class compatibility attribute. If the attribute is present, it extracts the auxiliary class information and places it back onto the object and removes the "unknown" type. This functionality allows an NDS 6.x and NDS 7.x server to reside in the same replica ring with an NDS 8 or eDirectory server without breaking synchronization.

This solution, however, does not come without problems. If the object that is extended with an auxiliary class is read through iManager, ConsoleOne, or any other directory management tool, the object will be read as an "unknown" object. As such, the management tools will not know what type of object it is displaying, so it will not be able to apply the applicable plug-in to that object. The end result is that the object cannot be managed when reading the object from NDS 7.x or NDS 8.x servers.

To get around this issue, NDS 6.x and NDS 7.x were updated. With the current releases of NDS 6.x and NDS 7.x, when any external utility requests that an object be read from these servers, the NDS agent checks for the auxiliary class compatibility attribute. If it finds the attribute, it converts the object back to its true form in memory and returns the valid "known" object to the requester. The end effect is that even though the object is still unknown in the database, the utilities that request to read the object see the object as a fully functional, known object.

Administration Options

With eDirectory 8.7.x, new ways of administration have been introduced. Also, some old ways of administering your NDS or eDirectory environment will no longer work. This section discusses the issues to be aware of when dealing with eDirectory administration.

NWAdmin

NWAdmin is an IPX- or IP-based tool that runs on a Microsoft Windows workstation. NWAdmin was the first tool that was developed by Novell to administer an NDS or eDirectory system. Although NWAdmin snap-ins are for the most part no longer being developed by Novell, some Novell applications still require the use of NWAdmin. Managing a BorderManager server and license management are some features that are not available through ConsoleOne. License management was added to iManager.

ConsoleOne

The latest versions of ConsoleOne are based off of JVM version 1.4.x. ConsoleOne will run on Microsoft Windows; NetWare; SLES 8 and 9; Red Hat 7, 8, and 9; AS 2.1 and 3.0; and Solaris 7, 8, and 9.

Novell is in the process of transitioning off of ConsoleOne. For most of the new products, such as the new features in Novell OES, only iManager plug-ins are being written. ConsoleOne is still supported with existing plug-ins, but new functionality is no longer being added to ConsoleOne.

The big product lines from Novell that do not have ConsoleOne plug-ins are BorderManager, Nsure Identity Manager 2 (formerly known as DirXML), Nsure Audit, latest LDAP snap-ins for eDirectory, and OES features such as Linux User Management LUM, etc.

iManager

Two versions of iManager are currently supported by Novell, namely, iManager 2.0.2 and iManager 2.5. Novell is writing new plug-ins only for iManager 2.5.

Note For more information about the product life cycle of all Novell products, see `http://support.novell.com/lifecycle/`.

iManager is a web-based product that has been built for seamless, cross-platform functionality. The biggest difference between iManager 2.0.2 and iManager 2.5 has to do with the framework. iManager 2.0.2 is dependent upon the Novell Extend Portal Services (NPS). iManager 2.5 is independent of NPS or eDirectory. It acts more like a true independent web application. For the most part, iManager 2.0.2 plug-ins work fine with iManager 2.5. For the exceptions, there are new iManager 2.5 plug-ins available on the Novell download site (`http://download.novell.com`).

Most all of the new products are manageable from within iManager. The exceptions are the following:

- GroupWise
- ZEN for Desktops 3.x
- ZEN for Servers
- iChain
- BorderManager
- File system management (file system trustees, viewing assigned rights, queue-based printing, etc.)

iManager is the future for Novell. It is recommended that, wherever possible, you use iManager 2.5 for your eDirectory management tool.

There are a few shortcomings with iManager 2.5 that you need to be aware of:

- iManager 2.5 cannot be used as a user portal for password self-management services. This was a feature that was available with iManager 2.0.2. iManager 2.5 can be used to administer password self-management, but you need to keep at least one iManager 2.0.2 server in your environment so that users can access their password self-management web page.
- iManager is IP-based. If you have servers that are exclusively IPX, iManager will not be able to manage them.
- iManager's partition and replica management plug-ins cannot be used if NDS 6.x is in the replica ring. In order for partition operations to be completed, all servers in the replica ring must be contacted. iManager uses new APIs to determine whether servers are available that are not supported if NDS 6.x (NetWare 4.x) is in the replica ring.

Protocol Considerations When Introducing Multiple Platforms

Because Linux, AIX, HP-UX, Solaris, Windows, and NetWare 6.x are all supported with eDirectory 8.7.x, the proprietary IPX protocol is becoming increasingly more obsolete. This can cause issues during a migration to eDirectory 8.7.x. This section points out most of the pitfalls involved with protocol issues.

The *nix platforms are becoming more and more popular as the platform of choice when using eDirectory. Novell just released a product called Open Enterprise Server (OES). The concept underlying OES is that the kernel is no longer a factor as far as an end user or administrator is concerned. In other words, regardless of whether you choose NetWare as your kernel or SLES 9 as your kernel, the administration tools, functionality, and product set are the same. Although this is good in concept, there are some differences.

OES ships NetWare 6.5 SP3 as the NetWare kernel solution. NetWare 6.5 supports both the IP and IPX protocols. So, you could bind both an IPX and an IP protocol to the same network interface card (NIC) and service both your IP-only servers and your IPX-only servers (such as NetWare 4.x). However, if you choose to deploy OES on SLES 9, you cannot bind the IPX protocol to the NIC and service both IPX and IP servers.

If you have a pure or mostly pure NetWare 4.x environment or you have NetWare servers that are set up to handle only IPX traffic, you will have eDirectory synchronization and access issues if you introduce eDirectory running on *nix platforms.

Before migrating your existing infrastructure, make sure that all servers migrated or introduced into the current environment have a way to communicate with all other servers within the same replica ring.

■ **Note** For name resolution and other tree walking requests, you may see problems if the server you are upgrading does not contain the entire tree and you have an IPX-only environment.

The best way to make sure that you do not run into protocol issues is to upgrade all IPX-only servers to a server platform that will support the IP protocol.

Important Although it is not recommended, you can upgrade to an IP-based platform only the server(s) that hold(s) the partition that contains the new or migrated server. However, if for whatever reason the eDirectory directory agent has to walk the tree, there may be conditions where communication fails and the request is denied.

PART 2

Administration

Part 2 of the eDirectory Field Guide addresses the day-to-day tasks you face when administering eDirectory. It does not give step-by-step procedures for various tasks in eDirectory. Rather, it provides you with real-life information that will assist you in performing the eDirectory administrative tasks successfully.

CHAPTER 4

Partition Operations

The following topics are covered in this chapter:

- Partition splits
  - Partition split best practices
  - Troubleshooting failed partition splits
- Partition merges
  - Partition merge best practices
  - Troubleshooting failed partition merges
- Move SubTree operations
  - Move SubTree best practices
  - Troubleshooting failed Move SubTree operations
- Tree merge
  - NetWare
  - Windows
  - Solaris, Linux, AIX, HPUX

Partition operations are the most complicated procedures in eDirectory. It is critical that you understand the procedure that takes place in each partition operation so that you can prepare the tree to successfully perform that operation.

Before proceeding further, it is important to establish some basic eDirectory terms. Consider the following:

- *Partition*: eDirectory has the ability to distribute different sections of the tree onto several servers. eDirectory accomplishes this by creating "partitions." A partition is a defined section of the tree.
- *Replica*: In order for partitions to be distributed to different servers, a replica of the partition is created and placed on one or more servers. The concept of replicas allows the partition, a collection of objects, to be duplicated on many servers for redundancy and to provide convenient access to the objects.
- *Partition boundary*: Partitions are defined by their topmost object in eDirectory. When a container (Tree Root, Organization, or Organizational Unit) has a partition root flag placed on it, the object becomes the partition boundary. All subordinate objects underneath the partition boundary are considered part of that partition until a subordinate container is assigned a partition root flag. The subordinate or child partition root boundary signifies the end of the parent partition.
- *Parent and child partitions*: All eDirectory trees always have at least one partition. The partition boundary is assigned to the Tree Root object. The [Root] partition is considered the topmost or parent partition. All partitions below [Root] are considered child partitions. Parent/child partition relationships are relative. Each child partition has one and only one direct parent partition. Each parent partition, with the exception of [Root], is a child partition to its direct parent partition.

Partition Splits

In eDirectory, the action of "creating a partition" is accomplished by splitting an existing partition into two partitions. The original partition boundary becomes the parent partition and the new partition boundary becomes the subordinate or child partition.

Three main tasks are performed by the eDirectory agent during a partition split:

- *Adds the partition flags and partition attributes to the new child partition root entry object*: The eDirectory agent places a partition root flag on the entry to specify a new partition boundary. In eDirectory, container objects are the only valid objects that can be partition boundary objects. Partition root objects require additional attributes that will be used for partition replication. A new partition root object is "extended" with an auxiliary class called "partition." This class allows partition-specific attributes to be assigned to the new partition root object.

Note The partition-specific attributes are Convergence, Partition Creation Time, Replica, Inherited ACL, Low Convergence Sync Interval, Received Up To, Synchronized Up To, Authority Revocation, Certificate Revocation, CA Private Key, CA Public Key, Cross Certificate Pair, Low Convergence Reset Time, High Convergence Sync Interval, Partition Control, Replica Up To, Partition Status, Transitive Vector, Purge Vector, Synchronization Tolerance, Obituary Notify, Local Received Up To, federationControl, syncPanePoint, syncWindowVector, authoritative, SAS:Security DN, masvLabel, and ndapPartition-PasswordMgmt.

- *Changes the partition ID*: The eDirectory agent changes the partition ID of all the subordinate objects underneath the new child partition to the EntryID of the child partition root object rather than to the EntryID of the old parent partition root object. For all partitions, other than subordinate reference partition boundaries, subordinate objects are assigned to that partition by simply changing the value in the partition ID field on the leaf entry object to point to the EntryID of the partition root object. When a child partition is created, the eDirectory agent changes the partition ID on the entry objects of all subordinate objects underneath that child partition.
- *Adds replicas*: The eDirectory agent adds a replica of the new child partition to all applicable servers. Any server that held a copy of the original parent partition is added to the replica ring of the child partition. The eDirectory agent on each replica adds the new partition record for the child partition and changes the partition ID on each subordinate entry to the new child partition.

Partition Split Best Practices

To ensure a successful partition split, do the following before you request the split:

- Run a treewide health check. NDS iMonitor provides a feature that allows you to evaluate the health of each server in the tree. As with any partition operation, time must be synchronized, communication between all applicable servers must be intact, schema must be synchronized, and replication with the affected partitions must be up to date. The treewide health check reports the status of these points of interest.

  To access the NDS iMonitor treewide health check, go to http://<*server address*>:<*httpstk port*>/nds/reportconfig. Click the Configure Report icon to the left of the Treewide report (see Figure 4-1).

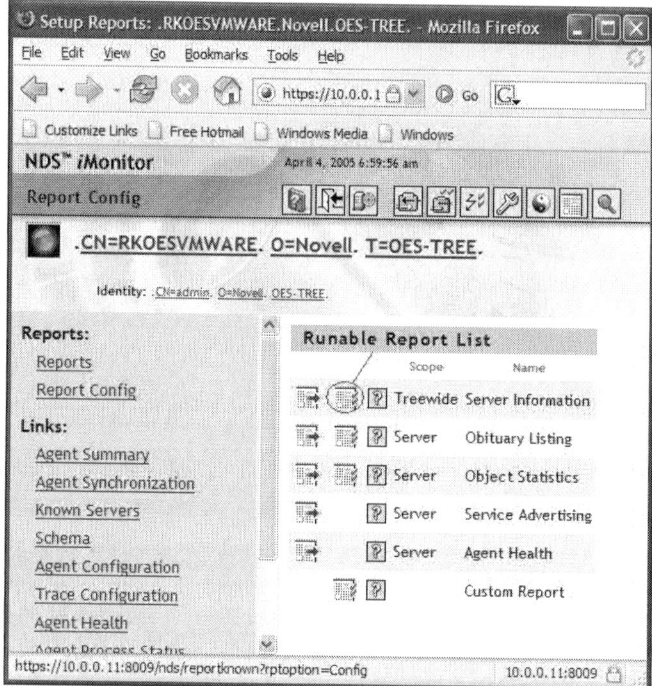

Figure 4-1. *Configure treewide report*

To decrease the amount of time that it takes to run the report, deselect the Health subreports. You need to resolve any error(s) that are listed in the resulting report, especially any errors that occur on the servers involved in the partition split.

■ **Note** If there are a lot of servers in the tree, the treewide health check may take a considerable amount of time to run. You can use DSREPAIR to verify that time is synchronized and replication is up to date with no errors on the servers involved in the partition split operation. A good practice would be to go to the master of the parent partition and run a Time Synchronization report as well as a Report Synchronization Status report from DSREPAIR.

- Make sure that the operating systems on all servers involved in the partition split are healthy. If a server is not communicating correctly, is out of memory, or is out of disk space, or if the processor is averaging over 90 percent utilization, the partition operation may be delayed or fail.

Troubleshooting Failed Partition Splits

The partition split operation should go through without issues if the health checks come back clean. However, if you forgot to run the health checks or the operating system on the servers involved in the partition split are not healthy, the partition operation may fail. Most failures occur because of health check problems.

Another factor that can complicate issues is replica rings that have older versions of NDS in the ring (i.e. NDS 6.x, NDS 7.x, NDS 8.x, etc). It is a good idea to upgrade all servers within the replica ring to the latest version of eDirectory (eDirectory 8.7.3.x). If this is not possible, ensure that at least the master of the partition that is being split is running eDirectory 8.7.3.x. eDirectory 8.7.3.x has several enhancements that will ensure successful partition operations. Since most of the partition operation is controlled by the master replica, having the latest version of eDirectory on that box will help significantly in ensuring a successful partition split.

If the partition split fails, don't panic and try to abort the operation. More issues can arise when incorrectly aborting a partition operation. Use DSTRACE at the console or in NDS iMonitor to watch the partition operation. The master replica of the original parent partition controls the operation. Run DSTRACE from the master server and search for errors. Select the following DSTRACE filters:

- + part (Partition)
- + misc (Miscellaneous)
- + lost (Lost Entries)
- + sync (Outbound Synchronization)

If troubleshooting DSTRACE errors does not resolve the issue, run a Report Synchronization Status report from DSREPAIR on the server holding the master of the parent partition (which is also the server that holds the master of the new child partition). Troubleshoot any replication errors.

If there are still issues, run a local repair against all servers involved in the partition split operation. If DSREPAIR does not solve the issue, you may need to cancel the operation. Use iManager or ConsoleOne to cancel the operation. If the operation has proceeded too far to safely abort the operation, iManager and ConsoleOne will not allow you to cancel it.

If all troubleshooting steps suggested thus far have failed, it is advisable that you call Novell Technical Support for assistance. You need to understand the ramifications of your actions when choosing the approach to cancel the operation. This should be an extremely rare condition. Typically, if you resolve the errors that are preventing the successful partition operation, the partition operation will continue to completion.

Partition Merges

The partition merge operation works exactly the opposite of the partition split. The root most partition boundary becomes the partition boundary, and the child partition boundary is simply removed. The child partition root entry is stripped of all partition information and becomes a regular container object that resides underneath the parent partition.

Three main tasks are performed by the eDirectory agent during a partition merge:

- Removes the partition flags and partition attributes of the child partition root entry object. The eDirectory agent also removes the partition auxiliary class from the child partition root entry object and removes all partition values.

Note The partition-specific attributes are Convergence, Partition Creation Time, Replica, Inherited ACL, Low Convergence Sync Interval, Received Up To, Synchronized Up To, Authority Revocation, Certificate Revocation, CA Private Key, CA Public Key, Cross Certificate Pair, Low Convergence Reset Time, High Convergence Sync Interval, Partition Control, Replica Up To, Partition Status, Transitive Vector, Purge Vector, Synchronization Tolerance, Obituary Notify, Local Received Up To, federationControl, syncPanePoint, syncWindowVector, authoritative, SAS:Security DN, masvLabel, and ndapPartition-PasswordMgmt.

- Changes the partition ID of all the subordinate objects underneath the old child partition to the EntryID of the parent partition root entry object.
- Replicates the change to all replicas of the child and parent partition.

Partition Merge Best Practices

To ensure a successful partition merge, do the following:

1. Run a treewide health check. NDS iMonitor provides a feature that allows you to evaluate the health of each server in the tree. As with any partition operation, time must be synchronized, communication between all applicable servers must be intact, schema must be synchronized, and replication with the affected partitions must be up to date. The treewide health check reports the status of these points of interest.

a. To access the NDS iMonitor treewide health check, go to http://*<server address>*:*<httpstk port>*/nds/reportconfig. Click the Configure Report icon to the left of the Treewide report (refer to Figure 4-1).

b. To decrease the amount of time that it takes to run the report, deselect the Health subreports. You need to resolve any error(s) that are listed in the resulting report, especially any errors that occur on the servers involved in the partition merge.

Note If there are a lot of servers in the tree, the treewide health check may take a considerable amount of time to run. You can use DSREPAIR to verify that time is synchronized and replication is up to date with no errors on the servers involved in the partition split operation. A good practice would be to go to the master of the parent partition and run a Time Synchronization report as well as a Report Synchronization Status report from DSREPAIR.

---

2. Write down all servers that will be involved in the partition merge:
   - All servers in the parent partition replica ring
   - All servers in the child partition replica ring

Note The best way to determine what servers will be involved in the merge is to identify the servers listed in the Backlink attribute that resides on the partition root object. The best way to view the Backlink attribute is through NDS iMonitor.

---

3. Make sure that the master of the parent and child partitions can communicate with all servers in the list generated in Step 2.

Note A quick way to verify communication is by performing a Repair Selected Server's Network Address from DSREPAIR on the master of the source partition.

WHAT IS A SUBORDINATE REFERENCE?

In order for eDirectory to walk down the tree to child partitions, the eDirectory agent needs a way to quickly determine where the next child partition boundary object resides. Due to eDirectory's distributed nature, the entire tree does not have to be contained on every server. Replicas of different partitions can be located on one or many different servers in the tree. Because the next child partition may not reside on the local server, the eDirectory agent needs a way to determine whether another server holds a partition that it does not know about. eDirectory uses the subordinate reference partition types to fulfill this need.

A subordinate reference object is automatically created on the local server if a parent partition resides on that local server but the child partition does not. The subordinate reference object is a partition root object that contains all the attributes of a regular partition. The difference is that all the subordinate objects underneath the subordinate reference object are not real objects; they are external reference objects that reside in the external reference partition. When the eDirectory agent needs to walk down the tree by partitions, it identifies the next partition root object. If that object is a subordinate reference object, it finds the Replica attribute on that object. The Replica attribute contains network addresses and names of all real copies of the partition. The local eDirectory agent selects one of these addresses and creates a connection to the remote server. The remote server can then continue to walk down the tree until the desired information is obtained.

4. Avoid making the partition merge operation have to add subordinate reference replicas. If replicas of the child partition do not exist, you need to create subordinate references in the child partition. To avoid the additional complexity during a partition merge operation, add replicas prior to the partition merge operation. The replica rings for the parent partition and child partition should be identical. There should not be any subordinate references in any of the replica rings.

5. Try to reduce the number of servers in the replica rings on all three affected partitions. The fewer servers involved in the move, the less potential for problems.

6. The NCP server object that holds the master of the source partition should not reside in the source partition. If the NCP server object of the server that holds the master of the source partition resides in the source partition, you should change one of the read/write replicas that does not reside in the source partition to master. Remember that the master of the source partition initiates the move and completes the move. If the NCP server object is being moved, timing scenarios can occur in which there is a temporary loss of communication as the NCP server object is being moved. If this occurs, stuck conditions could arise.

Note You can change a read/write replica to master through ConsoleOne, iManager, or DSREPAIR. For more information on how to perform this operation, refer to the *eDirectory Administration Guide.*

7. Try to make sure that at least the master of each partition that is affected in the Move SubTree operation is running eDirectory 8.7.x. There are many enhancements and bug fixes dealing with partition operations that will help with a successful move if the master is running the current versions of eDirectory. If at all possible, all servers in the replica rings should be on the latest version of eDirectory, but this is not as important as having the master on eDirectory 8.7.x.
8. Make sure that the operating system on all servers involved in the partition merge are healthy. If a server is not communicating correctly, is out of memory, or is out of disk space, or if the processor is averaging over 90 percent utilization, the partition operation may be delayed or fail.

Troubleshooting Failed Partition Merges

If the partition merge fails, don't panic and try to abort the operation. More issues can arise when incorrectly aborting a partition operation. Use DSTRACE at the console or in NDS iMonitor to watch the partition operation. The master replica of the original parent partition controls the operation. Run DSTRACE from the master server and search for errors. Select the following DSTRACE filters:

- + part (Partition)
- + misc (Miscellaneous)
- + lost (Lost Entries)
- + sync (Outbound Synchronization)

If troubleshooting DSTRACE errors does not resolve the issue, run a Report Synchronization Status report from DSREPAIR on the server holding the master of the parent partition (which is also the server that holds the master of the new child partition). Troubleshoot any replication errors.

If there are still issues, run a local repair against all servers involved in the partition split operation. If DSREPAIR does not solve the issue, you may need to cancel the operation. Use iManager or ConsoleOne to cancel the operation. If the operation has proceeded too far to safely abort the operation, iManager and ConsoleOne will not allow you to cancel it.

If all troubleshooting suggested thus far has failed, it is advisable that you call Novell Technical Support for assistance. You need to understand the ramifications of your actions when choosing the approach to cancel the operation. This should be an extremely rare condition. Typically, if you resolve the errors that are preventing the successful partition operation, the partition operation will continue to completion.

Move SubTree Operations

The Move SubTree operation is a useful feature in eDirectory. It allows you to move entire partitions from one area in a tree to another. Move SubTree is the most complicated partition operation within eDirectory. In the past, Move SubTree operations were "buggy," which caused many failed Move SubTree operations. Fortunately, eDirectory 8.7.x has no outstanding issues with Move SubTree. However, like any operation, if your tree is not healthy, the Move SubTree request may still fail.

To perform a Move SubTree operation, you simply go into ConsoleOne or iManager, highlight the partition root entry of the partition you want to move, and request a move object. If the object that you select is not a partition root entry, but rather is a container object, the request will be denied. If the object that you select is not a partition root entry and is not a container object, then the single object is simply moved. If the object that you select is a partition root entry, then all objects within that partition are also moved.

The following are some terms that you need to be familiar with to follow the discussion of the Move SubTree operations:

- *Source partition*: This is the actual partition root entry object as well as all subordinates that are within the said partition's boundary that are being moved.
- *Source parent partition*: This is the original parent root partition entry object to the source partition.
- *Target parent partition*: The source partition will become a child partition of the first partition boundary in the new location as you walk up the tree. The first partition boundary root object is the new target parent partition.

The high-level steps that occur during a Move SubTree operation are as follows:

1. All replica states are checked in the replica rings of the source partition, source parent partition, and target parent partition. If all replicas are not in an "On" state or the servers cannot be contacted, the requested Move SubTree operation is aborted and an error is returned.

2. A lock is placed on the source parent partition. The lock ensures that no other partition operations occur while the Move SubTree is in place.
3. The target parent partition master sets its replica state and the partition state to a Move State 0.
4. The source partition master sets its replica and partition state to a Move State 0.
5. The source partition master makes a list of all servers that will be involved in the move. This includes any servers in the Backlink attribute on the partition root entry, as well as any servers that hold a replica of the source partition.
6. The source partition master creates a Move Tree obituary attribute and synchronizes it to every server derived in Step 5.
7. The source partition master checks to see if there are any child partitions in its new location. If there are child partitions, and any server that holds a replica of the source partition does not hold a replica of the child partitions, subordinate references are created for those servers by the eDirectory agent.
8. The parent partition ID value on the source partition root entry object is set to the ID of the new parent partition ID.
9. All Move Tree obituaries are moved to a Purgeable state (4) and all locks are cleared.
10. All replicas and partitions are changed to an "On" state.

Move SubTree Best Practices

To ensure a successful Move SubTree operation, perform Task 4-1.

Task 4-1. Ensuring a Successful Move SubTree

1. Perform a complete health check, verifying time synchronization and partition replication on the source partition, source parent partition, target parent partition, and child partition of the source partition's new location (if there is one).
2. Write down all servers that will be involved in the Move SubTree operation:
    - All servers in the source partition replica ring
    - All servers in the target parent partition replica ring
    - All servers listed in the Backlink attribute (best viewed through NDS iMonitor) on the partition root object of the server that holds the master replica of the source partition

3. Make sure that the master of the source partition can communicate with all servers in the list generated in Step 2. (A quick way to verify communication is by performing a Repair Selected Server's Network Address from DSREPAIR on the master of the source partition.)
4. Avoid making the Move SubTree operation have to add subordinate reference replicas. If replicas of the source child partitions do not exist, you need to create subordinate references in the child partitions. To avoid the additional complexity during a Move SubTree operation, add replicas prior to the Move SubTree operation. The replica rings for the source parent partition, source partition, and target parent partition should be identical. There should not be any subordinate references in any of the replica rings. (See the sidebar "What Is a Subordinate Reference?" earlier in the chapter for more information about subordinate references.)
5. Try to reduce the number of servers in the replica rings on all three affected partitions. The fewer servers involved in the move, the less potential for problems.
6. The NCP server object that holds the master of the source partition should not reside in the source partition. If the NCP server object of the server that holds the master of the source partition resides in the source partition, you should change one of the read/write replicas that does not reside in the source partition to master. Remember that the master of the source partition initiates the move and completes the move. If the NCP server object is being moved, timing scenarios can occur in which there is a temporary loss of communication as the NCP server object is being moved. If this occurs, stuck conditions could arise.
7. Try to make sure that at least the master of each partition that is affected in the Move SubTree operation is running eDirectory 8.7.x. There are many enhancements and bug fixes dealing with partition operations that will help with a successful move if the master is running the current versions of eDirectory. If at all possible, all servers in the replica rings should be on the latest version of eDirectory, but this is not as important as having the master on eDirectory 8.7.x.

Troubleshooting Failed Move SubTree Operations

If the Move SubTree operation fails, don't panic and try to abort the operation. More issues can arise when incorrectly aborting a partition operation. Use DSTRACE at the console or in NDS iMonitor to watch the partition operation. The master replica of the original parent partition controls the operation. Run DSTRACE from the master server and search for errors. Select the following DSTRACE filters:

- + part (Partition)
- + misc (Miscellaneous)
- + lost (Lost Entries)
- + sync (Outbound Synchronization)

If troubleshooting DSTRACE errors does not resolve the issue, run a Report Synchronization Status report from DSREPAIR on the server holding the master of the parent partition (which is also the server that holds the master of the new child partition). Troubleshoot any replication errors.

If there are still issues, run a local repair against all servers involved in the partition split operation. If DSREPAIR does not solve the issue, you may need to cancel the operation. Use iManager or ConsoleOne to cancel the operation. If the operation has proceeded too far to safely abort the operation, iManager and ConsoleOne will not allow you to cancel it.

If all troubleshooting suggested thus far has failed, it is advisable that you call Novell Technical Support for assistance. You need to understand the ramifications of your actions when choosing the approach to cancel the operation. This should be an extremely rare condition. Typically, if you resolve the errors that are preventing the successful partition operation, the partition operation will continue to completion.

Tree Merge

DSMERGE is a tool that is included in eDirectory on all supported platforms. DSMERGE enables you to merge one tree (source tree) into another tree (target tree), resulting in one tree.

With eDirectory 8.7.3.x, seven main prerequisites need to be in place before DSMERGE will allow a tree merge to take place:

- Schema must be identical in both trees. Because objects from both trees will reside in one tree after the merge, and because schema is tree wide, before the two trees can be merged, both trees need to have all schema. The best way to accomplish this is to use DSREPAIR. Under Advanced Options ➤ Global Schema Operations, you would choose the Import Remote Schema option. You would need to do this from the master of the [Root] partition from both trees, specifying each other as the remote tree.

Note On the Linux, Solaris, AIX, and HPUX platforms, you must have SLP correctly configured for both servers that hold the master of [Root] in both trees. If you do not want to use SLP in your environment, you can use a hosts.nds file to specify a server that holds the master of [Root]. In the hosts.nds file, you need to list both the source and the target tree. The hosts.nds file should reside in the /etc directory in both the source and target server. On NetWare and Windows, if SLP is not configured, you can specify an IP address rather than a tree name.

- There can be only one server in the replica ring of the [Root] partition on both the target and the source tree. If more than one server exists in the replica ring of [Root], many complications arise. Thus, to prevent failures, DSMERGE will not allow you to merge two trees if more than one server is in the replica ring of the [Root] partition.
- The Organization (the "o") object must not have the same name in both trees. For example, if the source *and* the target tree both had an Organization object named o=novell, the tree merge would fail. The reason for this is that the Organization object from the source tree is added as an Organization object in the target tree. In eDirectory, you cannot have two objects in the same container with the same name.
- Time must be synchronized between the two servers that hold the master of [Root] in both trees. Time synchronization does not depend on eDirectory tree boundaries. You can configure both servers to be in the same time synchronization boundary. The servers' time must be synchronized before the merge can take place.
- The server holding the master of [Root] in both trees needs to be running eDirectory 8.7.3.x.
- The Security container should be removed from the source tree before the merge begins.
- All leaf objects in the source [Root] partition should be removed. During the merge, only the Organization objects are consumed. Because the [Root] partition in the source tree will be deleted, the leaf objects will not be retained. If you want to maintain these leaf objects, move them before you start the merge.

When the prerequisites are met, DSMERGE will merge the two trees. The following process is executed by DSMERGE:

1. A schema compare is executed to make sure that schema is identical between the two trees. If it is not, the operation is aborted.
2. The [Root] partition replica ring is checked on both the target and source server to verify that there is only one server in the replica ring. If more than one is present, the operation is aborted.
3. A time check is made to verify that the servers' time is synchronized. If it is not synchronized, the operation is aborted.
4. All Organization ("o") objects that are in the source tree become partition boundaries. In other words, the [Root] partition performs a partition split and the "o" becomes the child partition.
5. All copies of the [Root] partition are removed from the source tree.
6. A copy of the [Root] partition from the target tree is added to the server that held a copy of the [Root] partition of the source tree.
7. The tree name is changed on all servers in the source tree to the target tree name.

The end result of the preceding procedure is that the server that held the master of the [Root] partition on the source server now holds a replica of the [Root] object of the target tree. The source server will also hold subordinate references of all child partitions that reside under the [Root] partition of the target tree. The source server will hold a replica of its original "o" partition. The target server will hold an external reference of the source server's "o" and a real copy of its own "o".

If you do not want to have two Organization objects in your tree, you can partition off the organizational units underneath one of the "o"s and perform a Move SubTree operation to redesign your tree.

After the merge is complete, the security components on the source servers need to be updated. The user certificates, KMO objects, SAS objects, etc., are now invalid. To re-create these objects, perform the steps that follow for your specific operating system.

NetWare

1. Run **pkidiag** from the server console on every server that was in the source tree.
2. Delete all user certificates and re-create them.

Windows

1. Delete the SAS object for all servers that were in the source tree.
2. Delete the KMO object for each server that was in the source tree.

Solaris, Linux, AIX, HPUX

1. Delete the SAS object and KMO object associated with each server that was in the source tree.
2. Run **ndsconfig add –m SAS** on each server that was in the source tree.

CHAPTER 5

Backup and Restore Operations

The following topics are covered in this chapter:

- Types of backup options
  - Hot continuous backup (Backup eMTool)
  - Directory backup and restore in NWCONFIG
  - DIB backup through DSREPAIR
  - NDSBackup
  - TSA backup
  - File copy
  - DIBClone
- Backup and restore strategies
- Using hot continuous backup
  - The backup file header
  - Roll-forward logging
  - Using iManager to configure and perform backup and restore
- Backing up the security infrastructure

eDirectory has built-in fault tolerance. Because eDirectory is a multi-master directory, any read/write replica can become the master replica and distribute replicas to other servers. So, if a server fails because of a hardware problem or for any other reason, the eDirectory information can be re-sent from another server that holds a replica of the same data to the failed server after the failure has been resolved.

Even though eDirectory has built-in fault tolerance, it is a good idea to back up the eDirectory database on each server, especially if the server contains replicas of very large partitions. With large partitions, or a large number of objects broken up into many partitions, it will take a while to replicate all of the objects back to the server that failed. If you have made a backup of the local database, the backup can be restored fairly quickly, leading to less down time.

Types of Backup Options

There are several ways to back up the eDirectory database. Some of the methods are platform specific. This section covers the different backup methods and makes recommendations on which one to use and when to use it.

Hot Continuous Backup (Backup eMTool)

The Novell eDirectory Backup eMTool (hot continuous backup) is designed to give you a complete backup and restore solution of the database and associated files on an individual server. The eMTool will verify the state of other servers in the tree that hold replicas of the same partitions that the "bad" server held and will restore the replicas to the current state on the server that went down. The eMTool does this by restoring the last full backup and incremental backups taken and then re-executing any transactions that occurred after the last backup.

Advantages

- Same tool is used for all platforms.
- Backs up the database with the directory agent still running.
- Restores very quickly, for minimal down time.
- Provides remote task-management support, so you don't have to be at the server to use it.
- Supports unattended backups through scripts.
- Maintains partition boundary information.

■ **Note** For detailed information on the eMBox Backup tool, see "Backing Up and Restoring Novell eDirectory" in the *Novell eDirectory 8.7.3 Administration Guide*, at `http://www.novell.com/documentation/edir873/edir873/data/a2n4mb6.html`.

Disadvantages

- It is not very useful for a multiple-server outage. The exception to this is that if the whole tree is wiped out, one box can be restored with the entire tree and then eDirectory replication can be used to rebuild the other servers.
- Does not back up file system information.
- Roll-forward logs (RFLs) store all of the updated transactions, which can take up a lot of disk space.
- Does not support single-object backup or restore.

Directory Backup and Restore in NWCONFIG

This option is used for hardware upgrades. The migration utility in NetWare uses this method to back up an eDirectory database and move it to another server during the migration process.

Advantages

- Quick and efficient way to back up the database for hardware upgrades.

■ Note For more information on backup and restore options in NWCONFIG, see `http://support.novell.com/cgi-bin/search/searchtid.cgi?/10014282.htm`.

- Built into the eDirectory agent. No additional configuration is required.

Disadvantages

- Only available on NetWare.
- Does not back up the file system.
- Very rigid on restore. It is important that nothing is changed in the existing tree between backup and restore.
- Will lock the current database.

DIB Backup Through DSREPAIR

DSREPAIR has an option to back up the eDirectory database (creating an eDirectory archive).

Advantages

- Is quick and efficient.
- Can be automated.

Disadvantages

- Does not back up file system information.
- Only available on NetWare.
- No restore option is available through the product. Novell NTS must be used to restore the database.
- Most of the time, after the database is restored, all replicas must be removed and re-added to ensure data integrity across all replicas of the given partitions.
- Does not back up file system information.

NDSBackup

NDSBackup is a *nix (Linux, Solaris, HP-UX, AIX) solution. It is a powerful tool that allows the backup of a database with the NDSD process active or inactive.

■ **Note** For more information about NDSBackup, see `http://www.novell.com/documentation/edir873/edir873/data/a2n4mbo.html#advslf6`.

Advantages

- Allows for selective backup and restore.
- Can be scripted to run in unattended mode.

Disadvantages

- Only available on *nix platforms.
- Does not save partition information.

- If restoring, all other copies of the objects being restored must be removed from the other servers. The reason for this is that the object information is saved but the EntryIDs are not. On restore, a new object with the same name and information is created. If other copies of the old object are still present, collision renames will occur because you will have two objects with the same name but different creation time stamps.
- Does not back up file system information.

TSA Backup

Novell eDirectory provides APIs that will allow a TSA-enabled backup vendor to capture eDirectory data and store it on tape.

Advantages

- File system–specific data can be backed up.
- It allows for selective backup and restore.
- It can be scripted to run in unattended mode.

Disadvantages

- Only available for Windows and NetWare.
- Does not save partition information.
- If restoring, all other copies of the objects being restored must be removed from the other servers. The reason for this is that the object information is saved but the EntryIDs are not. On restore, a new object with the same name and information is created. If other copies of the old object are still present, collision renames will occur because you will have two objects with the same name but different creation time stamps.
- Requires a third-party TSA backup application.

File Copy

The Novell eDirectory database files can be copied to another server or directory for redundancy. If a server goes down, they can be copied back to the default location as a restore option.

Advantages

- Is quick and efficient.
- Can be automated.

Disadvantages

- Does not back up file system information.
- If a server fails, when new hardware is put in place, make sure that the server maintains the same name and addresses as it did before the crash.
- Most of the time, after the database is restored, all replicas must be removed and re-added to ensure data integrity across all replicas of the given partitions.

■ **Important** Do not restore the database unless you have experience doing so. You can create conditions where the entire partition with all of its replicas will no longer synchronize. It is highly recommended that you contact Novell NTS before executing this restore procedure.

DIBClone

DIBClone enables you to replicate an entire server with all of its partitions to another server. You do this simply by adding the new server's NCP server object into eDirectory and adding the new server to the replica ring and transitive vectors. The DIB from the original server is copied to the target server. The target server makes some modifications on bootup so that the DIB belongs to the target server rather than the source server. The result is that you now have two servers with the same partitions without having to replicate the objects over the wire.

Advantages

- Very fast way to replicate a server.
- Great for large-scale environments.

Disadvantages

- Must have another server with all of the partitions to make a copy.
- Only restores the NCP server object, so it is not a completely fault-tolerant solution. You would need to reinstall all the components, such as SAS, HTTP, LDAP, NMAS, etc.

Backup and Restore Strategies

The reason that there are several backup and restore options for eDirectory is that the disaster-recovery requirements change in each business environment. Your task is to determine which solution works best for you. To help you make that determination, this section provides some points of consideration and describes which backup and restore solution works best for each business case scenario. Review the different areas of interest and determine the best backup strategy for your environment.

The following are some backup and restore considerations, each of which is described in turn in the sections that follow:

- Automated backups
- No data loss
- Remote capabilities
- No additional configuration requirements after restore
- Size of the DIB in eDirectory
- Partitioning considerations
- Selective restore requirements
- File system considerations
- Multiple-server restore strategies

Automated Backup

If you want to automate your backups, the following options are available:

- *Partition replication*: By default, eDirectory replicates all data to all servers in a given replica ring. It is important in these cases to make sure that there are adequate copies of the partition. You should have at least three copies of any partition. Furthermore, one of those copies should be located at a different site in case of a loss of an entire site.
- *Hot continuous backup*: The Backup eMBox tool allows you to run backups in batch mode. Depending on the operating system, you can write a script with the command-line options. Also depending on the operating system, you can use automated applications like CRON to launch the script at different times of the day, week, month, or year.

Tip See `http://www.novell.com/documentation/edir873/edir873/data/agatd4y.html` for more information on backup options with the eMBox client.

- *DIB Backup through DSREPAIR*: DSREPAIR has command-line options in NetWare. Running the DSREPAIR –RC command will automatically execute a backup of the eDirectory database. This command can be written to an NCF file and executed in intervals using CRON.
- *NDSBackup*: NDSBackup is a command-line utility for Linux/Unix platforms. For more information on the available options, see the man pages for NDSBackup (type **man ndsbackup** from a Linux or Unix console). You can write a script with the desired options for NDSBackup. You can then automate execution of the script with applications like CRON.
- *TSA backup*: This option is vendor specific. Many TSA backup vendors provide automated procedures for backing up eDirectory.

No Data Loss

The sensitivity of lost data must be considered. If preventing data loss is extremely important to you because of the uniqueness or sensitivity of the data, you should put in place additional measures to prevent data loss. In the case of high data availability, the following backup and restore options are recommended:

- *Partition replication*: By default, eDirectory replicates all data to all servers in a given replica ring. It is important in these cases to make sure that there are adequate copies of the partition. You should have at least three copies of any partition. Furthermore, one of those copies should be located at a different site in case of a loss of an entire site.
- *Hot continuous backup*: Make sure that roll-forward logging is turned on so that all data is recovered.

Tip For more information on roll-forward logging, please see `http://www.novell.com/documentation/edir873/edir873/data/agavcur.html`.

- *File system trustee backup*: If file system trustees are critical, they should be backed up separately.
- *Security infrastructure backup*: If user certificates, trusted root containers, SSL connections, etc. are being used and are critical, you should back up the Certificate Authority Container object and the W0 object. For more information, see the following Novell resources:

- *Server keys*: See `http://support.novell.com/cgi-bin/search/searchtid.cgi?/10066559.htm` for information on and the location of NICI files for each platform.
- *Certificate Authority object*: See `http://support.novell.com/cgi-bin/search/searchtid.cgi?/10065921.htm` for information on the Certificate Authority object.
- *Tree key information*: See `http://support.novell.com/cgi-bin/search/searchtid.cgi?/10064202.htm` for information on how to manage the tree key.

Remote Capabilities

The following backup and restore options are available remotely:

- *Hot continuous backup*: Novell iManager enables you to execute the backup and restore options remotely. For more information, see `http://www.novell.com/documentation/edir873/edir873/data/af37xzc.html`.
- *TSA backup*: Depending on the vendor, the TSA backup option will allow you to do remote backup and restore operations.

No Additional Configuration Requirements After Restore

The following backup option should be used if you do not require additional configuration after the restore of the eDirectory database:

- *Hot continuous backup*: Hot continuous backup enables you to restore a server to the exact state it was in before it went down. The exception to this would be file system trustee assignments.

Size of the DIB in eDirectory

If the size of the DIB is large—2 to 3GB or greater—some backup and restore operations can take a while. Partition replication, TSA backup, etc. may not be the best options. The following is recommended in these cases:

- *Hot continuous backup*: This option is highly scalable. Novell testing has shown isolated cases where a 20GB database can be backed up in 10 minutes and restored in 15 minutes.

■ Important Because many variables will affect performance, your testing results may vary from those reported in the tests conducted by Novell.

- *DIBClone*: DIBClone was designed to duplicate a very large database quickly. In testing conducted by Novell, a 100-million-object tree was cloned on a second server in just a few hours.
- *NDSBackup*: This option could be a good solution if only part of the database is critical. A selective backup and restore could be performed using NDSBackup to save only the critical, irreplaceable data.

Partitioning Considerations

If your tree has extensive partitioning, TSA backup and NDSBackup are probably not good options. The reason for this is that those options do not save partition configurations. After a restore with TSA backup or NDS-Backup, all partitioning would have to be reconfigured, which could be very time consuming and costly. The following options should be considered if partitioning is a factor:

- Hot continuous backup
- DIBClone
- DIB backup through DSREPAIR

Selective Restore Requirements

The following options allow for selective restore:

- NDSBackup
- TSA backup (dependent on the third-party TSA solution)

File System Considerations

Most of the backup options do not back up the file system–specific information. The following options are available:

- TSA backup (dependent on the third-party TSA solution)
- File system trustee backup

Multiple-Server Restore Strategies

If multiple servers fail, typical backup and restore options may not apply. The purpose of this section is to recommend some disaster-recovery options to consider:

- *Hot continuous backup*: This option was designed to restore a single-server failure. The nature of this restore is to re-execute all changes made to eDirectory on the given server since the last backup of the database. If multiple servers are involved with the same changes, determining which server to restore first and how to synchronize the data can become very complex. If multiple servers fail at the same time and you are using hot continuous backup, Novell recommends restoring without verification a server that holds common replicas and restoring all other servers as external reference objects. For more information on these procedures, see `http://www.novell.com/documentation/edir873/edir873/data/agm7hq7.html`.
- *TSA backup*: This is a good option for a treewide disaster recovery. The TSA backup software allows the whole tree to be backed up to tape. The entire tree would be restored to one server. eDirectory partitions would be removed from all other servers in the tree. Partition boundaries would be re-established and then replicated to all servers in the tree.
- *NDSBackup*: With NDSBackup, a procedure similar to the one described in the preceding TSA backup option would be used.

Best Practice Recommendations

It is wise to use multiple backup strategies to ensure minimal data loss in case of hardware failure. It is also wise to ensure proper tree design and partition replication as the default method of backup and restore.

Tip For more information on Novell eDirectory replication, see `http://www.novell.com/documentation/edir873/edir873/data/a2iiie1.html`.

Secondarily, hot continuous backup is a great option for server-to-server backup and restore. It enables you to back up and restore a server to its exact state before the failure.

Although hot continuous backup is a great option, a wise administrator would not be satisfied with a potential single point of failure. There is always a chance that the hot continuous backup information could also be lost. For that reason, it is wise to also keep a reasonably current snapshot of the database. The frequency of this will vary, depending on the amount of changes that are taking place in the tree and the criticality of the data. Use options like the following to make sure a reasonably current version of the database is maintained:

- DIB backup through DSREPAIR
- File copy
- Export to an LDIF file
- NDSBackup

These backups should be stored off of the server on secondary media and possibly even offsite to ensure high availability in the case of a disaster.

Using Hot Continuous Backup

eDirectory ships with a Java-based toolbox called eDirectory Management Toolbox (eMBox). This Java client can access tools called eMTools. A very powerful and flexible eMTool called Backup is included. The Backup eMTool can be used to perform hot continuous backup. In most cases, it is recommended to use the hot continuous backup solution over the other backup solutions described in this chapter. Therefore, I will spend some time talking about how to configure and use the Backup eMTool.

■ **Note** For an exhaustive description of how to use this tool, please refer to the *eDirectory Administration Guide* at `http://www.novell.com/documentation`.

The following files are the primary files used for hot continuous backup solutions:

- *backuptl*: This file provides the user interfaces. It connects into the library backupcr. This file can be accessed by the eMBox Client by calling "backup" or by using the iManager eDirectory Maintenance backup and restore plug-in.
- *backupcr*: This is the core library that performs the actual backup and restore. It is called through the backuptl interface.

The Backup eMTool backs up the entire eDirectory database and stores it in an encrypted file. The filename is specified when you initiate the backup. eDirectory also provides a feature called *roll-forward logging* (see the section "Roll-Forward Logging" later in the chapter). This is a true database transactional backup. All modifications to the directory are stored in roll-forward logs (RFLs). The Backup eMTool has the ability to restore the backup, which is a snapshot in time, and then re-execute all of the modification transactions that are stored in the RFLs, putting the DIB back into the exact state before the failure that triggered the need to restore the database.

The Backup File Header

The backup file that is created is stored in an XML format. The Document Type Definition (DTD) is included at the beginning of the backup file. There is a lot of good information stored in the DTD that you can use to determine which backup file you are looking at. Refer to Table 5-1 for information about the data stored in the DTD.

Table 5-1. *The DTD*

Field	Description
backup version	Identifies the version of the backup tool that was used to perform the backup.
backup_type	Specifies whether the backup was incremental or a full backup.
idtag	Identifies the ID of the backup. The ID is a GUID that is based off of the time stamp when the backup was taken.
time	Stores the date and time when the backup was taken.
srvname	Identifies the Distinguished Name (DN) of the server that was backed up.
dsversion	Indicates the eDirectory version of the server that was backed up.
compression	Specifies whether or not the backup was compressed.
os	Records the operating system that eDirectory is running on. It is recommended that you restore the backup on the same operating system that it was backed up from.
current_log	Specifies the first RFL that the backup is expecting. This field helps you to identify which RFLs you need to restore a complete backup.
number_of_files	Indicates the number of files in this backup set. This value will only be set on the first file. One of the variables you can set is the backup file size. If you choose this option, you could potentially have more than one backup file.

Continued

Table 5-1. *Continued*

Field	Description
backup_file	Provides the full path and name of the backup file. If your backup spans multiple files, this field contains the name as well as a number indicating its order in the backup file set.
incremental_file_id	Identifies the file ID if the backup is incremental.
next_inc_file_id	Indicates the file ID of the next backup file if the backup is an incremental backup.
replica_partition_DN	Specifies the DN of each partition root entry that resides on this server. This is helpful to identify which partitions reside on this server.
modification_time	Lists the Transitive Vector value for this server at the time of the backup. This value is used by the restore process to ensure replication consistency after a restore. The values are stored in hexadecimal. The Transitive Vector value contains the number of seconds since January 1, 1970, as well as the replica number and event; for example, CB708641_r1_e1.
replica_type	Lists the replica type for each value in the replica_partition_DN field.
replica_state	Lists the replica state for each value in the replica_partition_DN field.
file_size	Indicates the file size of any files that are user files included in the backup.
file_name	Specifies the name and location of any user-included files.
file_encoding	Lists the algorithm used to encode the specified user-included file.
file_type	Lists the type of file included by the user.

Listing 5-1 includes a sample backup.log file and output.

Listing 5-1. *Sample backup.log File*

```
<?xml version="1.0" encoding="UTF-8" standalone="yes" ?>
<!DOCTYPE backup [
<!ELEMENT backup (file|replica)*>
<!ELEMENT file (#PCDATA)>
<!ELEMENT replica EMPTY>
<!ATTLIST backup version CDATA #REQUIRED
     backup_type (full|incremental) #REQUIRED
     idtag CDATA #REQUIRED
     srvname CDATA #REQUIRED
```

```
    dsversion CDATA #REQUIRED
    compression CDATA "none"
    os CDATA #REQUIRED
    current_log CDATA #REQUIRED
    number_of_files CDATA #IMPLIED
    backup_file CDATA #REQUIRED
    incremental_file_ID CDATA #IMPLIED
    next_inc_file_ID CDATA #IMPLIED>
<!ATTLIST file size CDATA #REQUIRED
    name CDATA #REQUIRED
    encoding CDATA "base64"
    type (user|nici) #REQUIRED>
<!ATTLIST replica partition_DN CDATA #REQUIRED
    modification_time CDATA #REQUIRED
    replica_type (MASTER|SECONDARY|READONLY|SUBREF ➥
|SPARSE_WRITE|SPARSE_READ|Unknown) #REQUIRED
    replica_state (ON|NEW_REPLICA|DYING_REPLICA|LOCKED ➥
||CRT_0|CRT_1|TRANSITION_ON|DEAD_REPLICA ➥
||BEGIN_ADD|MASTER_START|MASTER_DONE|FEDERATED|SS_0|SS_1|JS_0 ➥
||JS_1|MS_0|MS_1|Unknown) #REQUIRED>
]>
<backup version="2" backup_type="full" idtag="425AB288" ➥
| time="2005-4-11'T11:23:20" srvname="\T=RK_TREE\O=User\CN=rklinux"➥
dsversion="1055260" compression="none" os="windows" ➥
|current_log="00000001.log" next_inc_file_ID="1" ➥
number_of_files="0000001" backup_file="backup.bak">
<replica partition_DN="\T=RK_TREE\O=User\OU=DK" ➥
|modification_time="s425AB216_r3_e2" replica_type="SUBREF" ➥
|replica_state="ON" />
<replica partition_DN="\T=RK_TREE\O=User\OU=obit" ➥
|modification_time="s425AB0C0_r3_e2" replica_type="SUBREF" ➥
|replica_state="ON" />
```

```
|=================DSBackup Log: Backup================|
Backup type: Full
Log file name: backup.log
Backup started: 2005-4-11'T11:23:20
Backup file name: backup.bak
Server name: \T=RK_TREE\O=abendme\CN=rklinux
Current Roll Forward Log: 00000001.log
DS Version: 1055260
Backup ID: 425AB288
```

```
Starting database backup...
Database backup finished
Completion time 00:00:02
Backup completed successfully
```

Roll-Forward Logging

Roll-forward logging enables eDirectory to be a true journaling database. Each modification made to eDirectory is stored in the roll-forward logs (RFLs). eDirectory enables you to specify where the RFLs are stored. The only requirement is that the RFLs must be stored on a local drive.

By default, roll-forward logging is configured to overwrite the existing log when the size limit is exceeded. This implies that there could potentially be modifications that are lost if a database restore is required. If you use the Backup eMTool, it is recommended that you configure roll-forward logging to not overwrite the existing log when the size limit is hit. Configure the roll-forward logging to create a new file and continue logging. While performing a restore, the Backup eMTool will allow you to specify which RFLs to use and will re-execute all the transactions in those RFLs to bring the database back to the exact state before the database went down, causing the restore in the first place.

To allow roll-forward logging to create new files, you can use the eMBox Client. The procedure provided in Task 5-1 will enable roll-forward logging.

■ **Note** To use eMBox, Role-Based Services (RBS) must be set up in iManager. For more information on how to use eMBox, see Novell's documentation at `http://www.novell.com/documentation`.

Task 5-1. Enabling Roll-Forward Logging

1. Launch eMBox in interactive mode by typing **edirutil –i**.

■ **Note** On Windows, edirutil.exe is located in the directory where dhost.exe resides. By default, this is c:\novell\nds.

---

2. Log in to eMBox by typing the following at the eMBox Client prompt (if going nonsecure, you must specify the -n option):

```
login -s <server address> -p <http port i.e. 8008, 8028> ➥
| -u <user DN i.e. admin.novell> -w <password> -n
```

To determine the HTTP port, perform the following based on your operating system:

- *Netware*: The port is hard-coded to 8008 for nonsecure and to 8009 for secure.
- *Windows*: In NDSCons, click the Transports tab and then choose HTTP ➤ Bound Transports for nonsecure or HTTPS ➤ Bound Transports for secure.
- **nix*: At a terminal, type **ndsconfig get | grep http.**

3. Turn on logging by typing the following (the -s option starts a new file):

```
backup.setconfig -L(turns on logging) ➥
| -T(starts logging of streams files) -r<RFL directory> ➥
| -n<minimum size of RFLs> -m<max size of files> ➥
| -s
```

■ **Note** To see all of the options, type **list –t backup**.

When using roll-forward logging, you should address the following issues:

- Create a new partition on your disk for roll-forward logging. The RFLs are stored in the same directory as the eDirectory DIB. If, by mistake, you forget to remove the logs before you run out of space, you may create a condition in which eDirectory cannot open because it is out of disk space.
- Remove RFLs periodically and store them on an external storage device, such as a tape drive.
- Do not change the name of the RFLs.
- Removing eDirectory from a server will also remove the RFLs. Make sure the logs have been copied to another drive before you remove eDirectory when performing disaster recovery.
- During a restore, all RFLs must be located in the same directory.

Using iManager to Configure and Perform Backup and Restore

You can also use iManager to configure and perform eMBox backups. To access the tools from iManager, choose eDirectory Maintenance ➤ Backup Configuration, as shown in Figure 5-1. After you configure the backup, as shown in Figure 5-1, click Start to save your changes.

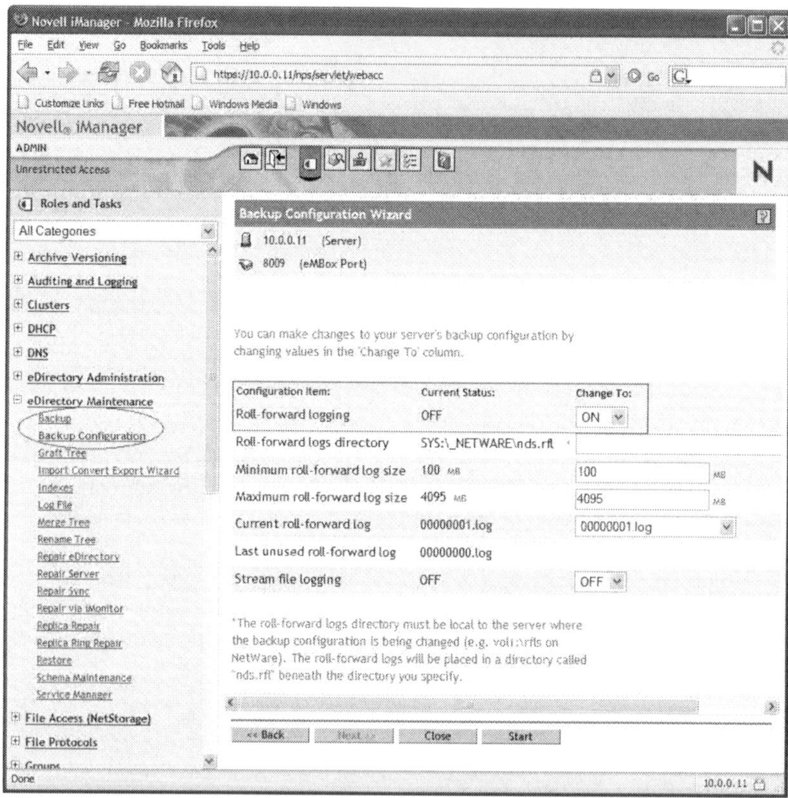

Figure 5-1. *Configuring the backup*

To initiate a backup through iManager, use the same eDirectory Maintenance role but use the Backup task instead, as shown in Figure 5-2.

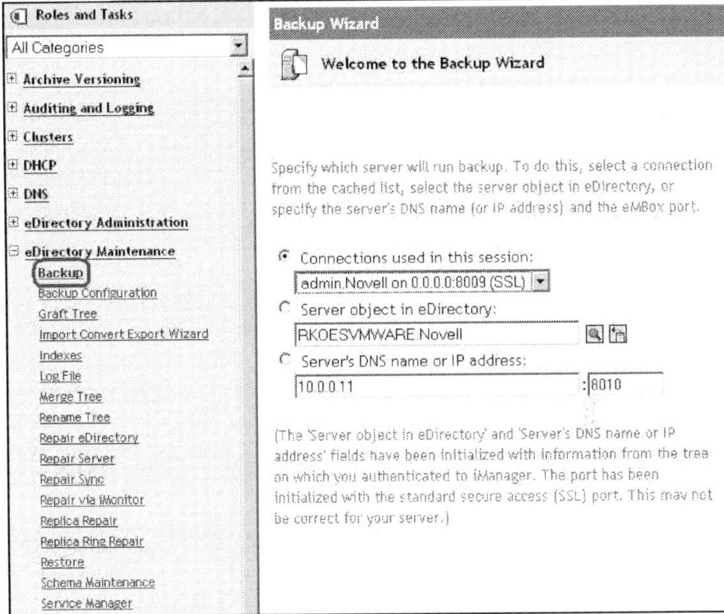

Figure 5-2. *Initiating a backup*

When creating a backup, you must specify, at a minimum, the names of the backup file and log file, similar to what is shown in Figure 5-3. You should specify the explicit directory as well.

Backup Wizard
0.0.0.0 (Server)
8009 (eMBox Port)

Specify backup file options. The backup file will contain information necessary to restore eDirectory to its current state.

Do an incremental backup
An incremental backup will back up only the changes to the database since the last backup (full or incremental) was performed.

* Backup file: sys:\bkFiles\edirbk0601.bk
Maximum size: MB
* Log file: sys:\bkFiles\edirbk0601.log

Figure 5-3. *Specifying the backup file and log file*

Click Next to finish configuring your backup options. When you are ready to begin, click Start.

■ Note Prior to the backup, you must create the directory in which the backup file and backup log will be stored. If the directory does not exist, an Error –2 will be returned and the backup will fail.

Backing Up the Security Infrastructure

You should also consider the security infrastructure when evaluating your backup needs. In general, the backup options described thus far do not back up file system information. Much of the security infrastructure is dependent on objects within Novell eDirectory as well as on the file system. It is important that the file system information also be backed up for disaster-recovery purposes. The following are some areas to consider:

- *Server keys*: Server keys are the core component of eDirectory's security infrastructure. If these keys are lost, all data that was encrypted directly or indirectly using the server keys will be lost. For more information on backing up the server keys, see `http://support.novell.com/cgi-bin/search/searchtid.cgi?/10066559.htm`.
- *Certificate Authority object*: The CA object has the trusted root information in it. If the CA object is lost, for whatever reason, all user certificates and server certificates will have to be reissued. For more information about backing up the CA object, see `http://support.novell.com/cgi-bin/search/searchtid.cgi?/10065921.htm`.
- *Tree key*: The tree key is used to encrypt user secrets. NMAS uses this extensively. Typically, all servers in the tree have a copy of the tree key, so it is not extremely critical if one server loses the key. It can by synchronized back. However, if all servers lose the tree key, all data (e.g., users' passwords) will be lost. For more information about backing up the tree key, please see `http://support.novell.com/cgi-bin/search/searchtid.cgi?/10064202.htm`.

CHAPTER 6

Schema Administration

The following topics are covered in this chapter:

- Schema synchronization
  - Monitoring schema synchronization
  - Controlling schema synchronization
- Schema comparison
- Schema modification
  - Extending schema
  - Modifying existing schema
  - Using auxiliary classes

Schema is a specific data type that defines how data is stored in a directory. eDirectory schema definitions are stored in a system partition called the *schema partition* within the eDirectory database. This chapter addresses the administration of the schema partition.

Schema Synchronization

Schema does not replicate in the same way that the user-defined partitions replicate within eDirectory. User partitions use a multimaster transitive synchronization algorithm. The tree can be broken up into partitions, and one or more servers can hold replicas of the partition. All servers that hold a replica are part of the "replica ring." The servers within the replica ring synchronize data among each other.

With schema, all servers in the tree contain the same schema definitions. Schema flows from the top of the tree down. Only servers that hold replicas of the [Root] partition can modify schema. These [Root] partition servers build what is called the *schema poll list*. This list contains all servers that are in direct child partitions to the [Root] server. As modifications to schema are made, the [Root] server synchronizes the schema to the other replicas of [Root]. Each replica for [Root] has its own poll list. These servers replicate to each server in the list. Each server in the list, in turn, has its own poll list. This process continues until all servers in the tree have received all schema changes.

The procedure in Task 6-1 outlines the process that the eDirectory Agent uses to build the schema poll list.

Task 6-1. Building a Schema Poll List

1. All servers that are in the replica rings of any partitions that are stored on the local server are added to the schema poll list.
2. Any subordinate reference servers that are listed from Step 1 are replaced with the master replica server of their particular partition.
3. The eDirectory Agent adds to the schema poll list all servers that do not contain any partitions (an external reference server) but whose NCP server object resides in a partition that the local server has a read/write or master replica of.

■ **Note** The servers listed in Step 3 are treated as special cases. They receive updates only if schema has been deleted or added. If schema is modified, the schema definitions are not replicated through the normal schema synchronization process. If you want modifications to be sent to external reference servers, you need to force this by issuing a "receive all" schema option, a "schema epoch," through the DSREPAIR advanced menu options, or by adding a replica of a partition to the external reference server. The need to send the modifications to the external reference object would be extremely rare. This stands to reason, keeping in mind that the external reference servers contain only external reference objects. External reference objects have limited attributes assigned to them.

Monitoring Schema Synchronization

NDS iMonitor has three different ways to view the status of schema:

- View the agent process status screens
- View the DSTRACE screens in NDS iMonitor
- View the Schema Sync attributes on the Schema partition object with NDS iMonitor

Each of these methods is described in turn in the sections that follow.

Agent Process Status

Each server in eDirectory contains in its local database an object called the pseudo server object. This object does not replicate to other servers. The purpose of the object is to maintain server-specific information. One of the key attributes on the pseudo server object is a pointer to the NCP object associated to the local server.

On the pseudo server object, there are several attributes that track the status of most of the background processes. After a background process finishes, the eDirectory Agent writes the completion code in its corresponding attribute on the pseudo server object. If the status is completed, just the time stamp of when it was completed is shown. If there was an error, the error is reported.

One of the background processes that stores its current status on the pseudo server object is Schema Sync. View the Schema Sync status through NDS iMonitor by going to the Agent Process Status (`http://<server address>:<http port>/nds/pstatus`) screen. On the Agent Process Status screen, there is a column named Schema Sync. If there is an error listed in the Error column, it means that an error occurred during the last schema synchronization attempt. If the Error column is blank, schema successfully synchronized. The Time field shows the time when the synchronization was completed.

DSTRACE

You can monitor the actual schema synchronization process through DSTRACE. To monitor schema synchronization, perform the steps in Task 6-2.

Task 6-2. Configuring DSTRACE

1. Open NDS iMonitor and go to the Trace Configuration (`http://<server address>:<http port>/nds/trace`) screen.
2. Clear all trace filters by clicking the Clear All button.
3. Select the following filters:
   - Schema
   - Schema Detail
4. Click Trace On.
5. In the left frame, click Trace History.
6. Click Trace Live.
7. Click Refresh On and then click Update.

At this point, when the schema synchronization process begins again, you should see the schema activity scroll across the screen. To capture the information, you can cut and paste the information into an editor. NDS iMonitor does store the trace files in an HTML file. If you wish to view the HTML file or send it to someone, you can retrieve it from the ~ndsimon/dstrace directory. Typically, the ndsimon directory is in the same location as the main DIB directories on Windows, Linux, Solaris, AIX, and HP-UX and in the SYS:\SYSTEM directory on NetWare.

Note You can use the command-line DSTRACE utilities to view the same information that you can see through the NDS iMonitor DSTRACE screens. For specific instructions on how to run these utilities on each platform, refer to the *eDirectory Administration Guide* at `http://www.novell.com/documentation`.

The Schema Partition Object

To view the Schema partition object in NDS iMonitor, go to Agent Configuration ➤ Agent Information (`http://`*`<server address>`*`:`*`<http port>`*`/nds/agent/info`). At the bottom of the screen, click the Schema Root link. On the Schema Root screen is an attribute called Synchronized Up To. This attribute stores a TimeStamp value, which shows the last time that schema was synchronized. During a schema synchronization cycle, if the modification TimeStamp (MTS) of any given schema value is newer than the Synchronized Up To attribute value on the Schema Root object, then the schema value is sent to everyone in the local server's schema poll list.

Controlling Schema Synchronization

You can control the schema background process in NDS iMonitor in several ways:

- *Enable/disable synchronization*: You can enable or disable schema synchronization in NDS iMonitor by going to Agent Configuration ➤ Schema Synchronization (`http://`*`<server address>`*`:`*`<http port>`*`/nds/agent?config=SSyncCtl`).
- *Change the schema sync interval*: You can change the schema sync interval in NDS iMonitor by going to Agent Configuration ➤ Background Process Settings (`http://`*`<server address>`*`:`*`<http port>`*`/nds/agent?config=BackCtl`).

- *Issue an immediate sync*: By initiating an "Agent Trigger," you can force immediate schema synchronization. To do this in NDS iMonitor, go to Agent Configuration ➤ Agent Triggers (`http://<server address>:<http port>/nds/agent`), select Schema Synchronization, and then click Submit.

You can also force schema synchronization from the DSTRACE command-line module. The following triggers can be used with a DSTRACE command:

- `*ss`: Triggers an immediate schema sync
- `*ssd`: Deletes the schema poll list
- `*ssa`: Creates a new schema poll list and sends a schema sync
- `*ssl`: Lists the current schema poll list

Note You can also view the schema list in NDS iMonitor by going to Schema ➤ Service List (`http://<server address>:<http port>/nds/schema/sync`).

For more information on how to issue these commands for each platform, see the *eDirectory Administration Guide* at `http://www.novell.com/documentation`.

Schema Comparison

NDS iMonitor has a powerful feature in which you can compare the schema of two servers. You can access the Schema Compare feature in NDS iMonitor by going to Schema ➤ Source List. You can compare schema between the local server (the server you are accessing through NDS iMonitor) and any other server in the local server's schema poll list. You can view these servers by looking at the Source List.

Note If you want to compare schema between the local server and a server that is not in the local server's schema poll list, you can modify the URL and put in the desired server's name and IP address after selecting the Class Compare or Attribute Compare option. See TID 10079971 (`http://support.novell.com/cgi-bin/search/searchtid.cgi?/10079971.htm`) for more details on how to do this.

When comparing schema, you have several configuration options. You can specify the following, as shown in Figure 6-1:

- *Full Compare*: You can select from the following types of schema:
  - *Difference*: The result of the comparison shows all schema differences except for known differences. Differences in schema definitions may occur if the source and target servers are not running the same version of eDirectory. Selecting this option will not include the Expected Differences in this type of condition.
  - *Expected Differences*: These are differences that are expected when the source and target servers are not running the same version of eDirectory.
  - *Base only*: Only the differences from the source server are displayed.
  - *Target only*: Only the differences from the target server are displayed.
  - *Equal*: Schema that is equal between the two servers is still returned. It is usually best to deselect this option so that you only see the differences and don't have to go through a large report to find the differences.
- *Filter by Health*: Even though schema shows that it is different between two servers, it is possible that the difference is not going to cause any issues. By using the Filter by Health option, you can display only the differences that you need to worry about. If you are troubleshooting schema issues, you may want to select the following Filter by Health options:
  - *Unknown*: A schema difference has been detected and the NDS iMonitor agent is not sure whether or not the difference is acceptable.
  - *Suspect*: A schema difference has been detected and the NDS iMonitor agent has determined that, in some situations, the difference needs to be resolved.
  - *Warn*: A schema difference has been detected and the NDS iMonitor agent has determined that, in most cases, the schema difference needs to be resolved.

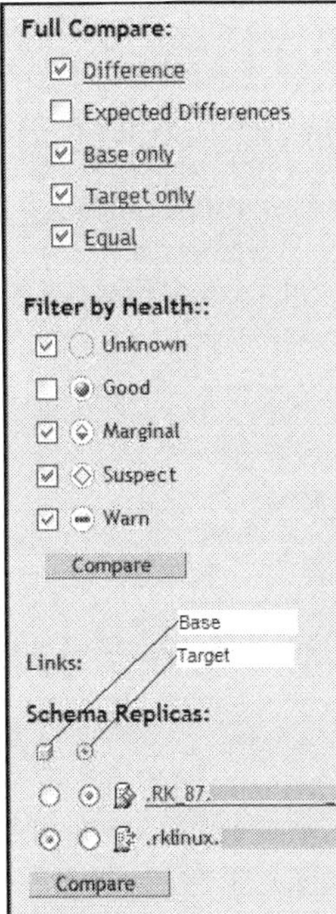

Figure 6-1. *Schema Compare options*

Schema Modification

eDirectory provides you with a few different ways to modify schema within eDirectory. You may want to "extend" schema, which means that you add new class and/or attribute definitions. You may also want to modify existing definitions. This section discusses in detail each of these activities.

Extending Schema

The term *extending schema* refers to the action of adding new attributes and/or classes to the existing eDirectory schema partition. By doing this, you can create your own custom objects and place your specific data in the custom attribute definitions. Two different methods that you can use to extend schema are discussed next.

Import Convert Export Utility

The Novell Import Convert Export (ICE) Utility is an LDAP client utility that ships on all platforms that support eDirectory. The syntax is the same regardless of the platform. For the purposes of adding schema into eDirectory, ICE uses two "handlers." LDIF is used as the source handler and LDAP is used as the destination handler. You can create an LDIF file that contains the new attribute definitions or class definitions that you would like to add to eDirectory. You can then import that LDIF file via ICE. A typical ICE command line would look something like this:

```
ice -S LDIF -f <ldif file> ➥
-D LDAP -s <server address> -p <LDAP port> -d <DN> -w <password>
```

The following is an example of the preceding syntax with specific values substituted for the placeholders:

```
ice -S LDIF -f /home/rk/schema.ldif ➥
-D LDAP -s 10.0.0.11 -p 389 -d cn=admin,o=novell -w novell
```

■ **Note** For specific information about the syntax for ICE, see the *eDirectory Administration Guide* at `http://www.novell.com/documentation`.

The format of an LDIF file is defined in the LDAP RFCs. The following is the basic LDIF format for modifying an attribute definition:

```
dn: cn=schema
changetype: modify
add: attributetypes (<OID> NAME <Name of Attribute> ➥
DESC <Description used for schema mappings> ➥
EQUALITY <type of comparison> ➥
SYNTAX <SYNTAX OID> <OPTIONAL ATTRS>)
```

The following is a sample LDIF file that will add uidSSN to eDirectory (the OID is not real):

```
dn: cn=schema
changetype: modify
add: attributetypes (1.8.1.1.1.1.1.0 NAME 'uidSSN' ➥
DESC 'Social Security Number' EQUALITY integerMatch ➥
SYNTAX 1.3.6.1.4.1.1466.115.121.1.27 SINGLE-VALUE)
```

The best way to find the SYNTAX value is to dump schema from eDirectory to an LDIF file and find a schema definition that has the same SYNTAX value as the syntax you want to use. To dump an eDirectory schema to a file using ICE, type the following:

```
ice -S LDAP -s <server address> -p <LDAP port> ➥
-d <DN of user to bind as> -w <password> -b cn=schema ➥
 -F objectclass=subschema -c base -D LDIF -f schema.ldif
```

Note If you get the error `ldap_simple_bind failed: 13(Confidentiality required)`, you need to bind securely or turn off Require TLS with Simple Binds on the LDAP group object.

To delete schema through an LDIF file, simply change the action to `delete`, as follows:

```
dn: cn=schema
changetype: modify
delete: attributetypes (1.8.1.1.1.1.1.0)
```

Adding a schema class through LDIF is similar in format. The difference is that the `add` request is dealing with `objectclasses` instead of `attributetypes`. A sample LDIF definition to add CCUser to eDirectory would look like this (the OID is not real):

```
dn: cn=schema
changetype: modify
add: objectclasses
objectclasses: (1.8.6.1.1.1.6.0 NAME 'CCUser' ➥
SUP top AUXILIARY DESC 'Credit Card User' ➥
MUST (cn $ title) MAY (uidSSN))
```

Note If any object or schema class is using the specific schema definition that you are trying to delete, the operation will fail. For instance, in the preceding example, if a user object had an attribute of type 1.8.1.1.1.1.1.0 or a schema class had an optional attribute of attribute type 1.8.1.1.1.1.1.0, then the preceding LDIF `delete` example would fail.

Make sure that all attributes that are defined in the class definition are already in eDirectory or else the class extension will fail. If you are not comfortable with the command-line switch, iManager has an ICE plug-in that you can access by going into iManager and choosing eDirectory Maintenance ➤ Import Export Converter.

■ **Note** Another typical schema file that is used is a SCH file. This file is similar to an LDIF file. However, you cannot use LDAP clients such as ICE to import a SCH file. eDirectory ships a utility called `ndssch` on all the platforms supported by eDirectory. For information on how to use this tool, please see the *eDirectory Administration Guide* at `http://www.novell.com/documentation`.

---

iManager

Typically, you will use ICE to import schema if you are provided an LDIF file from an application. If you simply want to add a few custom definitions, you will find that the iManager schema plug-in is a very easy tool to use. To access the schema plug-in, log into iManager and go to the Schema role on the left pane. You have options available to Add Attribute, Delete Attribute, Add Class, and Delete Class. Each of these options will take you through a wizard to define the schema definition.

Modifying Existing Schema

Modifying an existing schema definition through an LDIF file is very similar to adding a definition. The difference is that you must delete the existing definition first and then add the new definition. To avoid data loss, if you perform this operation in one transaction with a dash (–) separating the `delete` and `add` requests, existing values that are using the schema definitions will not be altered. The following is an example in which we can change uidSSN from SINGLE-VALUE to MULTI-VALUE by removing the SINGLE-VALUE syntax:

```
dn: cn=schema
changetype: modify
delete: attributetypes (1.8.1.1.1.1.1.0 NAME 'uidSSN' ➥
DESC 'Social Security Number' EQUALITY integerMatch ➥
 SYNTAX 1.3.6.1.4.1.1466.115.121.1.27 SINGLE-VALUE)
-
add: attributetypes (1.8.1.1.1.1.1.0 NAME 'uidSSN' ➥
DESC 'Social Security Number' EQUALITY integerMatch ➥
SYNTAX 1.3.6.1.4.1.1466.115.121.1.27)
```

Similarly, we can add the attribute Description as an optional attribute to the class CCUser by creating the following LDIF file:

```
dn: cn=schema
changetype: modify
delete: objectclasses
objectclasses: (1.8.6.1.1.1.6.0 NAME 'CCUser' ➥
SUP top AUXILIARY DESC 'Credit Card User' ➥
MUST (cn $ title) MAY (uidSSN))
-
add: objectclasses
objectclasses: (1.8.6.1.1.1.6.0 NAME 'CCUser' ➥
SUP top AUXILIARY DESC 'Credit Card User' ➥
MUST (cn $ title) MAY (uidSSN $ Description))
```

Using Auxiliary Classes

An auxiliary class is a special class. You cannot create an object in eDirectory with an auxiliary class. An auxiliary class is "extended" onto an existing object. When this occurs, all attributes that are associated with the auxiliary class are not valid attributes for the object that it was extended onto. For instance, if we were to "extend" CCUser to an object called cn=rkuser, ou=users,o=novell, where cn=rkuser is a user object, then cn, title, uidSSN, and Description would all be valid objects for that user, even if they were not defined in the user class.

The power of auxiliary classes is that you do not need to change default schema. You can simply choose an object and extend the object, allowing you to specify a valid attribute value for the auxiliary class on that object. If you want to remove the values, simply remove the auxiliary class from the object.

To create auxiliary classes, simply add the word AUXILIARY in the class definition in the LDIF file or click the Auxiliary Class option when creating the schema in iManager. To extend an object with an auxiliary class through LDIF, simply add an `objectclass` value with the auxiliary class name.

The following is a sample LDIF file that extends CCUser to a user called rkuser (assuming rkuser already exists in eDirectory):

```
dn: cn=rkuser,ou=users,o=novell
changetype: modify
add: objectclass
objectclass: CCUser
```

If you prefer, you can use iManager to extend an object with an auxiliary class. To extend the object, log into iManager. Go to the Schema role and choose the task called Object Extensions.

CHAPTER 7

LDAP

The following topics are covered in this chapter:

- LDAP binds
  - DN
  - Password
  - Server address and LDAP port
  - Connection method
- Understanding LDAP queries
  - LDAP filter
  - Scope
  - Base
  - Performance considerations
- Persistent Search
- Managing the LDAP objects
  - LDAP server object
  - LDAP group object
  - Creating and configuring the LDAP objects
- Walking the tree
  - Default referral
  - Conditions to use default referral
  - Referral options
- Access control
- Using ICE to bulk-load data

The Lightweight Directory Access Protocol (LDAP) is an industry-standard client-server protocol. LDAP provides a common interface in which LDAP-compliant clients can access data from within an X.509 database. Most directories on the market today are either partially or fully LDAP compliant. Because of this, developers can create LDAP clients that are capable of attaching to many LDAP directories, allowing for tremendous flexibility.

eDirectory provides an LDAP server, the purpose of which is to process LDAP requests from LDAP clients. The LDAP server does this by converting the requests into formats that the eDirectory Agent can understand and then forwarding the requests to the eDirectory Agent. The eDirectory Agent accesses the eDirectory database and retrieves or modifies the database based off of the request. The result is sent back to the LDAP server, which converts the message into an LDAP-compliant message that can be understood by the LDAP client, and then forwards the reply back to the client.

LDAP Binds

LDAP binds is an LDAP term that refers to the action of authenticating to an LDAP directory. The authentication methodology that is specific to each directory is irrelevant to the LDAP client that is making the bind request. Because the LDAP protocol is a standard protocol, the bind request packet is consistent, regardless of the LDAP directory.

Each LDAP client has its own method of collecting information from the user that is making the authentication request. Regardless of how the LDAP client gathers the information from the user, the following information needs to be sent to the LDAP server to perform a successful LDAP bind:

- *DN*: Distinguished Name of the user that is requesting the bind.
- *Password*: The user's password.
- *Server address*: The network address of the LDAP server that will complete the bind request.
- *Port*: The port that the LDAP server is listening to for LDAP requests.
- *Connection method*: There are two connection methods:
    - *Clear*: The data transmitted between the two entities that are connected is transmitted in clear text.
    - *Secure*: The data transmitted between the two entities that are connected is encrypted with an SSL encryption algorithm.
- *Path to the server certificate*: If the connection method is Secure, the location of the server certificate is necessary.

The items in the preceding list are described next in more detail.

DN

The DN has two components, the common name and the hierarchal location of the user object in the LDAP directory. It can have many containers and subcontainers. The format of the DN is as follows:

```
cn=<name>,ou=<subcontainer>,o=<container>
```

The following is an example DN:

```
cn=user1,ou=marketing,ou=provo,o=novell
```

Password

Through eDirectory's NMAS component, the password can be stored in several different encrypted formats. However, by default, a clear-text password is used with the bind request. The password is not stored in eDirectory. The password, however, is used along with a public key to create an encrypted hash. A hash is also stored on the user object in the database. If the encrypted message that was encrypted with the clear password can be unencrypted with the hash on the user object, then eDirectory allows the bind to complete.

Server Address and LDAP Port

The LDAP protocol uses the TCP protocol to transfer LDAP packets from the LDAP client to the LDAP server and vice versa. Therefore, the server address used for an LDAP bind must be an IP address.

By default, when the eDirectory LDAP server loads, it initializes LDAP listening ports on all available interfaces. LDAP will always initialize a clear-text listening port for clear-text LDAP requests. If configured to do so, the LDAP server will also initialize a secure listening port. By default, LDAP initializes the clear text listening port on 389 and the secure listening port on 636.

Connection Method

LDAP supports both clear-text and secure connections. If the LDAP bind occurs on the clear-text port, all communications between the LDAP client and the LDAP server will be sent in clear text. If the LDAP bind is secure, all communications between the LDAP client and the LDAP server will be sent in SSL-encrypted format.

Understanding LDAP Queries

Once a bind is established, the LDAP client can request the LDAP server to do the following:

- Retrieve a set of objects
- Retrieve one object
- Retrieve a specific value that resides on an object
- Check the existence of a specific value on an object
- Delete an object
- Add an object
- Add a value to an object
- Delete a value on the object

Regardless of the request made by the LDAP client, an LDAP query must be specified in order to identify the object or set of objects within the LDAP directory. The LDAP query consists of three basic components:

- LDAP filter
- Scope
- Base

Each of these components is discussed in detail next.

LDAP Filter

The LDAP filter defines what object or set of objects is requested. The LDAP protocol defines the syntax for the LDAP filter. The filter has two components. First, the filter specifies an attribute. The attribute is defined in schema and describes the syntax and type of data that are stored on the object. The second part of the filter is the specific content of the desired attribute. An example of an LDAP filter that finds all identities that contain an attribute called `objectclass`, the value of which equals `user`, would look like the following:

```
objectclass=user
```

A filter can test for the existence of any value of a specific attribute type. For instance:

```
NetworkAddress=*
```

The filter can show any type of expression, like =, >, <, or !=. The filter can be a simple or complex comparison. The ampersand (&) is used to require that both parts of an expression are true before an identity is returned. The pipe symbol (|) is used to specify that if at least one part of the expression is true, the whole expression is true. The following is an example of a complex query:

```
(&(objectclass=user) (!(CN=rkillpack))
```

■ **Tip** For detailed information about the filter syntax, refer to RFC 2254.

Scope

The scope defines how far down the LDAP tree to apply the filter. The valid entries for the scope are as follows:

- `base`: Only the object that is specified as the base is valid.
- `one`: Objects directly beneath the base are valid.
- `sub`: All objects, subcontainers, and objects under the subcontainers are valid.

Base

When an object meets the specific filter, it is verified that it is a subcomponent of the specified base and that it falls within the specified scope. If the object in question is not under the base or does not fall within the scope, the object is not returned to the requester.

Performance Considerations

Several factors affect the performance of LDAP queries. If you understand these factors, you can configure your system to achieve optimal performance during LDAP operations. This section describes the following factors and then describes how to measure query performance:

- Search order
- Indexing
- Schema syntax
- Partitioning

Search Order

Depending on your tree design, the order in which the components of the LDAP query are evaluated dramatically affects how fast results are returned to the LDAP client. eDirectory's database (FLAIM) has built-in algorithms that are designed to provide optimal search performance based off of the filter, not the tree design. The reason for this is that most large implementations of eDirectory are designed with thousands or possibly millions of user objects. The user objects are in a relatively flat container. In such cases, a loss of performance would incur if the base were considered before the filter.

The search order used by FLAIM for an LDAP query is as follows:

1. The filter is evaluated to find the smallest set of objects.

   If the filter is a simple query, with just one expression (e.g., `title=Manager`), the request with that expression is processed by the eDirectory Agent. If the query is complex, with more than one expression, each expression is calculated to find the smallest set of objects that needs to be evaluated. The smallest set of objects is chosen by evaluating the attribute indexes for each attribute in the expression. The smallest sets of objects that can be derived from the existing indexes are calculated. The expression that contains attributes for the index selected is the expression that is evaluated first.

   Another factor involved is whether the expressions are AND'ed or OR'ed. If the expressions are AND'ed, both expressions must be true. In the case of AND'ed expressions, if one expression does not return any entries, the entire query is stopped and no results are returned to the LDAP client.

   The following are a few examples of how FLAIM determines which expression to use:

   - `(&(objectclass=user) (title=engineer))`: If `title` is indexed and `objectclass` is not, `title` is evaluated first. If both attributes are indexed, the attribute that contains fewer values is used. A typical eDirectory tree has more users than objects that contain a `title` on the object. Therefore, in most cases, `title` would still be evaluated first.
   - `(|(objectclass=*) (title=engineer))`: This is a special type of query. Keeping in mind that `objectclass` is a mandatory attribute for all objects, `objectclass=*` would include all objects. Because this is an OR'ed operation, there is no need to evaluate `title` to return a true value. No index is used in this case, even if both attributes are indexed.

Note Requesting `objectclass=*` is not advisable, especially if performance is a concern. Because each object contains `objectclass`, indexes cannot be used. Every object in eDirectory will be evaluated against the scope and base. This can take a considerable amount of time and memory. If at all possible, it is advisable to narrow the query; e.g., `objectclass=user`.

2. The scope is evaluated to determine if the subset can be narrowed further. If the scope is set to `base` or `one`, the parent index of the base object can be applied against the subset returned from Step 1. This narrows the result list down even further. If the scope is set to `sub`, the result set cannot be narrowed.

Tip Whenever possible, use `one` as the scope rather than `sub`. If `one` is used, only the objects within the base will be evaluated, instead of all objects in the tree.

3. Each object in the return set is evaluated to make sure that it is within the base and scope. If an object is within the base and the scope, the object is returned to the LDAP server to send to the LDAP client. If the object does not fall within the base and scope, the object is not returned.

Indexing

Indexing is the most important factor that will alter performance when executing LDAP requests. An index key specifies an attribute or a combination of attributes. When an index key is applied, specific information is stored in an index container within the eDirectory database about all objects that have a value of the attribute(s) in the index key. The values are sorted alphabetically. The concept behind an index is that the eDirectory Agent does not need to scan each individual object to determine whether or not the object contains a value of the specified attribute type. Another benefit of the index is that the eDirectory Agent does not need to scan through all objects that do contain the attribute value. The values are alphabetical, so the eDirectory Agent can retrieve the index with the list of objects that contain the specific attribute value and skip down to the section that corresponds to the LDAP query.

To give you a better idea of how this works, let's consider an example. If the LDAP query were searching for all objects of a user-defined class type of `LDAPTestObject`, then the LDAP query would be `objectclass=LDAPTestObject`. In our scenario, suppose that `objectclass` has been indexed on the local server and that there are one million user objects and ten `LDAPTestObject` objects. In this example, the index would contain information about all one million and ten objects. However, because of the index, all ten objects of the type `LDAPTestObject` would be together and would come before all objects of the type `user`. With this example, only ten objects are evaluated. If `objectclass` were not indexed, all one million and ten objects would have to be analyzed to find the ten `LDAPTestObject` objects.

Indexing does take a little bit of overhead. It takes up additional FLAIM cache memory as well as time during certain operations. The benefits of indexes are most evident during large partition operations or bulk loads (importing data into the directory). Day-to-day transactions will experience insignificant delays as a result of indexing. With the additional overhead in mind, it is wise to index only what is queried on a regular basis. If there are specific LDAP queries that are performed on a regular basis, identify the attributes in the queries and create indexes for them. If you are not certain which attributes are being searched on a regular basis and what indexes are being used during the searches, there are two eDirectory features that can assist you:

- *DSTRACE*: DSTRACE has a filter called `+recm` (or Record Manager in NDS iMonitor and Windows). With this filter set, you can watch the LDAP queries being performed. As they are executed, the index that is being used will be written to the screen (and/or trace log, depending on how DSTRACE is configured).
- *Predicate Stats*: Predicate Stats can be enabled through ConsoleOne for any server. By default, a Predicate Stats object is created for every NCP server object in the same container in which the NCP server object resides. The default name of this object is *<server name>*–PS. If you right-click the Predicate Stats object, you can configure the specified NCP server to collect usage information. One of the items you can track is how often each attribute is accessed. The idea is that you can turn on Predicate Stats for a period of time during peak usage and identify the attributes you should index.

■ **Warning** Predicate Stats will take up a lot of processor time and memory. Do not run this on a continual basis. Configure the object to collect stats for a time period long enough to obtain the necessary data and then turn off the logging.

Knowing what type of index to create is as important as knowing what to index. There are three basic types of indexes:

- *Value*: Creates a list where the actual values are stored and sorted in the index file.
- *Presence*: Creates a list of objects that contain at least one value of the specified attribute type.
- *Substring*: Creates an extensive list of every possible combination of values or partial values for a specified attribute type. For example, the value joe would have the following entries: j, jo, joe, o, oe, and e.

With very few exceptions, you should always create a value index. There are few benefits to creating a presence index. If the value index contains an entry for a specified object, then the attribute is obviously present. For this reason, the eDirectory Agent will always use a value index if one is available, even if there are both presence and value indexes for a specified attribute. The worst index you could choose is the substring index. These indexes are very resource intensive and typically do not serve any real value. They are used if the left side of the value is not known (e.g., *illpack or *ill*). If your application requires this type of functionality, use a substring index. If, however, you do know the left side of the string but not the right side (e.g., rkill*), a value index will be used if present.

Indexes are server specific. You must set an index on each LDAP server that may perform the query. To set an index using iManager 2.5, perform Task 7-1.

Task 7-1. Creating Indexes in iManager 2.5

1. Log into iManager.
2. Select the eDirectory Maintenance role on the left pane.
3. Select the Indexes task.
4. Select the LDAP server from the list provided.
5. Click the Create button.
6. Fill in the Name field with a name that will describe the index.
7. Select the attribute to Index.
8. Select the rule.

■ **Tip** The Linux, Solaris, AIX, and HP-UX platforms include a utility called `ndsindex`. This utility provides a command-line interface to manage indexes. The power of this utility is apparent in its ability to quickly suspend or re-enable existing indexes. For more information about `ndsindex`, see the man pages on the respective platform.

Schema Syntax

LDAP queries can only perform string comparisons (or in the case of a presence index, a Boolean return). Be sure that when you select the attribute type, the syntax for the attribute is either Case Exact String (CE_String) or Case Ignore String (CI_String). Some schema files define attributes with Octet String. Octets, by definition, store the value in a binary format rather than in clear text. Very specific, exact matches can be executed against Octet Strings but wildcard searches cannot. For this reason, do not use attributes of Octet String unless absolutely required.

Partitioning

Partitioning does not really affect LDAP query performance. It is wise to make sure that the LDAP server contains real replicas of all objects that are accessed via LDAP. Make sure that you partition your directory so that the required replicas are replicated to the LDAP servers. LDAP does have the ability to walk the tree if the desired objects are not local; however, this will significantly impact performance.

Measuring Performance

It is important to measure LDAP performance correctly. The LDAP server will return the objects that fit the LDAP query as soon as the LDAP server receives the results from FLAIM. When measuring LDAP performance, a mistake is often made where the difference is measured from the time the query was requested to the time objects started to appear on the screen from the LDAP client output. This measurement is not accurate. FLAIM may be processing thousands of objects and discarding these objects because they do not meet the base and scope requirements. In these cases, the results are not sent back to the LDAP client.

Consider, for instance, a query against a tree with one million users, such as `objectclass=*`, with a base `ou=10users` and a scope set to `sub`. In this case, FLAIM has to process all one million objects to find the ten users in the `ou=10users`. If those ten users are toward the bottom of the database, the LDAP client output will show nothing for quite a while, skewing the LDAP performance measurements. However, if the ten objects are at the top of the database, the LDAP client may return the values fairly quickly, even though the query in the background continues on for a very long time. LDAP performance needs to be measured based on how long the query takes to complete, not on how fast the first objects are returned to the LDAP client.

The best way to test LDAP performance is to issue a very specific query, like `cn=rkillpack`. This will have a finite set of results. Run the query over and over and measure how many transactions are returned per minute, per second, and per hour.

Persistent Search

Persistent Search is an LDAP extension. This means that it is not part of the basic LDAP RFC. However, many of the industry-leading LDAP servers, including eDirectory, provide support for Persistent Search. The idea behind Persistent Search is to create a persistent connection. The LDAP client creates a connection with the LDAP directory. The client sends a query to the LDAP server and receives a result. It then leaves the connection open. Whenever a new object is added to the LDAP directory that fits the query, the object is automatically sent along the open connection and added to the already existing result set. Persistent Search can be used by an LDAP client to track changes within eDirectory.

To configure Persistent Search through iManager 2.5, perform Task 7-2.

Task 7-2. Configuring Persistent Search

1. Log into iManager.
2. Modify the LDAP server object.
3. Click the Search tab.
4. Configure Persistent Search.

After Persistent Search is enabled on the LDAP server, any LDAP client that supports Persistent Search can send a request to the LDAP server to create a Persistent Search connection.

Managing the LDAP Objects

During an eDirectory installation, eDirectory automatically creates all necessary LDAP objects and configures the objects to enable the LDAP server to listen on both the clear-text and secure ports. However, sometimes you may need to reconfigure and/or re-create the LDAP objects. Before you do so, you should have a good understanding of the purpose of the LDAP objects. If the LDAP objects are corrupt or unreadable, the LDAP server will fail to open the Listening ports.

There are two LDAP objects that are stored in eDirectory that you should be familiar with:

- LDAP server object
- LDAP group object

The LDAP objects can be configured in iManager, ConsoleOne, or through command-line utilities. In iManager 2.5, there is an LDAP role that has LDAP options to create LDAP objects as well as configure them. The following sections describe some of the information that can be configured.

LDAP Server Object

An LDAP server object is created by default for every NCP server object in the tree. By default, the LDAP server object resides in the same container as the NCP server object for the given server. The default name for the LDAP server object is LDAP Server–*<full DN of server>*.

The LDAP server object contains the following information:

- *General Information*: Lists the NCP server object. Specifies the NCP server object that the LDAP server is associated with. It also lists the LDAP group object that the LDAP server is associated to. It also has an option to dereference alias objects. This option is turned off by default.
- *Connections*: Describes how LDAP communicates. This is where you configure how LDAP will communicate over a secure channel. You can also configure the ports, timeout parameters, and bind restrictions.
- *Searches*: Defines how searches are executed. There are a few search options that you can configure to alter the default behavior of the LDAP server during searches.
- *Events*: Manages how events are handled. Any application can use the eDirectory SDK and create an application that registers for an event within eDirectory. Events like user adds, partition operations, etc. can be monitored. Depending on the event and the frequency of the event occurring, significant load can be placed on the server. The LDAP server allows you to both disable an application from registering an event through LDAP and configure how many events can be registered to the LDAP server.

- *Tracing*: Allows control over what DSTRACE messages are generated. By default, if you use the `+ldap` filter in DSTRACE, only LDAP errors will be traced to the screen. Sometimes you may want to trace general LDAP traffic to verify LDAP queries or measure performance by connection times. The LDAP server allows you to configure what type of information is sent to the DSTRACE output.
- *Referrals*: Allows you to control how the LDAP server finds objects in the tree. The LDAP server allows you to configure how to locate a requested object if that object does not exist on the local database.

LDAP Group Object

By default, an LDAP group object is created for every NCP server object. It is contained in the same container as the NCP server object and the LDAP server object. You can reconfigure this later to have multiple servers associated to one group. The advantage of this is that if you make a change to the LDAP group object, all associated LDAP servers will receive the change. By default, the LDAP group object is called LDAP Group–*<full DN of server>*. The LDAP group object contains the following information:

- *General Information*: Lists all LDAP servers that belong to a group. All LDAP servers associated to the group are listed here. There is also an option to require TLS binds only. You can also configure an LDAP proxy user for anonymous binds.
- *Referrals*: Manages how objects in the tree are located. As with the LDAP server object, you can configure how referrals are handled if the requested object is not on the local server. Further discussion about referrals will come later in this chapter.
- *Attribute Map*: Allows you to define LDAP alias attribute names. Standard LDAP attribute names often do not match up with eDirectory attribute names. To allow LDAP clients to request attributes with their default LDAP names, attribute maps are created. When the LDAP request comes in, the attribute map table is searched. If the LDAP attribute being requested is located in the table, the associated NDS name is used to fulfill the query.

- *Class Map*: Allows you to define LDAP alias class names. Standard LDAP class names often do not match up with eDirectory class names. To allow LDAP clients to request classes with their default LDAP names, class maps are created. When the LDAP request comes in, the class map table is searched. If the LDAP class being requested is located in the table, then the associated NDS name is used to fulfill the query. The most common example of this is inetOrgPerson, which is defined by LDAP to be the central user object. By default, inetOrgPerson is not defined in eDirectory schema. So, when an LDAP request is made to add an object of type inetOrgPerson, the LDAP server reads the class map table and sees that inetOrgPerson object is linked to the `user` schema class in eDirectory. The request is sent to the eDirectory Agent to create an object of type `user`.

Creating and Configuring the LDAP Objects

You can use ConsoleOne or iManager to create or configure the LDAP objects. For every version of the LDAP server, there is a corresponding version of LDAP objects in eDirectory as well as a specific version of a ConsoleOne snap-in or iManager plug-in. It is important that you don't try to administer your LDAP objects with an older version of the snap-ins. To avoid this issue, it is recommended that you use iManager. iManager ships with the latest LDAP plug-ins, which will work with the different versions of LDAP objects. If, for whatever reason, you need to re-create the LDAP objects, you can use one of the following tools:

- *iManager*: iManager includes an LDAP role, which has several tasks that allow you to create, delete, and modify LDAP server objects and LDAP group objects. It is important to remember that after you make changes to the LDAP server object or the LDAP group object, you need to go to the Information tab on the LDAP server and click Refresh.
- `ndsconfig`: The Linux, Solaris, AIX, and HP-UX platforms include a utility called `ndsconfig`. If you are missing LDAP objects in eDirectory, you can re-create the LDAP objects with the default configuration by issuing `ndsconfig add -m LDAP`.

■ **Note** For more information on the `ndsconfig` utility, see the man pages for `ndsconfig`.

- `ldapconfig`: The Linux, Solaris, AIX, and HP-UX platforms also include a utility called `ldapconfig`. If LDAP objects already exist and you want to configure them from the command line, you can use `ldapconfig`. The following are a few basic commands that you can use for `ldapconfig`:
  - `ldapconfig get`: Use to display all possible parameters and their values. You can use these exact parameters in the `ldapconfig set` command.
  - `ldapconfig set` <*parameter*>=<*value*>: Use to set specific parameters and values. (Use `ldapconfig get` to discover all of the available parameters.) An example of this command would be `ldapconfig set 'Screen Level Options'=all`.

If you re-create LDAP objects, you need to know what LDAP extensions were installed on the original objects. *LDAP extensions* are programs that are outside of the LDAP server that are called by the LDAP server. If an application writes an LDAP extension, it can make their specific calls to the extension through the LDAP server. Many default Novell applications use LDAP extensions.

When you re-create your LDAP server objects, you will not have the extensions any longer and you may break your LDAP applications. The extensions can be re-created. Typically, if you know what application used the extensions, that application will have an LDAP extension installation program that you can use to re-extend the LDAP server object. If you do not know what LDAP extensions are on the original LDAP server object, you have a couple of options. You can view the current extensions on any LDAP server in either of two ways:

- *iManager*: If you go to the eDirectory Administration ➤ Modify task, you can browse for the LDAP server and modify it. If you use the Modify task instead of the LDAP Options task, one of the available tabs is Other. In this tab, you will see an attribute called `extensioninfo`. If you click the Edit button for this attribute, you will see that it is multivalued with several extensions added. You can write down each extension value on the old LDAP server object before you delete it. After creating the new LDAP server object, you can go back to the same attribute and add the missing values.

Note If the old LDAP server object is already deleted, you can view an LDAP server object from another server that is running the same applications to get the extension information.

- *RootDSE*: The RootDSE is a special record that is loaded into memory every time an LDAP server is loaded. This record contains all extensions, controls, versions, etc. about that server. LDAP clients can query the RootDSE to find out what it can and cannot support. If you dump the RootDSE, part of the record will be a list of all the currently supported extensions. You can make a list of these extensions. After creating the new LDAP object, you can put the list of extensions into an LDIF format and import the LDIF file into eDirectory. This will add the applicable values back onto the LDAP server object.

The following is the query that you would use from the command-line version of ICE to dump the RootDSE:

```
ice -S LDAP -s <server address> -p <LDAP port> ➥
-d <DN of user to bind as> -w <password> -c base ➥
-F objectclass=* -D LDIF -f rootdse.ldif
```

The following is an example of the preceding query with the placeholders replaced with specific values:

```
ice -S LDAP -s 10.0.0.11 -p 389 -d cn=admin,o=novell -w novell ➥
-c base -F objectclass=* -D LDIF -f rootdse.ldif
```

Next is a sample LDIF file called extension.ldif that you could use to import the extensions onto the new LDAP server object:

```
version: 1
dn: cn=LDAP Server - rkOESServer,o=Novell
changetype: modify
add: extensionInfo
extensionInfo: E#2.16.840.1.113719.1.39.42.100.19#nmasldap.nlm
extensionInfo: E#2.16.840.1.113719.1.39.42.100.21#nmasldap.nlm
```

Notice that `E#` is added to the front of each extension OID and that `#<module name>` is added to the end. When you dump the RootDSE, you will not see these. You will only see the OID. Make sure that you add these values to the OID that was exported with the RootDSE before you reimport the data. If you prefer to use iManager, make sure that you edit the value and type in the HEX value, not the ASCII values. For LDIF import, you would use the ASCII value, not the HEX value. Make sure that the extensions that you add through LDIF do not already exist on the new LDAP server object or else the import will fail.

You could use the following ICE command to import the extension.ldif file, which would modify the LDAP server object:

```
ice -S LDIF -f extension.ldif -D LDAP -s <server address> ➥
 -p <LDAP port> -d <DN of user to bind as> -w <password>
```

■ **Note** As you can see from the preceding discussion, adding extension information back to an LDAP object is very time consuming. For this reason, don't delete the LDAP server object unless there is no other choice. If you do delete it, your first plan of attack should be to go through each of the extensions and identify the modules. This should give you a good idea of what applications are using the extension (e.g., #nmasldap.nlm would be the NMAS product). Reinstall the given product or run the product's LDAP extension installation rather than manually modifying the LDAP server object.

Walking the Tree

It is highly recommended that all objects that will be accessed through LDAP operations reside on the LDAP server. eDirectory is a powerful, multimaster, distributed directory. This means that eDirectory can distribute its objects over several servers. If, for some reason, your LDAP server does not hold all objects that will be required to fulfill the LDAP operations that are requested from an LDAP client, the LDAP server will need to find a server that does contain the required objects.

The LDAP server allows you to configure how remote servers are contacted to obtain desired objects within the directory. In iManager, when you are modifying the LDAP server object, a Referrals tab is available with the following options:

- Default Referral
- Conditions to Use Default Referral
- Referral Options

Default Referral

The default referral, commonly known as the federated boundary, is a way to provide connection of disparate LDAP systems. For instance, the LDAP client can make a request to the eDirectory LDAP server. Based off of the policies that are set, if the DN is not present or the eDirectory servers are down, you can redirect the request to a remote LDAP server. This remote server does not necessarily need to be running eDirectory. It must, however, be an LDAP server that is listening for LDAP requests. When one of the conditions to use

Default Referrals (described next) is met, the LDAP server contacts the remote LDAP server based on the server address specified in the Default Referral field.

Conditions to Use Default Referral

You may want the Default Referral field to be used only if the server is not available. Or, if the object is not on the LDAP server, you will want to use the Default Referral field to resolve the address. This field allows you to set up the referral policies.

Referral Options

The Referral Options let you specify whether you want the LDAP server to "chain" or return referrals of other directory servers to the LDAP client. These options really depend on the LDAP client. If the LDAP client does not have the ability to receive server referrals and to attempt a connection with one of the servers in the referral list, then chaining is probably the better option. With chaining, the LDAP server passes the request to the eDirectory Agent. If the required objects are not on the local directory server, the eDirectory Agent acts like a client and makes the request on behalf of the LDAP client to a remote server that contains the desired object(s).

The advantage of chaining is that the LDAP client does not need additional logic to handle the reconnection with the remote servers. The disadvantage is that if eDirectory is acting like the client, you cannot control which servers it chooses to contact to obtain the objects. Potentially, it may even stretch across a WAN link to a remote server to get the desired information specified in the LDAP request sent by the LDAP client.

Access Control

When performing anonymous binds, you can configure the LDAP server to use an existing eDirectory user as the "proxy user" or you can bind using the hard-coded [public] user. As with any ACL in eDirectory, the user that you bind as will determine what ACL rights you have to resources within eDirectory.

By default, all eDirectory objects inherit the ACL from [public] (which gives all users Entry Browse rights to the entire tree). It is not advisable to alter the default ACLs for [public], because several applications rely on the default ACL of being able to browse all objects in the tree. If you alter these rights, you potentially will break some applications. To get around the issue of not being able to modify the ACLs for [public], you can create a user in eDirectory that does not contain a password. You can configure the LDAP group object to use that specified LDAP proxy user. With the proxy user object, you cannot assign specific ACLs to limit what an LDAP client can see with an anonymous query.

One exception to this rule is that if an attribute is marked as Public Read, that attribute can be explicitly asked for in an LDAP query and the value will be returned, regardless of the ACL rights set for the proxy user. What does this mean? Consider the following example.

Suppose that you created a proxy user called ldapproxy. You set a filter for all containers in the tree so that ldapproxy has no rights to browse or write to any object in the tree. With this configuration, if you perform an LDAP query and search, for instance, for `objectclass=*`, nothing would be returned. However, if you perform an LDAP query on a Public Read attribute, like `surname`, the value would be returned. So, the LDAP query would do something like find all objects where `surname=killpack`. All objects with a surname of killpack would be returned. The only way to avoid this would be to alter the ACL of [public], which would break applications. Just be aware of this and do not store sensitive data in schema attributes that are marked as Public Read.

Another way of protecting your server from unwanted anonymous LDAP queries is to disallow anonymous binds. In iManager, under the LDAP Server ➤ Connections tab, there are options to disallow anonymous binds. Be cautious with this. If the LDAP client wants to query basic information without authenticating, they will use anonymous binds. By disabling the ability to bind anonymously, you will break these applications. The following are a couple of examples of clients that do this:

- *NetWare Client 32 for Windows version 4.9.x*: Includes a feature to perform contextless logins. The client finds the context for the user by doing an anonymous query against the LDAP database.
- *eGuide*: Performs much of its functionality with anonymous binds. These will no longer work if this feature is disabled.

Using ICE to Bulk-Load Data

Chapter 6 briefly discussed ICE and its ability to modify objects within eDirectory through an LDIF file. ICE is a very powerful tool that will export data into LDIF or CSV formats. It will also import LDIF files to modify schema, add objects, or modify existing objects. If you are building a very large tree, the quickest way to build the tree is to create an LDIF file with all of the users and their values. You can then use ICE to bulk-load in these attributes. For more information on ICE, refer to the *eDirectory Administration Guide* at `http://www.novell.com/documentation`.

Summary

eDirectory provides an LDAP server to process LDAP requests from LDAP-compliant clients, which gives eDirectory great flexibility to provide data to a variety of clients. eDirectory's LDAP server supports Persistent Search, enabling LDAP clients to track changes within eDirectory through a persistent connection. You can manage LDAP objects by using iManager, which enables you to create or configure LDAP objects. Placement of eDirectory replicas plays a key role in LDAP performance.

CHAPTER 8

Management and Monitoring Tools

The following topics are covered in this chapter:

- iManager: Managing your eDirectory system
- NDS iMonitor: Monitoring your eDirectory system
- SNMP: Monitoring the eDirectory event system

Novell eDirectory provides many tools that will allow you to manage and monitor your eDirectory system. The three main eDirectory tools are iManager, NDS iMonitor, and SNMP, which are the focus of this chapter.

iManager: Managing Your eDirectory System

iManager is the primary administration console for most of Novell's products. iManager is a web-based application that runs under the Tomcat servlet engine, which by default is hooked into the Apache Web Server. Many plug-ins are available for iManager, which provide a way to manage many different Novell solutions as well as non-Novell products. iManager is installed by default if you install NetWare 6.x. It is also included in Novell's OES bundle for Linux. iManager is free and can be downloaded from `http://download.novell.com`.

There are two different types of iManager. You can download the full-blown version and run it from a server. Or you can download Mobile iManager. Although this is a full-scale version of iManager, Tomcat and Apache, which run underneath, are stripped of most features. Mobile iManager runs on a self-contained embedded version of Tomcat and utilizes the libraries found in both Internet Explorer and Firefox for its web browser interface. You can download Mobile iManager, unzip the archive to a directory, and execute a batch file on Windows or a shell script on Linux. When you run Mobile iManager, it launches a scaled-down version of Tomcat and integrates with embedded browser libraries and launches iManager for you. When you close Mobile iManager, Tomcat is shut down and the browser is closed. Mobile iManager gives you the ability to have a standalone web application on your laptop or workstation that will administer your entire network.

Regardless of which iManager plug-in you use, you need to run only one copy of iManager for your entire network (although you can run as many copies as you need from as many servers as you like). It should be noted that although Novell is trying to make iManager platform independent, there are some plug-ins that work only on Linux and other plug-ins that work only on NetWare. For this reason, if you have a mixed Linux and NetWare environment, you probably should run at least one iManager instance on each platform. However, all of the eDirectory-based plug-ins are platform independent, so you can administer your mixed-platform, mixed-eDirectory-version environment from one instance of iManager.

Within iManager, there are two basic views for configuring and manipulating objects. You can use either the Roles and Tasks view or the View Objects view, each of which is described in detail next.

Roles and Tasks View

A role in iManager is a collection place for tasks. Tasks are specific operations. For instance, a role may be called Users, which may contain a task called Add User. Roles enable you to collect common tasks for ease of administration. The default roles are sufficient for most cases. However, iManager provides you with an interface wherein you can create your own roles and assign any task you want to the role. iManager plug-ins can contain one or many roles and tasks. When you install a plug-in, iManager copies the role XML files and the task binaries onto the file system under the iManager directories. Because roles and tasks are stored in the file system on the server running iManager (or workstation, in the case of Mobile iManager), you must install a desired plug-in into all instances of iManager to get access to the plug-in's roles and tasks from all instances of iManager. In other words, iManager plug-ins do not synchronize between instances of iManager.

By default, iManager runs in Unrestricted Access mode. This means that everyone who has rights to eDirectory can launch iManager and see all roles that are installed in that instance of iManager. Keeping in mind that tasks are just an interface into the directory, you must ensure that you have sufficient ACL rights to whatever object you are trying to read or configure through that task. If you do not have sufficient rights to execute whatever that task performs, an eDirectory error will be returned and you will not be able to complete the task.

iManager has the ability to automatically set up the rights that you need to perform a specific task. If you configure Role-Based Services (RBS) within iManager, you can assign any user, set of users, container, Organizational Role, or group to a role. By doing so, iManager will assign the necessary rights in eDirectory for that user, group, or Organizational Role to perform the specific tasks. When assigning roles to users, you are asked for a Scope. The Scope is a container. iManager will set sufficient rights to administer whatever task is in that role from the container specified in the Scope and all of its subordinates. If the tasks within the role require Read and Write rights to the entries and attributes, each user assigned to the role that contains that task will get Supervisor rights to the container specified in the Scope and all of its subordinates. By default, most of the eDirectory-related roles require Supervisor rights.

■ **Note** For more information about Role-Based Services and how to configure it, please refer to the *iManager Administration Guide* at `http://www.novell.com/documentation`.

Although there are many iManager plug-ins that you can use to administer most of your Novell applications, for the purposes of keeping in the scope of this chapter, this section describes only the roles that are specific to administering your eDirectory environment.

Groups

The Groups role enables you to create new groups, either static or dynamic. You can view the membership of the group. If you are using Dynamic Groups, you can actually view the current membership. When you request to view the membership of a Dynamic Group, iManager performs an LDAP query based off of the Dynamic Group's Member Query attribute.

LDAP

This role allows you to select and configure all of your current LDAP server and LDAP group objects. Specific information about this role was discussed in previous chapters.

NMAS

Novell Modular Authentication Services (NMAS) is a great feature that is part of eDirectory. With NMAS, you can define different methodologies for authenticating to eDirectory. NMAS is extendable, which means that a non-Novell vendor can write an NMAS method that plugs into the NMAS server. The NMAS method can store and retrieve method-specific data from eDirectory as its authentication methodology.

Novell ships several NMAS methods with eDirectory. One of the most popular methods is the Universal Smart Card (USC) method. The USC method allows user credentials to be stored on a card, similar to a credit card. When the user puts their USC into a card reader, the card reader extracts the data from the card and sends the information to NMAS. NMAS compares the data sent to it from the USC with the data stored in special attributes on the user object within eDirectory. If the data matches, the eDirectory Agent tells NMAS that the user is authenticated.

The NMAS role contains tasks that allow you to define what users have what NMAS methods available to them. The NMAS role also has tasks that allow you to define what combinations of methods constitute a successful login. For detailed information about NMAS, see the *NMAS Administration Guide* at `http://www.novell.com/documentation` or refer to the online help in iManager.

Novell Certificate Access

Novell has built-in security. One of the features of this security infrastructure is the ability to issue and administer user certificates. User certificates are used to prove to an application that the user trying to use the application is really that user. For instance, if you are using GroupWise and you want to make sure that all e-mail messages that you send and receive actually came from the user listed in the From line, you could issue user certificates to yourself and to all users that send you e-mail. You can configure GroupWise to use these certificates for all send and receive operations. If the certificate that is attached to the e-mail message is not valid, the e-mail message is discarded. There are many applications that can utilize this type of security. The Novell Certificate Access role allows you to administer user certificates.

Novell Certificate Server

The Novell Certificate Server role allows you to administer your entire security infrastructure. You can create your certificate authority, server certificates (KMOs), user certificates, etc.

Partition and Replica Management

All partition operations can be executed from this role. Viewing replica rings, creating partitions, merging partitions, and moving partitions are among the partition operations that can be executed from within this role.

Passwords

When you install iManager, with the exception of OES, the Passwords role is not available. You must download and install the eDirectory Password Management plug-in from `http://download.novell.com`. (If you do a keyword search for "Password Management," you will find the plug-in.) The Password Management plug-in is part of the Nsure Identity Manager suite. You do not need to install or run Nsure Identity Manager to use the Password Management plug-in. The plug-in allows you to create and administer Universal Password policies.

The Universal Password is an NMAS password. It allows you to set extensive password policies. It is called "Universal" because Identity Manager has the ability to distribute the Universal Password to other directories, keeping passwords synchronized between disparate systems.

Another task available in the Password Management plug-in enables you to administer your password self-provisioning solution. With password self-provisioning, you may allow users to define password hints as well as challenge and response questions. If a user forgets their password, they can view their hints. They can also change the password, if they have forgotten it, by answering questions to the challenges that are defined.

■ **Note** With iManager 2.0.2 installed on a server, if password self-provisioning is configured, a user can enter the Novell Portal Services (NPS) URL (e.g., `https://`*`<server address>`*`/nps`) to automatically launch the password self-service interface. The user can change their password through the challenge and response screens or view their password hints. This same functionality is not available with iManager 2.5. iManager 2.5 can be used to administer password self-service, but in order for your users to have a self-service portal, you need to have at least one instance of iManager 2.0.2 that the users can access. Another alternative for password self-service is available with the Novell Client 3.2 or 4.91. With this client, the user can view their hints. However, at the time of this writing, users cannot manage challenge and response questions to change their passwords.

Rights

This role allows you to view effective rights, set trustee assignments, set inherited rights filters, and perform other tasks related to rights.

Schema

The Schema role gives you the ability to view schema as well as define new schema attributes and classes.

Time Synchronization

Time Synchronization is a NetWare-only plug-in. This plug-in allows you to convert a NetWare server's time-synchronization solution from the legacy TIMESYNC.NLM to the open-source NTP.

Users

All user-type tasks, like creating, deleting, and modifying users, are available in the Users role.

eDirectory Administration

You can perform all of the tasks available in the previously defined roles through the eDirectory Administration role. Using the specific roles just described and using the generic administration tasks in the eDirectory Administration role both have advantages and disadvantages. The specific roles give you a view of tasks that would be used on a day-to-day basis. They are designed for a help desk user. The eDirectory Administration role provides tasks that give you additional tabs when modifying objects. For instance, if you modify a user through the Users role, you get all the applicable tabs to administer a user. If you modify a user through the eDirectory Administration ➤ Modify Object task, you have to browse through all objects to find the user (not just user objects). You will, however, have additional tabs available to you. The most common view is the Other tab. This shows you all attributes that are assigned to that user. The "other" tab is not available if you select the Modify User task under the Users role.

eDirectory Maintenance

The eDirectory Maintenance role enables you to maintain your eDirectory database. A majority of the tasks available give you an easy-to-use web interface to launch the command-line eMTools. You can repair, merge, back up, and restore your eDirectory database through this role. You can easily execute these tasks on any eDirectory server in your tree. Other tasks give you an interface into other eDirectory tools, like NDS iMonitor and ICE.

View Objects View

The View Objects view does not use roles or tasks. You can access this screen by clicking the fourth icon from the left from within iManager (see Figure 8-1).

Figure 8-1. *iManager View Objects view*

The way in which you browse objects in the View Objects view is similar to the way in which you browse objects in ConsoleOne. You can walk through the tree from container to container. When you have found the object that you want to modify or the container in which you want to add a new object, you can click on the object. A menu is then presented that gives you all related tasks for the specific object type (see Figure 8-2).

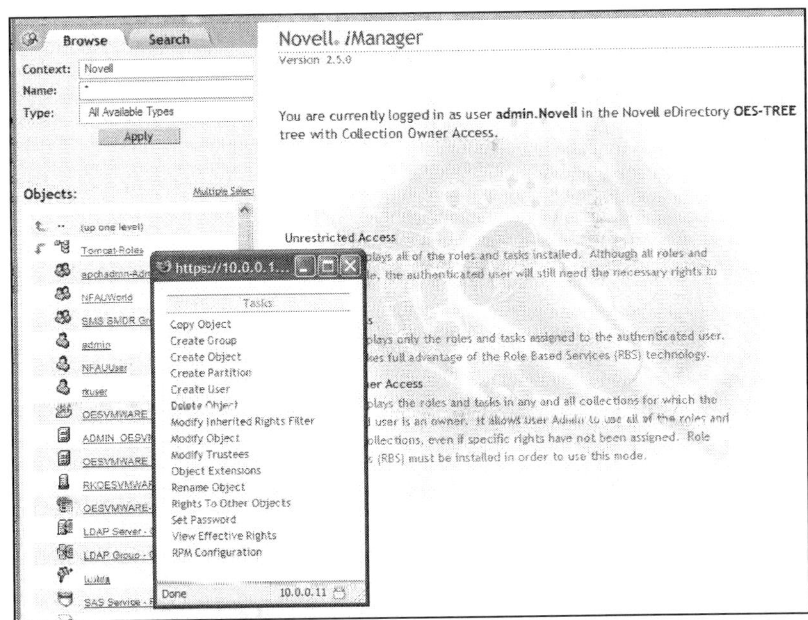

Figure 8-2. *iManager View Objects View Tasks window*

NDS iMonitor: Monitoring Your eDirectory System

Whereas iManager is Novell's primary cross-platform, web-management application to manage eDirectory, NDS iMonitor is Novell's primary cross-platform, web-monitoring application to monitor eDirectory. There are certain views in NDS iMonitor that allow you to configure eDirectory, but it is primarily a proactive monitoring and reactive troubleshooting tool. Unlike iManager, iMonitor does not run on Apache or Tomcat. NDS iMonitor has its own HTTP stack daemon for Windows, Solaris, Linux, HP-UX, and AIX. iMonitor runs on top of Novell's HTTPSTK.NLM on NetWare.

The trickiest part of iMonitor is figuring out what port the HTTP stack is listening on. Depending on the platform, the procedure is different. The following are the different ways to determine what port the HTTP stack is listening on:

- *NetWare*: The HTTPSTK.NLM is configured to listen on port 8008 for clear-text connections and 8009 for secure connections.
- *Windows*: Launch NDSCons. Go to the Transports tab. Click HTTP ➤ Bound Transports and HTTPS ➤ Bound Transports, respectively, to locate the clear-text and secure ports. By default, clear text is 8008 and secure is 8010.
- *Linux, Solaris, HP-UX, AIX*: At a terminal, type **ndsconfig get | grep http**. This gives you output of all HTTP settings in the nds.conf file. The clear-text port and secure port are listed in the output. By default, the clear-text port is on 8008 and the secure port is on 8010. The exception to this is OES on SLES 9. On this install, the defaults are 8028 for clear text and 8030 for secure.

Once the HTTP port is identified, you can access NDS iMonitor by going to `http://<server address>:<clear-text port>/nds` or `https://<server address>:<secure port>/nds`.

The following sections introduce the main NDS iMonitor views, providing a brief description of the primary use of each screen. Each screen is simply a hyperlink. If you know the screen filename, you can just append it to the URL or simply click the hyperlink. For instance, you could access the main summary page on a NetWare server with an address of 10.0.0.9 by typing the following in the URL line of your browser:

```
http://10.0.0.9:8008/nds/summary
```

Agent Summary

The Agent Summary view has three sections. Each section is a hyperlink to other pages within NDS iMonitor. The Agent Summary view provides information about the following pages:

- Agent Synchronization
- Known Servers
- Agent Process Status

The direct URL is http://<*server address*>:<*clear-text port*>/nds/summary or https://<*server address*>:<*secure port*>/nds/summary.

Agent Synchronization

This screen shows you all partitions that are stored on the local server as well as the partition status, synchronization status, and errors for the partition.

■ **Note** The server being viewed can be directly accessed via NDS iMonitor or indirectly accessed through proxy mode.

The direct URL is http://<*server address*>:<*clear-text port*>/nds/ssync or https://<*server address*>:<*secure port*>/nds/ssync.

Known Servers

The Known Servers view allows you to view and administer all servers within eDirectory. eDirectory is designed to be able to communicate with any server that contains an eDirectory database within the same tree, regardless of how many replicas of partitions the local server contains. eDirectory accomplishes this task by holding either a real object or an external reference of all NCP server objects in the tree.

■ **Note** It is possible, with the loosely consistent nature of eDirectory as well as communication variables, that the local server will not see all other servers in the tree.

The direct URL is http://<*server address*>:<*clear-text port*>/nds/known or https://<*server address*>:<*secure port*>/nds/known.

Schema

In eDirectory, the schema partition is a mandatory system partition. This special partition contains the attribute and class definitions. NDS iMonitor allows you to view schema objects through the Schema view. One of the most powerful features of the NDS iMonitor Schema view is the ability to perform a schema comparison. The Schema Compare feature is discussed in detail in the troubleshooting sections of this manual.

The direct URL is `http://<server address>:<clear-text port>/nds/schema` or `https://<server address>:<secure port>/nds/schema`.

Agent Configuration

The Agent Configuration page is your main configuration page. You can view and manipulate the background processes; view and configure the eDirectory database cache; and control the eDirectory replication and schema synchronization processes.

Note Additional configuration options are available if the Advanced Options are turned on. You can turn on the Advanced Options by clicking the NDS iMonitor icon in the top left of the screen. If the Advanced Options are turned on, you can view and change the Permanent Settings.

The direct URL is `http://<server address>:<clear-text port>/nds/agent/info` or `https://<server address>:<secure port>/nds/agent/info`.

Trace Configuration

NDS iMonitor is a cross-platform tool. This means that NDS iMonitor does not care what operating system or platform eDirectory is running on. Regardless of the platform, NDS iMonitor gives you the same look and feel. The Trace Configuration page is a good example of this. The command-line utility DSTRACE is available on each platform in which eDirectory runs. The command-line utility will have a different name and different syntax depending on the platform. In eDirectory environments in which you have multiple platforms, trying to remember which tool does what can get confusing. If you use NDS iMonitor, the DSTRACE configuration looks exactly the same.

The trace that is captured will be recorded in an HTML page. An archive of HTML traces is maintained. The exact location of the HTML files will depend on the platform in which you are running eDirectory. However, regardless of platform, the HTML pages will always be located in the relative directory, dstrace. On NetWare, the relative directory is located in SYS:\SYSTEM\NDSIMON. In Windows, it is located in the \novell\nds\ndsimon directory. On Linux, Solaris, HP-UX, and AIX, the relative directory is in the /var/nds directory.

The direct URL is http://<*server address*>:<*clear-text port*>/nds/trace or https://<*server address*>:<*secure port*>/nds/trace.

Agent Health

The Agent Health view is designed to give you a quick overview of the health of the server currently being viewed. NDS iMonitor reports the current status of replication as well as general eDirectory Agent statistics. NDS iMonitor displays symbols indicating whether replica and agent health is

- Good (green button)
- Marginal (green and white diamond)
- Warning (red hyphen)

NDS iMonitor gives you the ability to drill down into each section to find detailed information about why it determined the status.

The direct URL is http://<*server address*>:<*clear-text port*>/nds/health or https://<*server address*>:<*secure port*>/nds/health.

Agent Process Status

eDirectory stores the last result of each background process for a server on the pseudo server object within the server's local eDirectory database. The Agent Process Status screen displays the status values that are stored on the pseudo server object. This view is a quick way to determine the status of all background processes.

The direct URL is http://<*server address*>:<*clear-text port*>/nds/pstatus or https://<*server address*>:<*secure port*>/nds/pstatus.

Agent Activity

The Agent Activity view contains detailed information about the current activity of the eDirectory Agent. The following information is available:

- Verb statistics
- Synchronization information
- Background process information
- Event statistics

The direct URL is `http://<server address>:<clear-text port>/nds/activity` or `https://<server address>:<secure port>/nds/activity`.

Connections

The Connections view displays detailed information about every inbound and outbound eDirectory connection that is being made to an eDirectory server. Detailed information about each connection is displayed. Information such as who requested the connection and what type of connection is created is available. This page is useful if you think that there are too many connections to the directory or you are getting connection errors.

The direct URL is `http://<server address>:<clear-text port>/nds/cons` or `https://<server address>:<secure port>/nds/cons`.

Error Index

NDS iMonitor has most of the currently possible errors that eDirectory may encounter. The Error Index view gives you the error number, the description, and troubleshooting hints on how to solve the error.

The direct URL is `http://<server address>:<clear-text port>/nds/error` or `https://<server address>:<secure port>/nds/error`.

SNMP: Monitoring the eDirectory Event System

The Simple Network Management Protocol (SNMP) is a standard protocol that allows you to hook to specific events defined by the application. If the events are triggered, you can configure SNMP to send e-mail messages to individuals, write the status of the event to a database or file, or use any other method of communication.

eDirectory ships with an SNMP subagent. The subagent has a precompiled MIB, which contains all of the available traps. A "trap" is a request to capture a certain event in eDirectory. For instance, if you want to capture every instance in which a user changes their password, you could set a trap 51 (ndsChangePassword). iManager contains a role called SNMP that allows you to create SNMP group objects as well as configure specific traps. The eDirectory SNMP agent cannot run on its own. It must be configured to use a Master Agent (like Zen for Servers on NetWare). For more information about SNMP, see the *eDirectory Administration Guide* at `http://www.novell.com/documentation`.

PART 3

Troubleshooting eDirectory

Part 3 of the *eDirectory Field Guide* identifies common issues that can arise in an eDirectory system. This section also discusses in depth the suggested tools to use to troubleshoot and remedy eDirectory issues.

CHAPTER 9

Troubleshooting with NDS iMonitor

The following topics are covered in this chapter:

- NDS iMonitor page descriptions
- Troubleshooting NDS iMonitor
    - Understanding the iMonitor process
    - Determining the HTTP ports
    - Understanding the HTTP server object
    - Using DSTRACE to troubleshoot NDS iMonitor issues
- Troubleshooting Unknown objects
    - Identifying the Unknown objects
    - Determining why the object is Unknown
    - Resolving the condition that created the Unknown object
    - Reassigning the correct object type to the object
- Troubleshooting schema
    - Finding the schema issue
    - Deciding which server contains valid schema
    - Using NDS iMonitor to remedy schema issues
- Troubleshooting obituaries
    - Processing obituaries
    - Using NDS iMonitor to identify obituaries
    - Using NDS iMonitor to resolve obituary issues

- Troubleshooting processor high utilization
    - Using Agent Activity
    - Using Trace
    - Using Agent Configuration

NDS iMonitor is Novell's primary cross-platform, web-monitoring application to monitor eDirectory. NDS iMonitor is primarily a proactive monitoring and reactive troubleshooting tool.

You can access NDS iMonitor by going to `http://`*<server address>*`:`*<clear-text port>*`/nds` or `https://`*<server address>*`:`*<secure port>*`/nds`.

NDS iMonitor Page Descriptions

This section provides a brief description of the primary views in NDS iMonitor.

Agent Summary

The Agent Summary view is the default home page for NDS iMonitor. It has the following three sections, each of which is a hyperlink to other pages within NDS iMonitor:

- Agent Synchronization
- Known Servers
- Agent Process Status

The direct URL is `http://`*<server address>*`:`*<clear-text port>*`/nds/summary` or `https://`*<server address>*`:`*<secure port>*`/nds/summary`.

Agent Synchronization

The Agent Synchronization view shows you all partitions that are stored on the local server as well as the partition status, synchronization status, and errors for the partition.

Note The server being viewed can be directly accessed via NDS iMonitor or indirectly accessed through proxy mode.

The direct URL is `http://`*<server address>*`:`*<clear-text port>*`/nds/ssync` or `https://`*<server address>*`:`*<secure port>*`/nds/ssync`.

Known Servers

The Known Servers view allows you to view and administer all servers within eDirectory. eDirectory is designed to be able to communicate with any server that contains an eDirectory database within the same tree, regardless of how many replicas of partitions the local server contains. eDirectory accomplishes this task by holding either a real object or an external reference of all NCP server objects in the tree.

■ **Note** It is possible, with the loosely consistent nature of eDirectory as well as communication variables, that the local server may not see all other servers in the tree.

The direct URL is `http://`*<server address>*`:`*<clear-text port>*`/nds/known` or `https://`*<server address>*`:`*<secure port>*`/nds/known`.

Schema

In eDirectory, the schema partition is a mandatory system partition. This special partition contains the attribute and class definitions. NDS iMonitor allows you to view schema objects through the Schema view. One of the most powerful features of the NDS iMonitor Schema view is the ability to perform a Schema Compare. The Schema Compare feature is described in detail in the troubleshooting sections of this manual.

The direct URL is `http://`*<server address>*`:`*<clear-text port>*`/nds/schema` or `https://`*<server address>*`:`*<secure port>*`/nds/schema`.

Agent Configuration

The Agent Configuration page is your main configuration page. You can view and manipulate the background processes; view and configure the eDirectory database cache; and control the eDirectory replication and schema synchronization processes.

■ **Note** Additional configuration options are available if the Advanced Options are turned on. You can turn on the Advanced Options by clicking the NDS iMonitor icon in the top left of the screen. If the Advanced Options are turned on, you can view and change the Permanent Settings.

The direct URL is `http://`*<server address>*`:`*<clear-text port>*`/nds/agent/info` or `https://`*<server address>*`:`*<secure port>*`/nds/agent/info`.

Trace Configuration

NDS iMonitor is a cross-platform tool. This means that NDS iMonitor does not care what operating system or platform eDirectory is running on. Regardless of the platform, NDS iMonitor gives you the same look and feel. The Trace Configuration page is a good example of this. The command-line utility DSTRACE is available on each platform in which eDirectory runs. The command-line utility will have a different name and different syntax depending on the platform. In eDirectory environments in which you have multiple platforms, trying to remember which tool does what can get confusing. If you use NDS iMonitor, the DSTRACE configuration looks exactly the same.

The trace that is captured will be recorded in an HTML page. An archive of HTML traces is maintained. The exact location of the HTML files will depend on the platform in which you are running eDirectory. However, regardless of platform, the HTML pages will always be located in the relative directory, dstrace. On NetWare, the relative directory is located in the SYS:\SYSTEM\NDSIMON directory. In Windows, it is located in the \novell\nds\ndsimon directory. On Linux, Solaris, HP-UX, and AIX, the relative directory is in the /var/nds directory.

The direct URL is `http://`*<server address>*`:`*<clear-text port>*`/nds/trace` or `https://`*<server address>*`:`*<secure port>*`/nds/trace`.

Agent Health

The Agent Health view is designed to give you a quick overview of the health of the server currently being viewed. NDS iMonitor reports the current status of replication as well as general eDirectory agent statistics. NDS iMonitor displays symbols indicating whether replica and agent health is

- Good (green button)
- Marginal (green and white diamond)
- Warning (red hyphen)

NDS iMonitor enables you to drill down into each section to find detailed information about why it determined the particular status.

The direct URL is `http://`*<server address>*`:`*<clear-text port>*`/nds/health` or `https://`*<server address>*`:`*<secure port>*`/nds/health`.

Agent Process Status

eDirectory stores the last result of each background process for a server on the pseudo server object within the server's local eDirectory database. The Agent Process Status view displays the status values that are stored on the pseudo server object. This view is a quick way to determine the status of all background processes.

The direct URL is http://<server address>:<clear-text port>/nds/pstatus or https://<server address>:<secure port>/nds/pstatus.

Agent Activity

The Agent Activity view contains detailed information about the current activity of the eDirectory agent. The following information is available:

- Verb statistics
- Synchronization information
- Background process information
- Event statistics

The direct URL is http://<server address>:<clear-text port>/nds/activity or https://<server address>:<secure port>/nds/activity.

Connections

The Connections view displays detailed information about every inbound and outbound eDirectory connection that is being made to an eDirectory server. Information such as who requested the connection and what type of connection was created is available. This page is useful if you think that there are too many connections to the directory or you are getting connection errors.

The direct URL is http://<server address>:<clear-text port>/nds/cons or https://<server address>:<secure port>/nds/cons.

Error Index

NDS iMonitor has most of the currently possible errors that eDirectory may encounter. The Error Index view gives you the error number, the description, and troubleshooting hints on how to solve the error. This page also displays error codes used by other Novell products such as NMAS and NCP.

The direct URL is http://<server address>:<clear-text port>/nds/error or https://<server address>:<secure port>/nds/error.

Troubleshooting NDS iMonitor

NDS iMonitor runs as an application in NetWare and as a module within the NDSD (dhost) process space on Windows, Linux, Solaris, AIX, and HP-UX. Before you can use NDS iMonitor as your troubleshooting tool, you need to make sure that it is running and know what TCP ports that it is listening on. This section presents critical items that are associated with NDS iMonitor that you should be familiar with to ensure that NDS iMonitor is running and configured correctly.

Understanding the iMonitor Process

The NDS iMonitor process is associated to different binaries on each operating system. The first step in verifying that NDS iMonitor is running is to check the status of the process. The command to verify the status will vary based on the platform. Table 9-1 presents the commands that you would use for each platform to verify the status of the NDS iMonitor module, as well as the HTTP stack that NDS iMonitor is registered to use.

Table 9-1. *Viewing the Status of the NDS iMonitor and HTTP Stack Module*

Operating System/Platform	HTTP Stack Command	NDS iMonitor Module Command
NetWare	`modules httpstk.nlm`	`modules ndsimon.nlm`
Windows	Check the Status column in NDSCONS next to httpstk.dlm	Check the Status column in NDSCONS next to ndsimon.dlm
Linux/Solaris/ AIX/HP-UX	`ndstrace -c modules | grep httpstk`	`ndstrace -c modules | grep imon`

■ **Note** You can launch NDSCONS by going to c:\Novell\NDS\ndscons.exe or by clicking the Novell eDirectory Services icon in Control Panel.

If the status of NDS iMonitor or the HTTP stack shows that it is not running, load the module by using the commands provided in Table 9-2.

Table 9-2. *Commands to Load the HTTP Stack and NDS iMonitor Modules*

Operating System/Platform	HTTP Stack Command	NDS iMonitor Module Command
NetWare	`load httpstk /SSL /keyfile:"<ssl certificate>"`	`load ndsimon.nlm`
Windows	Select httpstk.dlm in NDSCONS and click Start	Select ndsimon.dlm in NDSCONS and click Start
Linux/Solaris/ AIX/HP-UX	`ndstrace -c "load httpstk"`	`ndstrace -c "load imon"`

Determining the HTTP Ports

iMonitor runs on top of its own HTTP stack daemon for Windows, Solaris, Linux, HP-UX, and AIX. iMonitor runs on top of Novell's HTTPSTK.NLM on NetWare.

The trickiest part of iMonitor is figuring out what port the HTTP stack is listening on. Depending on the platform, the procedure is different. The following are the different ways to determine what port the HTTP stack is listening on:

- *NetWare*: HTTPSTK.NLM is configured to listen on port 8008 for clear-text connections and on 8009 for secure connections.

■ **Note** The port for HTTPSTK.NLM on NetWare is written into the SYS:_NETWARE\HTTPSTK.DAT file. Unfortunately, this is a binary file and cannot be read or modified by a regular editor. You can view the port and manage it through the registry editor that is located in Novell Remote Manager. To access Novell Remote Manager, log onto the NetWare HTTPSTK with a browser by going to `http://`*`<server address>`*`:8008`.

- *Windows*: Launch NDSCONS. Go to the Transports tab. Click HTTP ➤ Bound Transports and HTTPS ➤ Bound Transports, respectively, to locate the clear-text and secure ports. By default, clear text is 8008 and secure is 8010.
- *Linux, Solaris, HP-UX, AIX*: At a terminal, type **ndsconfig get | grep http**. This gives you output of all HTTP settings in the nds.conf file. The clear-text port and secure port are listed in the output. By default, the clear-text port is on 8008 and the secure port is on 8010. The exception to this is OES on SLES 9. On this install, the defaults are 8028 for clear text and 8030 for secure.

Once you have determined what port the HTTP stack is listening on, you need to verify that the port is listening and accepting requests. To verify that the port is listening, you can use the `netstat` command.

Table 9-3 provides the syntax for `netstat`, per platform, that you can use to determine whether or not the port is listening.

Table 9-3. *The netstat Syntax per Platform*

Operation System/Platform	Command	Notes
NetWare	`netstat -aL`	Lists all ports that are listening as well as what network address they are listening on. If the address is an asterisk (*), all IP addresses are listening on that port.
Windows	`netstat -an | more`	All ports are listed. The ports that are listening can be found by reading the State field and looking for LISTENING. The port number is listed in the Local Address field. If the Local Address field starts with 0.0.0.0, then all IP addresses bound on the server for all interfaces are listening on that port.
Linux, Solaris, AIX, HP-UX	`netstat -an | grep -i listen`	Lists all ports that are listening. If an * is used, all IP addresses are listening on the specified port.

Understanding the HTTP Server Object

For every NCP server object in the eDirectory tree, there is an associated HTTP server object. This statement is not true, however, for NetWare servers. On NetWare, NDS iMonitor registers to the existing NetWare HTTPSTK. The NetWare HTTPSTK uses the NetWare registry to store its information, not eDirectory. On all other platforms, the eDirectory HTTPSTK is used, which stores its configuration information in eDirectory.

The default object name is Http Server – <*server name*>. For the Windows, Linux, HP-UX, AIX, and Solaris platforms, the configuration information for the HTTPSTK is also stored on the file system in configuration files. The configuration file for Windows is located in c:\Novell\NDS\DIBFiles\config.acs. The easiest way to view and configure this file is through NDSCONS.

On the other non-NetWare platforms, the HTTPSTK information is stored in the nds.conf file, which is located in the /etc directory. The best way to view and configure the nds.conf file is to use the `ndsconfig get/set` command. For instance, if you want to see all the HTTPSTK settings, type **ndsconfig get | grep http**. This displays the following types of information:

```
http.server.interfaces=@8008
http.server.sadmin-passwd=
http.server.module-base=/usr/lib/nds/nds-http/
http.server.request-io-buffer-size=8192
http.server.request_timeout-seconds=300
http.server.keep-timeout-seconds=15
http.server.threads-per-processor=2
http.server.session-exp-seconds=900
http.server.trace-level=2
http.server.clear-port=8028
http.server.tls-port=8030
http.server.auth-req-tls=1
https.server.interfaces=@8010
http.server.cached-cert-dn=SSL CertificateDNS - rkvmoeslinux.novell
http.server.cached-server-dn=
```

Table 9-4 maps each setting in the nds.conf file (`ndsconfig get`) to the corresponding attribute name that resides on the HTTP object in eDirectory, and describes how the parameter is used.

Modifying the HTTP Object Through iManager

All of the HTTP parameters can be configured by changing the values on the HTTP object in eDirectory using iManager. To do this, use the eDirectory Administration ➤ Modify Object task. When modifying the HTTP object, click the Other link under the General tab. You will see all the attributes that were specified in Table 9-4. You can make changes to any of the values.

Modifying the HTTP Object Through ndsconfig

You can use the `ndsconfig set` command to change any of the HTTP settings. The syntax is as follows:

```
ndsconfig set <nds.conf setting>=<value>
```

The following is an example:

```
ndsconfig set httpDefaultTLSPort=8130
```

The changes made are permanent and are written to the /etc/nds.conf file.

Table 9-4. *HTTP Object Attributes*

eDirectory Attribute	Nds.conf File Setting	Description
None	http.server.interfaces	If you want to limit which IP addresses listen to the specified port, you can specify them with this parameter. By default, all bound interfaces listen on the specified HTTP port.
None	http.server.sadmin-passwd	You can configure a SADMIN for the HTTP stack. This user is not stored in eDirectory. The password can be specified with this parameter. This is used if you need to access the directory to troubleshoot it and you cannot authenticate.
None	http.server.module-base	Specifies where the libraries for the HTTP stack are kept.
httpIOBufferSize	http.server.request-io-buffer-size	Indicates the size of packet that can be used when requesting information through iMonitor. By default, it is set to 8192 bytes.
httpRequestTimeout	http.server.request_timeout-seconds	Specifies the amount of time allowed after a request is sent with no reply. If the time is hit, the request is aborted.
httpKeepAliveRequestTimeout	http.server.keep-timeout-seconds	Sets the ping interval to verify that the session is still alive.
httpThreadsPerCPU	http.server.threads-per-processor	Specifies how many threads per CPU can be used to fulfill the requests.
httpSessionTimeout	http.server.session-exp-seconds	Indicates the number of seconds that the session can be kept alive without activity.

eDirectory Attribute	Nds.conf File Setting	Description
httpTraceLevel	http.server.trace-level	Determines how much output will be given when the +http filter is set in DSTRACE. The possible values are 1 to 5. The default is 2.
httpDefaultClearPort	http.server.clear-port	Identifies the port on which the HTTP stack will listen for clear-text requests.
httpDefaultTLSPort	http.server.tls-port	Identifies the port on which the HTTP stack will listen for TLS requests.
httpAuthRequiresTLS	http.server.auth-req-tls	If you want to make sure that all authorization requests into the HTTP stack are secure, set this to 1. Otherwise, set it to 0. By default, it is set to 1.
None	https.server.interfaces	Specifies which IP interfaces to bind to the HTTPS listening port. By default, all IP interfaces are enabled.
httpKeyMaterialObject	http.server.cached-cert-dn	Indicates the full DN of the server certificate object (KMO) for the specified server. This is used for secure connections.
httpHostServerDN	http.server.cached-server-dn	Indicates the full DN of the NCP server object that is associated to the server that is running NDS iMonitor.

Modifying the HTTP Object via LDAP

You can also use LDAP to modify the HTTP object within eDirectory. You can use any LDAP client that allows you to modify objects via LDAP. A common open-source utility is LDAPSearch. The following is an example of how to use LDAPSearch to dump to screen the values for the httpHostServerDN, httpDefaultTLSPort, and httpDefaultClearPort attributes:

```
ldapsearch -h <server address> -D <bind DN> -w <password> -x -LL ➥
objectclass=httpserver dn httpHostServerDN httpDefaultTLSPort ➥
httpDefaultClearPort
```

The following is an example:

```
ldapsearch -h 192.168.1.1 -D cn=admin,o=novell -w novell -x -LL ➥
objectclass=httpserver dn httpHostServerDN httpDefaultTLSPort ➥
httpDefaultClearPort
```

To modify the httpDefaultTLSPort attribute, for instance, you could use the LDAPModify utility. The following is an example of the `ldapmodify` syntax:

```
ldapmodify -h <server address> -D <bind DN> -w <password> -x
```

A specific example follows:

```
ldapmodify -h 192.168.1.1 -D cn=admin,o=novell -w novell -x
```

Modifying the HTTP Server in NetWare

By default, you do not have much control over the HTTP server object in NetWare. Most of the configuration information is stored in SYS:_NETWARE\HTTPSTK.DAT. This is a binary file and cannot be edited directly. There is an interface through Novell Remote Manager that will allow you to change the configuration of this file. For more information on this interface, see the *Novell Remote Manager Administration Guide for NetWare* at `http://www.novell.com/documentation`.

You can control whether or not the HTTP stack on NetWare will accept or require an SSL connection. If SSL is enabled, you can also specify the certificate by using the keyword `keyfile`. The following is a typical `load` statement in the autoexec.ncf file that enables SSL for the HTTP stack:

```
load httpstk.nlm /ssl /keyfile:SSL CertificateDNS - rkserver1
```

The following is an example load statement in which SSL is enforced:

```
load httpstk.nlm /sslonly /keyfile: SSL CertificateDNS - rkserver1
```

Configuring SADMIN

SADMIN is a special account that allows you to access most of the NDS iMonitor pages without authenticating to eDirectory. The idea is that if something is wrong with eDirectory and you want to use NDS iMonitor to troubleshoot, you may not be able to authenticate. SADMIN gives you limited access to some of the pages to try and find the problem.

Note With SADMIN, you have limited abilities, so you may receive errors such as `-672 Access_Denied` when trying to perform some of the tasks in NDS iMonitor.

On the Windows, Linux, Solaris, HP-UX, and AIX platforms, you can access the configuration page for the HTTP stack by going to: `http://`*`<server address>`*`:`*`<http port>`*`/dhost/httpstk`. This page enables you to set the SADMIN password and enable the account. On the Linux, Solaris, HP-UX, and AIX platforms, you can use the `ndsconfig` utility with the following syntax:

```
ndsconfig set http.server.sadmin-passwd=<your password>
```

An example follows:

```
set http.server.sadmin-passwd=sadminpwd
```

On NetWare, you can go to `http://`*`<server address>`*`:`*`<http port>`*`/SAdminPW/ENABLE`. You will be prompted to log into the directory as a user that has Supervisor rights to the server. After a successful authentication, you will be prompted to set the SADMIN password. Once the password is set, the account is enabled. To disable the SADMIN account, go to `http://`*`<server address>`*`:`*`<http port>`*`/SAdminPW/DISABLE`.

Note If you did not enable the SADMIN account and you can't authenticate to the directory to enable the account, you can temporarily enable it by typing `NRMDEBUG` *`<your password>`* at the console prompt. This enables SADMIN temporarily. The next time the HTTPSTK.NLM is loaded, the account will be disabled.

Using DSTRACE to Troubleshoot iMonitor Issues

There are two DSTRACE filters that you can set to track HTTP stack problems and NDS iMonitor problems. These filters are `+http` and `+imon`.

Troubleshooting Unknown Objects

Unknown objects are objects in which no specific schema class definition is assigned to the object. In these cases, the Unknown class is assigned to the object. There are three conditions that will cause an object to go Unknown:

- *Mandatory attributes are missing*: If an object does not contain all the attributes defined as mandatory for the specific object type (defined by the schema class definition that is assigned to the object), the object will be assigned as object type Unknown.
- *A class definition is undefined*: Objects are defined with a specific object type by attaching an `objectclass` attribute to the object. The `objectclass` value is the name of a schema class definition. The flags on the `objectclass` attribute will be "base class." An example would be a user object. A user object would be assigned the `objectclass user`. If the schema class specified in the `objectclass` attribute does not exist in the schema partition on the local server, the specified object is assigned the Unknown object type.
- *A collision occurs*: eDirectory requires that each object in the tree have a unique tuned name. An object is identified by two components:
    - *Fully qualified distinguished name (DN)*: Consists of the object's common name and its hierarchal position in the tree. For instance, if an object's common name is jdoe and jdoe resides in a subcontainer called provo, which is contained in an organization container called novell, then the fully qualified DN for joe would be cn=jdoe.ou=provo.o=novell.

      Creation time stamp: Contains the time, to the second, that the object was created, along with an event ID and the replica number of the replica in which the object was created.

  If two objects contain the same fully qualified DN or contain the same creation time stamp, eDirectory renames one of the objects *<number of collisions>_<replica number that created collision>* (e.g., 1_1) and marks the object as Unknown.

Note If the second number is a 0, such as 1_0, then it is an external reference.

Because schema must replicate to all servers, it is possible to have a situation where schema has not yet synchronized all the way down the tree. You may encounter situations in which servers lower in the tree do not have the most current schema definitions, which can cause the conditions previously described. For instance, if your tree contains a user-defined class definition called Wagons, and Wagons does not define any mandatory attributes, you could create an object with the object type Wagons and put it in only the mandatory attributes that are inherited from Top. You could then change schema at the top of the tree and define a mandatory attribute for Wagons called `color`. After schema has replicated to the server lower in the tree that contain the object of object type Wagons, the specified object no longer fits the schema class definition's rules. If a DSREPAIR is run or that object is synchronized, it will be assigned an Unknown object type.

It is important to understand that eDirectory has many safeguards to ensure that these types of scenarios do not occur. For instance, if an object is sent to a remote server through the synchronization process, before that object is received by the remote server, the remote server verifies that it contains all the necessary schema definitions for that object. If it is missing some of the schema definitions (schema class or attribute definitions) or if the schema definitions contained by the remote server have rules that do not agree with the incoming object, an error is returned and the object is not synchronized to the remote server's database. The errors will vary based on the schema violation. Typical errors would be the following:

- –603: ERR_NO_SUCH_ATTRIBUTE
- –604: ERR_NO_SUCH_CLASS
- –608: ERR_ILLEGAL_ATTRIBUTE
- –609: ERR_MISSING_MANDATORY
- –611: ERR_ILLEGAL_CONTAINMENT
- –613: ERR_SYNTAX_VIOLATION

A three-step process is required to resolve Unknown objects. NDS iMonitor can be used for all three steps. The following are the suggested steps, which are described in depth in the sections that follow:

1. Identify the Unknown objects.
2. Determine why the object is unknown.
3. Resolve the condition that created the Unknown object.
4. Reassign the correct object type back to the object.

Identifying the Unknown Objects

NDS iMonitor has a predefined report that lists all objects that are Unknown for the local server or for the entire tree. To access the reports, click the Reports icon, as shown in Figure 9-1.

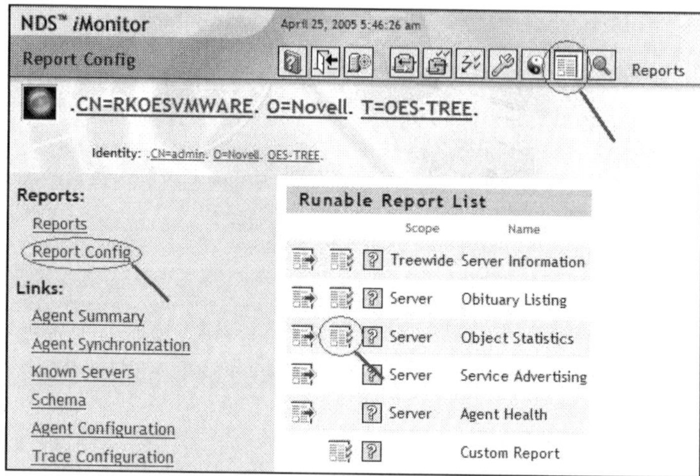

Figure 9-1. *Accessing reports*

The Object Statistics report allows you to find all Unknown objects for the specified server or the tree, as shown in Figure 9-2.

Object Statistics Configuration

Select desired options; some options may increase the time the report takes to complete — Complete Sub-Report, Partition Sub-Report

Entry Flag Sub-Reports:	Alias	Container	Damaged
	New Entry	Not Present	Partition Root
	Present	Reference	Verify Creation Time
External Reference Sub-Reports:	Backlinked	Cached Partition Root	Not Backlinked
	Temporary Reference		
Object Class Sub-Reports:	Auxiliary Class	BaseClass Summary	BaseClass Listing
	Unknown		
Additional Sub-Reports:	Empty Container	Name Collision	Obituary
Future Timestamp Sub-Reports:	Modification Timestamp		
	1 Days Hours		
Future Timestamp Sub-Reports:	Check Entry Only	Check Minimum Attributes	Check All Attributes

Scope Options

Start at:	OES-TREE. — Select a base ob
Scope of:	Base, Subordinate, Partition, Subtree
	Include external references

Run Report — Reset

Figure 9-2. *Object Statistics report*

To run the report, you click the Run Report button. After the report finishes, a report is generated that lists all Unknown objects in the tree, as shown in Figure 9-3.

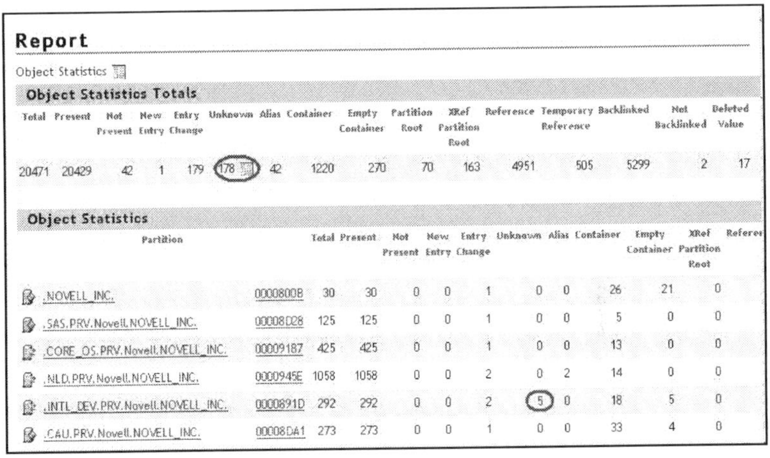

Report

Object Statistics

Object Statistics Totals

Total	Present	Not Present	New Entry	Entry Change	Unknown	Alias	Container	Empty Containes	Partition Root	XRef Partition Root	Reference	Temporary Reference	Backlinked	Not Backlinked	Deleted Value
20471	20429	42	1	179	178	42	1220	270	70	163	4951	505	5299	2	17

Object Statistics

Partition		Total	Present	Not Present	New Entry	Entry Change	Unknown	Alias	Container	Empty Container	XRef Partition Root	Referer
.NOVELL_INC.	0000800B	30	30	0	0	1	0	0	26	21	0	
.SAS.PRV.Novell.NOVELL_INC.	00008D28	125	125	0	0	1	0	0	5	0	0	
.CORE_OS.PRV.Novell.NOVELL_INC.	00009187	425	425	0	0	1	0	0	13	0	0	
.NLD.PRV.Novell.NOVELL_INC.	0000945E	1058	1058	0	0	2	0	2	14	0	0	
.INTL_DEV.PRV.Novell.NOVELL_INC.	0000891D	292	292	0	0	2	5	0	18	5	0	
.CAU.PRV.Novell.NOVELL_INC.	00008DA1	273	273	0	0	1	0	0	33	4	0	

Figure 9-3. *Unknown objects report*

Determining Why the Object Is Unknown

As discussed previously, there are three conditions that generate an Unknown object:

- A collision occurs
- A class definition is undefined
- Mandatory attributes are missing

Before you can remedy the Unknown object, you need to resolve the condition that rendered the object Unknown. The following sections describe each of the conditions, in order from easiest to hardest to resolve, and the resolution methods that you can use to determine why the object is Unknown.

A Collision Occurs

It is very easy to identify whether an object is a collision rename object. All collision rename objects have the pattern *<number of collisions>_<replica number>*, such as 2_3. If the Unknown object has a name similar to this, it is unknown because it has the same DN or creation time stamp as another object in the tree. Most of the time, some of the attributes listed on the object will give you an idea of what object it collided with.

Mandatory Attributes Are Missing

Each object in eDirectory is assigned a base class, which defines the object type. The base class is a schema class definition added to the object in the `objectclass` attribute. The attribute is flagged with a "base class" flag.

The class definition that is defined as the base class defines what attributes are mandatory for the specified object. If an object is missing mandatory attributes, the object will be set to Unknown.

To identify whether or not the specified object is Unknown because of a missing mandatory attribute, using the Unknown Object report previously generated, execute Task 9-1 in NDS iMonitor.

Task 9-1. Verifying Missing Mandatory Attributes

1. Click the Unknown subreport (see Figure 9-4).

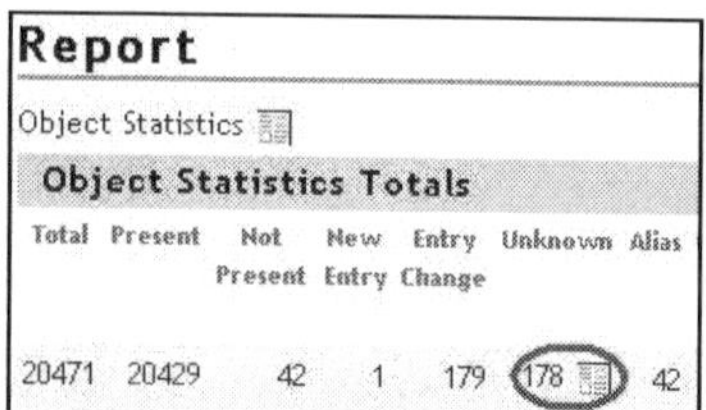

Figure 9-4. *Unknown subreport*

2. Select one of the Unknown objects (see Figure 9-5).

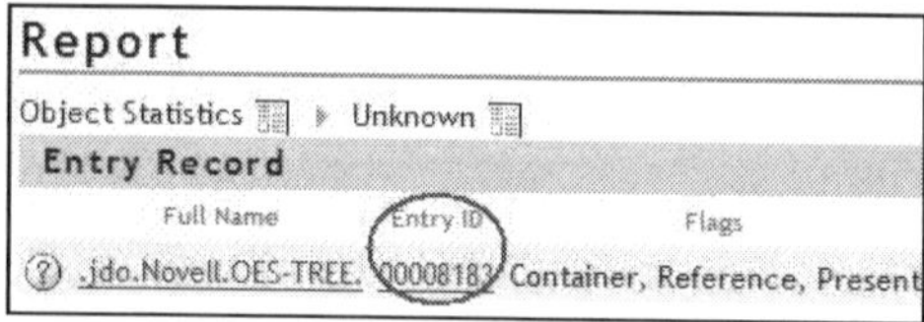

Figure 9-5. *Selecting an Unknown object*

3. In the left pane, under Attributes, click Unknown Base Class, as shown in Figure 9-6.
4. In the right pane, click the class that is listed under Unknown Base Class.
5. Under Attribute Rules, make a note of all Required attributes.
6. Click the browser's Back button to go back to the Unknown object.
7. In the Attributes list in the left pane, verify that all attributes that you noted in Step 5 are present.

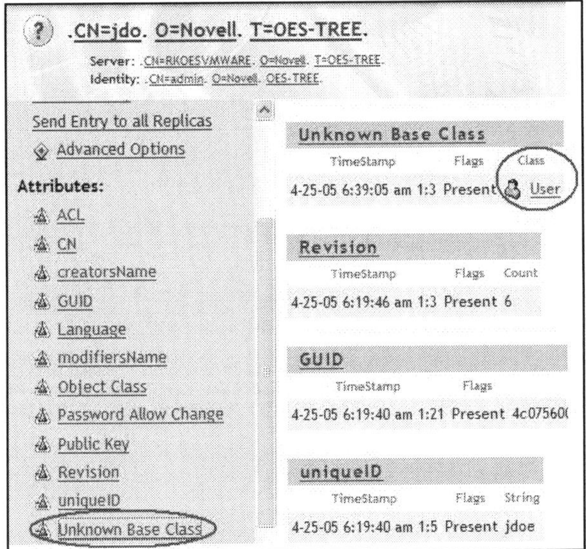

Figure 9-6. *Unknown Base Class section*

If one (or more) of the attributes noted in Step 5 is not present, you have verified that the object became Unknown because of a missing mandatory attribute. If all the attributes are present, the object became Unknown for another reason.

A Class Definition Is Undefined

If you find, while performing Task 9-1 Step 3 or Step 4, that there is not a class listed under the Unknown Base Class attribute, the most likely reason is that the schema class definition for that object type is not present on the local server. This condition would be extremely rare. There are a lot of checks in eDirectory to ensure that this type of condition does not occur. However, due to database corruption or manual intervention, this condition is possible.

■ **Note** One other condition that can occur that will cause objects to go Unknown is a condition in which auxiliary classes are being used in a partition that contains NDS 7.x or NDS 6.x. These conditions are normal and the Unknown objects should not be resolved. For more information of these conditions, see TID 10083622, "How to enable/disable auxiliary class support for DS 6.x and 7.x servers," in the Novell Knowledgebase at `http://support.novell.com`.

Resolving the Condition That Created the Unknown Object

Which of the three conditions previously described created the Unknown object determines which tasks you must perform to resolve the condition so that you can restore it to its original schema type:

- *Collision rename*: To resolve a collision rename, you must delete, rename, or move either the collision object or the real object. If the object is an object that is easily re-created, like a user object, deleting the collision rename object and adding any missing information on the remaining object usually is the simplest option.

  If the object is more critical, like an NCP server object or a container object, you should spend due diligence and verify each attribute to determine which object should be kept. If the object you decide to keep is the object that was not renamed, you can simply delete the collision rename object. If you determine that the collision rename object should be kept, you need to delete the other object and then rename the collision rename object to the original name.
- *Missing mandatory object*: To resolve the condition where there is a missing mandatory object, through iManager, you need to add the missing mandatory attribute back to the user object. This can be performed by using the iManager eDirectory Administration ➤ Modify object task. Use the "Other" tab to add the missing mandatory attribute.
- *Undefined class definition*: Perform Task 9-2 to locate a valid object in another replica.

Task 9-2. Locating a Valid Object in Another Replica

1. Make sure that you are currently viewing the Unknown object Entry Information in NDS iMonitor by browsing for the object or selecting the object from the Object Statistics report summary.
2. In the bottom-left pane, in the Replicas section, click each server link, one at a time.
3. Observe the Entry Information section of the specified object on each replica. If you find a replica that has a valid class in the BaseClass field, note the server that is currently selected and continue to click each server in the replica frame.

4. If you found a valid object on one of the other replicas, you can continue with the next step. If you did not, there is not much you can do. You need to delete the object from the tree.
5. Go back to one of the replica severs noted in Step 3 or 4 and click the Advanced Options link. From there, you can select Timestamp Entry. This will send this entry to all replicas, including the replica with the Unknown object.
6. If Step 5 does not work, depending on the state of the Unknown object, you can run DSREPAIR with a `-p` option from the server that contains the Unknown object. This marks the Unknown object as a reference object, which tells the directory agents that if the object is synchronized through an inbound synchronization process, they should ignore the local definition and all synchronization to overwrite the object.

Reassigning the Correct Object Type to the Object

Once the condition that generated the Unknown object is resolved, you can reassign the correct object type back to the object. NDS iMonitor provides an easy mechanism for accomplishing this task, called *mutating the object.* To mutate the object, perform Task 9-3.

Task 9-3. Reassigning the Correct Object Type

1. Make sure that Advanced Mode is On in NDS iMonitor. You can turn on Advanced Mode by clicking the NDS iMonitor icon, located in the top-left corner of the NDS iMonitor screen.
2. View the Entry Information for the Unknown object by clicking the object name in the Unknown Object report.
3. Click Advanced Options, as shown in Figure 9-7.
4. Select Mutate Entry and then click OK to mutate the object.
5. Verify that the object is now a Known object.

Note If a –603 error occurs, the object cannot be mutated and will probably need to be deleted. If a –609 error occurs, you are still missing a mandatory attribute.

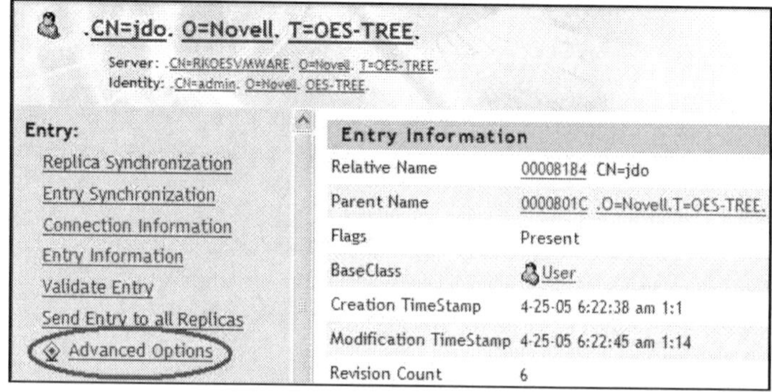

Figure 9-7. *Advanced Options link*

Troubleshooting Schema

The most common schema issue that you will experience is errors in schema synchronization. There are three main steps when troubleshooting schema:

1. Find the schema issue.
2. Decide which server contains valid schema.
3. Use NDS iMonitor to remedy the issue.

Finding the Schema Issue

You can detect schema errors by running a treewide health check. While performing the treewide health check, make sure that you check the Generate Health subreport option. If there are any schema errors, they will show up in the Agent Process subreports.

There are also server-specific tools that you can use to detect schema issues. In NDS iMonitor, one of the main menu items in the left pane is Agent Process Status. In you select this view, you see a Schema Sync Status, which shows you the last time schema was synchronized as well as any errors that occurred during the last synchronization. If schema synchronization is in progress, it also shows you to which server the connected server (the server you are connected to either directly or through proxy mode in NDS iMonitor) is sending schema updates at the current time. If the Error field is blank, then the last schema synchronization was successful.

Note Although the Schema Sync Status is accurate most of the time, it is dependent on the fact that the status is written to the schema status attribute on the pseudo server object. Another way to manually verify schema status is to run DSTRACE with the `+schema` filter. If there are any errors, they will appear in the DSTRACE console.

Another not-so-obvious schema issue can occur during regular object synchronization. If an object is sent from the local server to a remote server and the remote server does not have matching schema, it is possible that the object will not synchronize and an error will be generated. Typically, these errors will be schema related. The following are most of the typical errors that would occur that are schema related during object synchronization:

- –603: ERR_NO_SUCH_ATTRIBUTE
- –604: ERR_NO_SUCH_CLASS
- –608: ERR_ILLEGAL_ATTRIBUTE
- –609: ERR_MISSING_MANDATORY
- –611: ERR_ILLEGAL_CONTAINMENT
- –613: ERR_SYNTAX_VIOLATION

Deciding Which Server Contains Valid Schema

The most common mistake made by eDirectory administrators when they see a schema error is to make wrong assumptions about which server has valid schema, make that server authoritative, and push schema to all servers. If their assumption is incorrect and the server they chose to be authoritative has bad schema, the end result could be disastrous, potentially even data loss. With this in mind, it is imperative that you use due diligence to verify which server has valid schema before you take action to fix the schema issue.

Almost every schema issue can be narrowed down to two conditions:

- The source server contains schema that does not reside on the target server.
- The source server and target server contain the same schema definitions but the rules differ.

In either of these conditions, you must determine which server has the correct schema and which one is incorrect. The best way to accomplish this is to use NDS iMonitor's Schema Compare functionality.

NDS iMonitor has a powerful feature with which you can compare the schema between two different servers. To access the Schema Compare feature, choose Schema ➤ Source List. You can compare schema between the local server (the server you are accessing through NDS iMonitor) and any other server in the local server's schema poll list (you can view these servers by looking at the Source List).

■ **Note** If you want to compare schema between the local server and a server that is not in the local server's schema poll list, you can modify the URL and put in the desired server's name and IP address after selecting Class Compare or Attribute Compare.

When comparing schema, you have several configuration options. You can specify the following, as shown in Figure 9-8:

- *Full Compare*: You can select the following Schema Compare options:
  - *Difference*: The result of the Schema Compare shows all schema differences except for known differences. Differences in schema definitions may occur if the source and target servers are not running the same version of eDirectory. Selecting this option does not include the Expected Differences in this type of condition.
  - *Expected Differences*: These are differences that are expected when the source and target servers are not running the same version of eDirectory.
  - *Base only*: Only the differences from the source server are displayed.
  - *Target only*: Only the differences from the target server are displayed.
  - *Equal*: Schema that is equal between the two servers is still returned. It is usually best to deselect this option so that you only see the differences and don't have to go through a lot of schema to find the differences.
- *Filter by Health*: Even though schema shows that it is different between two servers, it is possible that the difference is not going to cause any issues. By using the Filter by Health option, you can display only the differences that you need to worry about. If you are troubleshooting schema issues, you may want to select the following Filter by Health options:

- *Unknown*: A schema difference has been detected and the NDS iMonitor agent is not sure whether or not the difference is acceptable.
- *Suspect*: A schema difference has been detected and the NDS iMonitor agent has determined that, in some situations, the difference needs to be resolved.
- *Warn*: A schema difference has been detected and the NDS iMonitor agent has determined that, in most cases, the schema difference needs to be resolved.

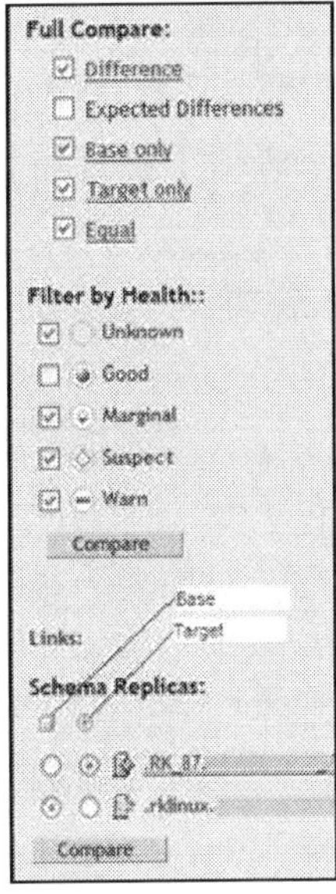

Figure 9-8. *Schema Compare options*

The best way to determine whether or not schema is valid for the specified server is to compare it against several other servers in the tree. Typically, you will find that one server or a few servers have different schema than the rest of the tree. In these cases, you can assume that the few servers that are different have the outdated or invalid schema. An exception to this rule would be in the case where a server with a copy of [Root] contains classes or attributes that other servers do not have. In these cases, you must push the schema down from the servers that do contain the disparate classes and/or attributes to everything else in the tree. Occasionally, this condition will occur because time is not synchronized when the schema was originally added.

Using NDS iMonitor to Remedy Schema Issues

After you have determined which server has valid schema, you can force schema from that server to be synchronized to the other servers. There are several ways in which you can do this within NDS iMonitor. The following are the most common ways to remedy schema issues through NDS iMonitor (click the Advanced Options link from the Schema page to access these options):

- *Reset Schema*: Resetting schema on a specific server removes the schema Synchronized Up To attribute and clears the time on all schema entries on the specified server. Because the time stamp is less than the schema Synchronized Up To value, one of the servers in the Schema Sources list will resend all schema to the specified server.

  To access the Reset Schema option in NDS iMonitor, perform Task 9-4.

Note You cannot reset schema on a server that contains the master of the root-most partition. If you need to reset a server that holds the master partition, designate another server in the replica ring to be the master replica, and then you can reset schema on the original master server.

- *Request Schema*: Requesting schema is similar to resetting schema with the exception that the Synchronized Up To attribute is not cleared nor is schema reset. The local server simply requests schema from the master of the partition. The master partition sends all schema. Only the schema definitions from the source server that have newer time stamps will be accepted by the target server. This is a less-intrusive feature; however, in a case where both servers have all schema definitions but differ in definition, this option will not resolve the issue.
- *Schema Epoch*: Using this option requires extreme caution. This option makes the server that the epoch is declared from authoritative. If the source server is missing schema, that schema will be deleted from all other servers in the tree. This option zeros out all schema entries on all servers in the tree. If misused, data loss can occur. This is an absolute last-resort option. It should be used *only* if schema has a future time stamp or if many servers in the tree have schema mismatch issues.

Warning Use the Schema Epoch option with extreme caution.

- *Timestamp Schema Entry*: This option simply timestamps a specific schema entry, making that schema entry authoritative. Because the time stamp is newer on the local server, the attribute will be synchronized down the tree. This is an effective option if just one or two schema attributes are not present on other servers or have a different configuration. This option is available only on attributes, not on class definitions. To execute this option, perform Task 9-5.
- *Timestamp All Classes and Attributes*: This works exactly the same as executing the Timestamp Schema Entry option with the exception that it will timestamp all schema entries on the specified server, not just one entry. This option differs from the Schema Epoch option in that the schema entries on the remote servers are not reset and schema is not removed if it is present on the remote server but not on the local server.

Task 9-4. Resetting Schema

1. Make sure that Advanced Mode is turned on in NDS iMonitor.
2. Click the Schema link in the left pane.
3. Click the Advanced Options link.
4. Select Reset Schema.

Task 9-5. Selecting Timestamp Schema Entry

1. Make sure that Advanced Mode is turned on in NDS iMonitor.
2. Click the Schema link in the left pane.
3. At the end of the URL, add the parameter ?attr=<*attribute name*>; for example, https://<*server address*>:<*http port*>/nds/schema/attribute?attr=surname.
4. Click the Advanced Option link on the left side of the screen.
5. Select Timestamp Schema Entry.

Troubleshooting Obituaries

eDirectory ensures that state changes to an object are replicated to all servers in the changed object's partition replica ring through the obituary process. When an object's state is changed, an obituary is placed on the object in the master replica of the partition where the object resides. The master replica for the partition processes the obituary throughout the other servers in the replica ring. Until the obituary process is finished, no other changes can occur on the specified object. The following are the main obituary types that are tracked with the obituary process:

- *Restored*: Used to re-create an obituary on an object.
- *Dead*: When a delete object request is issued to the directory agent, this obituary is placed on the specified object.
- *Moved*: Placed on an object when the object is moved. This obituary is placed on the original object, which is nonpresent, not on the moved object.
- *Inhibit move*: When an object is moved, this obituary is placed on the new object to ensure that it cannot be modified before the move is completed.
- *Backlink*: This obituary is called a secondary obituary. It is associated with the primary obituary. The primary obituary is placed on the original object on the master replica. The Backlink obituary is placed on all other replicas of the specified object.
- *Old RDN/New RDN*: These obituaries come in pairs. When an object is renamed, two obituaries are placed on the object. The Old RDN contains the old name and the New RDN contains the new name. In versions of the directory older than NDS 8, two objects were created. The original object was made nonpresent and the New RDN obituary was placed on the object to link the old object to the new object. A new, renamed object was created and the Old RDN was placed on it to link the new object back to the original, nonpresent object. With NDS 8 and higher, the original object is simply renamed and both obituaries are placed on the object for backward compatibility.
- *Tree old RDN/Tree new RDN*: These obituaries have the same purpose as the Old RDN/New RDN obituaries with the exception that they are used only on the [Root] object or Tree name. If the Tree is renamed, these obituaries ensure that the change is reflected to all servers.
- *Moved tree/Moved from*: These are also referred to as Moved SubTree. When an entire partition is moved from one parent to another in the tree structure, the Moved SubTree obituary is used.

- *Used by*: Also known as Type C obituaries, these are special obituaries that are used by the Distributed Reference Link (DRL) process. The DRL process is a secondary Obituary background process that was introduced in eDirectory 8.5. This process is more efficient in that it does not need to evaluate each object when looking for state changes. The Used by obituary is placed on the object and a reference to it is placed on the partition root object. The DRL process simply looks to the partition root object to find any object that has had a state change. The drawback to the DRL process is that Used by obituaries can be placed only on real objects. External reference objects do not get the state change. Because of this, both the DRL process and the standard Obituary process are used to track state changes.
- *Object version*: This is used typically on a Dead obituary to help in the synchronization process.

■ **Note** When running an Obituary Report in NDS iMonitor, one of the obituary types shows up as Unknown. This is not really an obituary type. It is placed in the report to identity any invalid obituary types.

Processing Obituaries

In order for an obituary to be processed or deleted from the system, it must go through several states. Each obituary (with the exception of Inhibit move, Used by, Tree old RDN, and Tree new RDN) must go through the following states:

- Initial State or Issued (0)
- Notified (1)
- OK to Purge (2)
- Purgeable (4)

Before an obituary can move from one state to another state, every obituary in the backlink list must see the current state. The backlink list is a list of servers that have a replica of the object that has been modified or have an external reference of the object that was modified. The master replica of the partition with the specified object that contains the obituary maintains this list. The obituary process for an object deletion is as follows:

1. An object state is modified.
2. The master replica that contains the object is notified of the deletion.
3. The master replica marks the object nonpresent.
4. The master replica places a Dead obituary onto the object.
5. The master replica builds a backlink list of all servers in the replica ring of the given partition as well as any server that is in the Backlink attribute of the given object (external reference servers).
6. The master replica adds a Backlink obituary value to the specified object. One value is added for each server in the backlink list.
7. The master replica synchronizes the nonpresent object with the obituary to all replica servers.
8. The master replica uses the Backlink process to send the obituaries to the external reference servers.
9. After the master verifies that all servers in the backlink list have seen the Initial State (0), the master flips the obituary value's states to Notified (1).
10. The entire process is repeated.
11. Once all servers have seen the Notified (1) state, each server independently moves its own states to OK to Purge (2), Purgeable (4), and then removes the obituary. Each server moves from one state to the next after a successful outbound sync, or in the case of an external reference server, after it reaches a Notified (1) state.

■ **Note** Previous to eDirectory 8.7.1, Step 11 was not executed. Each obituary had to contact the master, which then handled the state changes.

Most of the primary obituaries go through the preceding steps. The Moved obituary, however, has one more additional step in that it adds an Inhibit Move (tracking obituary) onto the new object that was moved. After the primary Moved obituary is changed to a state of OK to Purge (2), the Inhibit Move obituary is removed. The Used by, Tree old RDN, and Tree new RDN obituaries also have variations from the preceding steps. For more information on these obituaries, see the *eDirectory Administration Guide* at `http://www.novell.com/documentation`.

Using NDS iMonitor to Identify Obituaries

Obituaries are not always bad things. They are a necessary part of eDirectory to keep referential integrity of objects between replicas during modifications. However, if your tree is not healthy, it is possible that obituaries will not process through the different states and effectively be "stuck" on the object. You can use the reporting feature of NDS iMonitor to identify "stuck" obituaries and remedy the issue. To get a listing of all obituaries present on the local server, click the Reports icon (circled in red in Figure 9-9) at the top, click Report Config on the left, and then select the Configure Report icon for the Obituary Listing report.

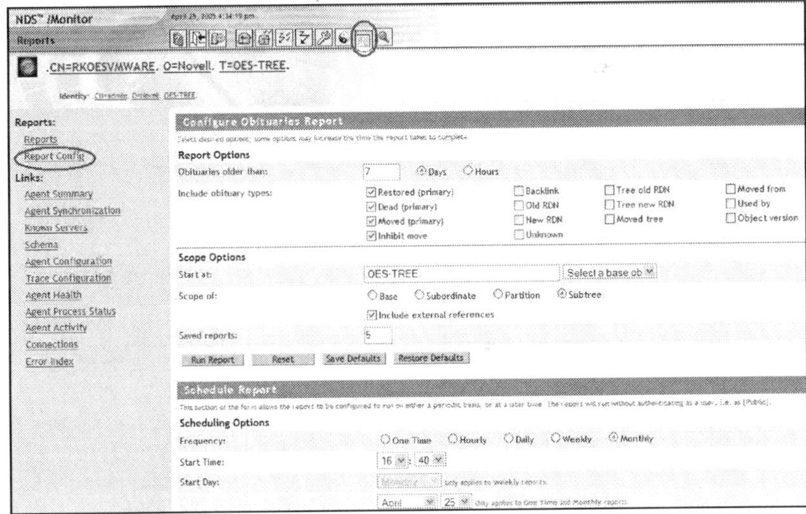

Figure 9-9. *Clicking the Reports icon*

If you use the Obituaries older than field in the Report Options section (see Figure 9-9), you can limit the report to only obituaries that seem to be stuck. Depending on the size of the system and how often synchronization occurs, it can take several hours to process obituaries. Keep in mind that if any server within a replica ring is down, the obituary process will not be able to continue.

You should be able to identify from the obituary report which obituaries may be old. The obituary report shows you the state of each obituary. Typically, which server is holding up the obituary process will be obvious, because all servers' obituaries will have a specific state and the problematic server will have an older state, similar to the example shown in Figure 9-10.

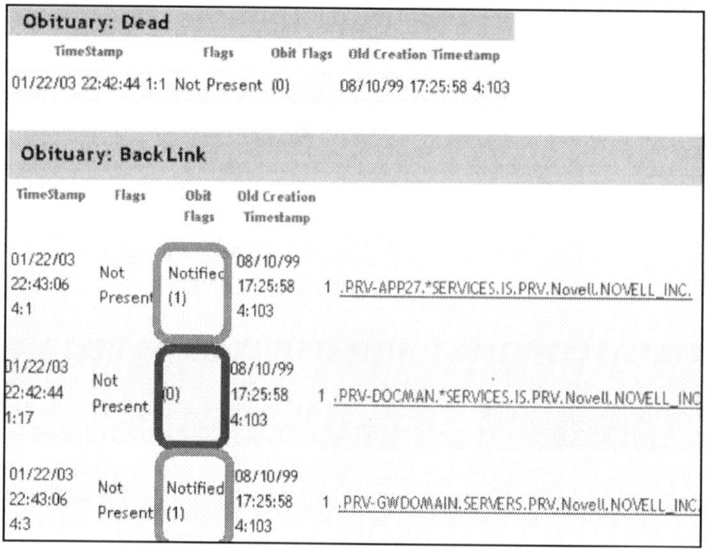

Obituary: Dead

TimeStamp	Flags	Obit Flags	Old Creation Timestamp
01/22/03 22:42:44 1:1	Not Present	(0)	08/10/99 17:25:58 4:103

Obituary: BackLink

TimeStamp	Flags	Obit Flags	Old Creation Timestamp		
01/22/03 22:43:06 4:1	Not Present	Notified (1)	08/10/99 17:25:58 4:103	1	.PRV-APP27.*SERVICES.IS.PRV.Novell.NOVELL_INC.
01/22/03 22:42:44 1:17	Not Present	(0)	08/10/99 17:25:58 4:103	1	.PRV-DOCMAN.*SERVICES.IS.PRV.Novell.NOVELL_INC
01/22/03 22:43:06 4:3	Not Present	Notified (1)	08/10/99 17:25:58 4:103	1	.PRV-GWDOMAIN.SERVERS.PRV.Novell.NOVELL_INC.

Figure 9-10. *Viewing the state of servers*

Using NDS iMonitor to Resolve Obituary Issues

Once you identify the problematic server, you need to resolve why the server has an issue. Typically the cause has to do with communication. The specified server may be having communication errors with all the other servers. If this is not the case, you may have problems with the specified server's database. You can run DSREPAIR on the object to try to resolve these types of problems. If none of these options works, the specified server may not know, for whatever reason, that it needs to synchronize the obituary. In these cases, you can use the NDS iMonitor Advanced Options to try to synchronize the obituary.

NDS iMonitor does a very good job of trying to show you what issues are holding up the obituary process as well as giving you some useful tools for troubleshooting obituaries. When you are viewing a specific obituary, if there are any synchronization errors, etc. on the partition that contains the obituary, the error will be displayed, similar to the example shown in Figure 9-11.

Obituary Status

Version	Flags	Time	Error	Activity	Partition	Target Server ID	Target Server		Entry Id	Entry
0		03/06/03 10:23:35	-625	Dead	0000800D	000080DC	.PRV-DOCMAN.*SERVICES.IS.PRV.Novell.NOVELL_INC.	Agent Summary, Agent Configuration, Agent Health	00017704	.Administrator.PRV.Novell

Figure 9-11. *Viewing synchronization issues*

If you suspect that an obituary is stuck because the entry is invalid, NDS iMonitor will validate the entry for you, allow you to timestamp the entry, and even repair the entry if necessary (see Figure 9-12).

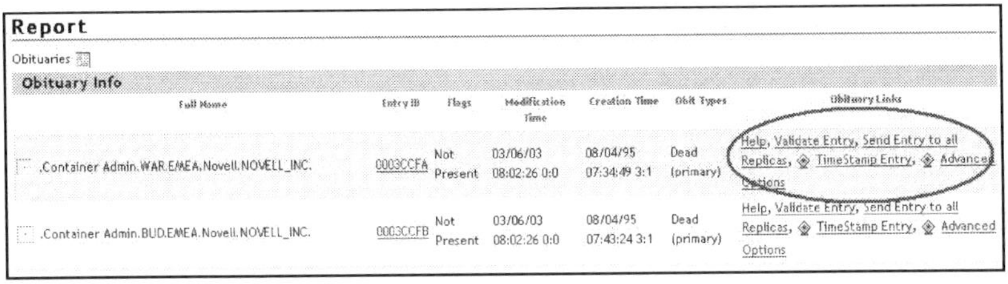

Report

Obituaries

Obituary Info

Full Name	Entry ID	Flags	Modification Time	Creation Time	Obit Types	Obituary Links
.Container Admin.WAR.EMEA.Novell.NOVELL_INC.	0003CCFA	Not Present	03/06/03 08:02:26 0:0	08/04/95 07:34:49 3:1	Dead (primary)	Help, Validate Entry, Send Entry to all Replicas, TimeStamp Entry, Advanced Options
.Container Admin.BUD.EMEA.Novell.NOVELL_INC.	0003CCFB	Not Present	03/06/03 08:02:26 0:0	08/04/95 07:43:24 3:1	Dead (primary)	Help, Validate Entry, Send Entry to all Replicas, TimeStamp Entry, Advanced Options

Figure 9-12. *Validating the entry*

Troubleshooting Processor High Utilization

All applications, regardless of the platform, require processor time to execute. eDirectory is a multiple-thread application. Each thread requests time from the processor (or processors) to execute the instructions that come through that thread. In certain conditions, hundreds of threads are all fighting for time on the processor. In other scenarios, one thread with a very large request can take over the processor and not release it for other threads to execute. In either of these conditions, the end result is that almost 100 percent of the processor time is used, not allowing information to process. The fallout from this condition is that the server appears to "hang" and does not process any new requests.

One of the tasks involved in troubleshooting high utilization is to determine which application is taking up most of the processor time. NDS iMonitor does not have the ability to monitor the entire server and all of its applications. You need to rely on the platform's native tools to determine whether or not eDirectory is the offending process. There are many tools available to use. Some common tools, per platform, follow:

- *NetWare*: MONITOR.NLM
- *Windows*: Task Manager
- *Linux*: `top`
- *Solaris, AIX, HP-UX*: `pstat`

Note If you cannot determine whether or not eDirectory is taking up most of the processor time in a high-utilization scenario, you can simply unload eDirectory and monitor processor utilization. If the processor utilization goes down, then eDirectory or an application that is running in the eDirectory space or accessing eDirectory is taking up most of the processor time.

If you have determined that eDirectory is directly or indirectly taking up most of the processor time, you can use NDS iMonitor to try to determine what eDirectory is executing (or being executed on) that is requiring significant amounts of processor time. Three key features of NDS iMonitor that can be used to monitor current processes are Agent Activity, Trace, and Agent Configuration. Each of these options is discussed in further detail next.

Using Agent Activity

To access the Agent Activity screen, simply click the Agent Activity link on the left side of the NDS iMonitor screen or go to `http://`*`<server address>`*`:`*`<clear-text port>`*`/nds/activity` or `https://`*`<server address>`*`:`*`<secure port>`*`/nds/activity`. The Agent Activity screen allows you to view the currently running verbs, events, and synchronization. It also allows you to see historical information.

To determine what eDirectory is currently executing, you can view the Activity link under the Verbs section in the left pane. You can also select the Activity link under the Events section, as well as the Current link under the Synchronization section. If you are experiencing high utilization, go to these pages and monitor the current activities. If an activity is taking up a lot of processor time, the specified activity will be in the Activity screen for long periods of time or will repeat many times.

Note One of the caveats of NDS iMonitor is that it too must receive information from the server to be able to display the information to you. If the server is experiencing high utilization, it may take a while for NDS iMonitor to load and display the information. Be patient and the data should be processed eventually. If the high utilization is severe enough that it appears to be locked, you may need to start guessing what is causing the utilization by disabling background processes like schema synchronization, replication, etc. You can do this with command-line utilities specific to each platform. For more information on these tools, see the *eDirectory Administration Guide* at `http://www.novell.com/documentation`.

The historical data is also very useful when troubleshooting high utilization. The Statistics link under both the Verbs and Events sections tells you what the averages are as well as high usages of each verb or event. To help identify the offending process, you can scan through the verbs and events, looking for an inordinately high number of requests for a particular verb or event. For instance, if someone turned on Predicate Stats without anyone knowing, it possibly could cause high utilization because eDirectory collects predicate information. In this case, the Verb Statistics page would show that the BK_PREDICATE_STATS verb has a high usage count.

Using Trace

The Trace option in NDS iMonitor is another useful tool to try to find high-utilization issues. To access the Trace screen, click the Trace Configuration link on the left side of the NDS iMonitor screen or access it directory by going to `http://`*`<server address>`*`:`*`<clear-text port>`*`/nds/trace` or `https://`*`<server address>`*`:`*`<secure port>`*`/nds/trace`. The following are some common Trace Configuration options that you can use to troubleshoot high-utilization scenarios:

- *Schema*: If schema is synchronizing over and over, high processor utilization will occur. You can monitor this with the Schema option.
- *Backlinker*: The Backlink process can cause high processor utilization if there are a lot of external references on the server.
- *Distributed References*: The continuously running DRL background process scans all reference attributes and resolves them. It also scans the Used by obituaries on the partition root object. This process does have low priority, but if there are a lot of reference values from large groups, etc., this process can take up processor time.
- *Emulated Bindery*: Bindery requests require a scan of the database. If there are a lot of bindery requests, you can experience high utilization.
- *LDAP*: A lot of LDAP requests and/or large LDAP requests can cause high utilization. Another way to verify LDAP would be to unload the LDAP module and see if utilization goes down.
- *Outbound Synchronization*: If objects are synchronizing over and over, high utilization can occur.

Using Agent Configuration

Regardless of the platform, the only real way to find high-utilization issues is to eliminate variables. You can unload modules one at a time and disable background processes until the processor utilization returns to normal.

Once you have found the offending thread, you can take action to eliminate the condition that created the high utilization.

The Agent Configuration screen enables you to configure processes. To access the Agent Configuration screen, click the Agent Configuration link on the left side of the NDS iMonitor screen or go to `http://<server address>:<clear-text port>/nds/agent/info` or `https://<server address>:<secure port>/nds/agent/info`.

Through the Agent Configuration ➤ Agent Synchronization option, you can enable or disable synchronization. You can also specify how many threads to use for synchronization. If you are experiencing high utilization, you may want to limit the synchronization threads if you find that synchronization is the cause of the processor high-utilization condition.

You can also disable schema synchronization through Agent Configuration ➤ Schema Synchronization. To quickly test whether or not schema synchronization is the issue, disable schema synchronization and monitor the processor utilization.

If you find that high utilization occurs during login times, it may be that you are writing to disk and the disk is creating a bottleneck, which indirectly will cause high utilization. Under Agent Configuration ➤ Login Settings, you can delay or disable the Login Update writes to the directory. The Login Updates are statistics like Last Login Time and the Network Address used to connect to eDirectory. If you don't care about these statistics, you can save a lot of processor time and disk I/O by disabling the Login Updates during authentication.

Summary

NDS iMonitor is a powerful tool that allows you to troubleshoot most conditions that occur within eDirectory. Although there are equivalent command-line tools available, NDS iMonitor will reduce the cost of ownership by providing an easy-to-use, remote-access, web-based interface to monitor and troubleshoot eDirectory issues.

CHAPTER 10

Common Command-Line Utilities

The following topics are covered in this chapter:

- DSREPAIR
    - Launching DSREPAIR
    - DSREPAIR command-line options
- DSTRACE
    - Understanding the different DSTRACE modules
    - Monitoring the DSTRACE operations
- NDSConfig
- LDAPConfig
- EDIRUTIL
- ICE

iManager and NDS iMonitor are the key cross-platform tools for eDirectory. They are web-based tools, which means you do not need to have direct access to the server console. They are also operating system–independent, which decreases costs because you do not need to train your personnel on different tools based on the operating system. However, for the power administrator, sometimes it is quicker and more efficient to use the command-line utilities to perform monitoring and maintenance on the directory.

This chapter discusses the most prevalent command-line tools that come with eDirectory. This chapter does not go into full detail about all the options of each tool. To obtain full information about the tools, refer to the *eDirectory Administration Guide* at `http://www.novell.com/documentation` or refer to the man pages for the specified tool on the Linux, Solaris, AIX, and HP-UX platforms.

DSREPAIR

The DSREPAIR utility is designed to check the eDirectory database for inconsistencies. There are many different checks that can be performed against the database. DSREPAIR checks for things like future time stamps, structural errors, object value violations based off of the current schema, time synchronization, replica synchronization, etc.

DSREPAIR also has limited abilities to administer the database. You can cancel partition operations, import schema, change master replicas to read/write replicas, remove replicas from the system, remove other servers from the replica rings, declare epochs, etc.

■ **Warning** You should use DSREPAIR as an administration tool only as a last resort. Your default administration tool should be iManager or ConsoleOne. DSREPAIR does not have as many built-in checks to verify that it can perform the administrative task that is requested. DSREPAIR has the perspective of the local database only. It is possible to damage your tree structure and possibly experience data loss by performing the wrong option at the wrong time in DSREPAIR. Make sure that you know what you are doing before performing administrative options.

Launching DSREPAIR

The methodology for running DSREPAIR changes for each platform. Tasks 10-1 to 10-3 provide the steps to launch DSREPAIR from each of the eDirectory-supported platforms.

Task 10-1. Accessing DSREPAIR from NetWare

1. Go to a system console prompt.
2. Type **sys:\system\dsrepair.nlm** ***<any command-line option>*** (e.g., `sys:\system\dsrepair.nlm -rd`).

■ **Note** Although the command line in Step 2 of Task 10-1 lists the full path, most of the time, the path is defined in the environment and you need to type only the command itself. For example, instead of typing sys:\system\dsrepair.nlm, you could type `dsrepair`.

Task 10-2. Accessing DSREPAIR from Windows

1. Browse to the %SystemDrive%:\Novell\Nds\ directory.
2. Run NDSCons.exe. (Note that there is a shortcut to NDSCons.exe in the Control Panel, called Novell eDirectory Services.)
3. Select dsrepair.dlm.
4. If there are any command-line options (e.g., `-rd`), put them in the Startup Parameters field.
5. Click Start.

Task 10-3. Accessing DSREPAIR from Linux, Solaris, AIX, and HP-UX

1. Go to a terminal prompt.
2. Type **/usr/bin/ndsrepair** <***desired command-line option***> (e.g., `/usr/bin/ndsrepair -R`).

■ **Note** When executing Task 10-1 on NetWare and Task 10-2 on Windows, an application is launched with menu options to choose from. However, on the Linux, Solaris, AIX, and HP-UX (*nix) platforms, by executing Task 10-3, you only get a help screen with a list of options. `ndsrepair` on the *nix platforms is actually a script that calls into the actual binary located in a different directory. You must pass options to the command-line script for `ndsrepair` to execute. The different options are discussed later in this chapter. If you do not want to memorize all the options, Novell has published a "wrapper" that gives you a TUI menu that is very similar to what you would see when running DSREPAIR on NetWare. To download the DSREPAIR wrapper for the *nix platforms, go to `http://support.novell.com` and search for **dsrepair menu wrapper**.

DSREPAIR Command-Line Options

DSREPAIR has the ability to accept command-line options on all platforms. The command-line options instruct DSREPAIR to execute specific operations. You can use the command-line options to automate repair. On NetWare, for instance, you could create an NCF file that executes the following command:

```
sys:\system\dsrepair.nlm -rd
```

When this NCF file is executed, a local repair of the database is performed. When the repair is completed, `dsrepair` will terminate. You could configure the NCF file to run as a cron job every night at midnight, for instance. With this type of power, you can automate your database maintenance.

Although most options are available on all supported platforms, the option itself varies. Table 10-1 describes the different configurable parameters for DSREPAIR as well as the associated option on each platform.

Make sure that you understand what you are doing before using any of the switches in Table 10-1. A lot of them will not even prompt you for data. They will, however, write to the log files so that you can view the results.

Table 10-1. *DSREPAIR Options*

Parameter	NetWare/Windows	*nix	Description
Advanced mode	`-a`	`-Ad`	Enables additional functionality that is not present in standard mode.
Modify schema syntax	`-a0`	`-R -Ad -A0`	Renames the modifiersName and creatorsName attribute schema definitions as uniBadModifier and uniBadCreator, respectively. It then deletes all values of attribute type creatorsName or modifiersName. DSREPAIR then deletes the renamed attribute schema definitions. After these definitions have been deleted, it re-creates the modifiersName and creatorsName attribute schema definitions with the correct syntax: SYN_CI_STRING. It does not perform a schema check before it performs the operation. It assumes that the schema definitions listed above need to be removed.
Disable reference checks	`-ab -rd`	`-R -c no`	Disables reference checking, which is time intensive.

Continued

Table 10-1. *Continued*

Parameter	NetWare/Windows	*nix	Description
Disable replica ring check	`-ad -rc`	NA	By default, DSREPAIR does not contact every server in the replica ring before it makes an archive of the database. In older versions of DSREPAIR, it would contact every server in the replica ring before it could make an archive, which delayed the process considerably. To revert to the old method and contact every server in the replica ring before locking the database, use the `-ad` switch. This option is not available on the Windows and *nix platforms.
Copy stream files	`-af -rd`	`-R -u yes -Ad -af`	If the option to create a temporary file while performing a local repair is enabled, this option enables DSREPAIR to copy stream files when creating the temporary file.
Add Audit:File object containment	`-ao`	`-R -Ad -ao`	The NAAS product requires that the Audit:File Object class be included in the containment rule on all container class definitions. This switch adds this containment if it is not already present.
Scan all objects during reference check	`-ar -rd`	`-R -Ad -ar`	The newer versions of DSREPAIR walk through the DRL list on the partition root entry when performing a reference check. This is a more scalable, quicker process than the old method. Older versions of DSREPAIR would scan every object in the local database, looking for reference attributes to verify. This switch enables the old method.

Parameter	NetWare/Windows	*nix	Description
Verify operational schema's superclasses	`-as`	`-R -o yes -Ad -as`	Verifies the superclass list for all operational schema. A common use of this switch would be to remove the class Top from the superclass rules. The Top class is assumed to be a superclass and should not necessarily be explicitly assigned as a superclass. In NetWare and Windows, run a local repair and choose to rebuild operational schema.
Check for duplicate time stamps	`-at -rd`	`-R -Ad -at`	Checks for duplicate modification or creation time stamps on attribute values. The creation time stamp is used as the unique ID for a specified value, so it must be unique within the local database.
Repair default ACLs	`-aua -rd`	`-R -Ad -aua`	Each schema class can have a default ACL template assigned to it. The ACL template is applied to any object of that schema type on object creation. In versions of DSREPAIR prior to eDirectory 8.6.2, DSREPAIR would automatically repair all default ACL values on schema objects. Starting with eDirectory 8.6.2, NDS iMonitor enables you to modify the default ACL template. For this reason, the default behavior for DSREPAIR is to not repair default ACLs. If you use the `-aua` option, the default ACLs are repaired on the schema class objects.

Continued

Table 10-1. *Continued*

Parameter	NetWare/Windows	*nix	Description
Skip disk space check	`-av -rd`	`-R -Ad -av`	By default, DSREPAIR checks your available disk space to make sure there is enough space to run the repair. Some file systems report invalid data, in which case DSREPAIR cannot run. This option allows you to bypass the disk space check.
Repair volume objects	`-ax -rd`	`-R -Ad -ax`	Once in awhile, during a migration, the volume IDs are reused by another object. This will generate errors in DSREPAIR and could potentially cause a loss of trustee assignments. The -ax switch zeros out the volume IDs on the file system and then writes a valid volume ID from a valid replica back to the file system.
Fix schema syntax	`-az -rd`	`-R -Ad -az`	Renames the modifiersName and creatorsName attribute schema definitions as uniBadModifier and uniBadCreator, respectively. It then deletes all values of attribute type creatorsName or modifiersName. DSREPAIR then deletes the renamed attribute schema definitions. After these definitions have been deleted, it re-creates the modifiersName and creatorsName attribute schema definitions with the correct syntax: SYN_CI_STRING. It does not perform a schema check before it performs the

Parameter	NetWare/Windows	*nix	Description
Fix schema syntax *(continued)*			operation. Unlike the `-a0` switch, used with the Modify Schema Syntax option, the `-az` switch verifies that schema needs to be modified before it performs the operation.
Disable schema flag repair	`-anf -rd`	`-R -o yes -Ad -anf`	By default, DSREPAIR changes schema flags on base schema back to defaults. If you have modified some of the schema flags, you will want to run DSREPAIR with the `-anf` switch when rebuilding operational schema.
Check transitive vectors	`-ant -rd`	`-R -Ad -ant`	In eDirectory 8.7.1, DSREPAIR does not check transitive vectors, by default, because cosmetic errors often occur while checking transitive vectors. This can be a nuisance when you are trying to determine what is valid and what is not valid. Compounding the problem is that to truly fix transitive vector issues, DSREPAIR must be run on every server in the replica ring with synchronization disabled. If you do not do this, DSREPAIR will resolve the issue but another replica will simply synchronize the incorrect vector back into the local replica. If you need to check transitive vectors, use the `-ant` switch.

Continued

Table 10-1. *Continued*

Parameter	NetWare/Windows	*nix	Description
Specify nondefault DIB to repair	`-d <ext>`	`-R -Ad -d <ext>`	Through DSDump, you can make a copy of a DIB with a new three-letter extension. Also, when you specify that you want DSREPAIR to create a temporary file during the repair process, DSREPAIR creates a backup and names it with an extension of .ndt. If you wish to run a repair against the backed-up DIB, you could use the `-d` option. For example, `dsrepair -dndt` would run a repair against the temporary database.
Destroy selected replica	`-dr -a`	`-P -Ad -dr`	By default, DSREPAIR attempts to contact the master replica before you can delete the replica on a selected server. You should always use iManager or ConsoleOne to remove a replica from a server. The only time you would use the Destroy Selected Replica option in DSREPAIR would be in the case where the replica is bad and you cannot cleanly remove it through the typical administrative interfaces. In such cases, the local agent most likely can not contact the master replica. The `-dr` switch allows you to bypass the requirement to contact the master replica and allows you to remove the replica. If you use this switch, you need to manually remove the server from the replica on the master server. When you specify this switch with the specified command-line syntax,

Parameter	NetWare/Windows	*nix	Description
Destroy selected replica *(continued)*			DSREPAIR will launch. You need to go to the Partition and Replica section, select the desired partition, and select the option to Destroy the Selected Replica.
Generate a new key pair	`-gkp -rd -a`	NA	Creates a new private and public key pair for the local NCP server object. If the local server is not the master of the partition in which the NCP server object resides, this switch is ignored. This option is available only on NetWare.
Update schema	`-ins`	NA	Automatically executes the Post NW 5 Schema Update option from the command line. This switch should be used only from NetWare.
Configure log file location	`-l` *<log filename>*	`-F` *<log filename>* `-A yes`	Allows you to specify a different log filename and path. You cannot use this option by itself. You need to specify an operation as well. For instance, to run a local repair and specify a log file for that repair on Linux, you would run `ndsrepair -R -F/home/admin/repair.log`.
Reports move inhibit obituaries	`-m -rd -a`	`-R -c yes -Ad -m`	Reports all Move Inhibit obituaries that are located on the server.

Continued

Table 10-1. *Continued*

Parameter	NetWare/Windows	*nix	Description
Clear network addresses	-rd -a -n *<# of days>*	-R -Ad -n *<# of days>*	The network address attribute is placed on each user object when a user logs into the network. This address is used to enforce the concurrent user login policy. If, for instance, the concurrent login policy is set to two connections, when a user logs in, if there is more than one network address attribute on the user object, the user will not be able to authenticate. In rare conditions, the network address may remain on a user object after the user logs out. The -n switch allows you to purge the network address attributes off all users in the local database. If you select 0 for the number of days, all network address values are purged from all users.
Remove NLS certificate values	-rd -a -nls	-R -Ad -nls	NLS has the ability to store common certificate values that were used in an attribute called NLS:Common Certificate. It is possible to have thousands of these values on the certificate object. This can cause high utilization during synchronization. To remove these values, use the -nls option.

Parameter	NetWare/Windows	*nix	Description
Timestamp obituaries	`-rd -a -ot`	`-R -Ad -ot`	Timestamps all obituary values on the local database, making them authoritative. This option is rarely used with the current versions of eDirectory. In the past, conditions could occur in which obituaries would not be able to be processed. The only way to retrigger the obituary process was to timestamp the obituaries. These issues have been solved with the latest versions of eDirectory.
Flag unknown objects as reference	`-rd -p`	`-R -Ad -p`	If an object is marked as Reference, it is nonauthoritative and will not synchronize to other servers. In the case of Unknown objects, you can flag them as Reference and then request to send all data from another replica to the local replica (through DSREPAIR or through iManager). Because the local Unknown object is marked as Reference, all of its data is overwritten by the valid inbound object.
Back up the database	`-rc`	NA	Makes an archive of the eDirectory database as well as all associated files (logs, streams, etc.). This option is valid only on NetWare and requires a Novell dial-in to restore the archive if necessary.
Run a local repair	`-rd`	`-R`	Launches a local repair with default options from the command line.

Continued

Table 10-1. *Continued*

Parameter	NetWare/Windows	*nix	Description
Run a local repair and lock the database	-rdl	-R -l yes	Locks the database and launches a local repair.
Repair server addresses	-ri	-N	Repairs the remote IDs for all known servers to this database.
Reset log files	-rl *<log filename>* -rd	-R -Ad -F *<log filename>*	Defines the log filename and deletes any existing logs.
Designate new master	-rm *<Partition Root ID>*	-P -Ad	Designates the specified partition on the local server to be master. This option should be used only on a read/write replica.
Repair known servers to the database	-rn	-N	Repairs all known server addresses that are known by the local eDirectory agent.
Repair replica ring	-rr *<Partition Root ID>*	-P -Ad	Repairs the specified partition replica ring.
Repair volume objects	-rv	NA	Repairs all volume objects from the command line. This option is available only on NetWare.
Repair volume objects and trustees	-rvt	NA	Repairs the volume objects and performs a trustee check on each volume. This option is available only on NetWare.
Disable the check attributes	-sc -rd	-R -Ad -sc	Disables the check attribute functionality while running a DSREPAIR.
Check the partition record	-si -rd	-R -Ad -si	Checks the partition record. By default, the partition records are not checked.

Parameter	NetWare/Windows	*nix	Description
Single object repair	`-so` *<EntryID>*	`-J` *<EntryID>*	DSREPAIR repairs only the specified object. Make sure that you use the 32-bit EntryID; e.g., 00008023, not 8023.
Reset local schema	`-sr`	`-S -Ad`	This option can be very dangerous. It resets schema on the local server and allows other servers to synchronize schema back in. You are counting on the fact that the sending servers have valid schema. This switch will not work on the server that holds the master of the root partition.
Unattended full repair	`-u`	`-U`	Issues an unattended full repair on the database.
Ignore API versions	`-v -rd`	`-R -Ad -v`	Instructs DSREPAIR to ignore API versions during repair checks. Warning: This is potentially a dangerous switch. The API version protects the data by ensuring that older versions of the directory do not alter the data sets. By disabling this feature, you are trusting that the eDirectory versions in your environment are up to date and that the DSREPAIR utility is of the same version as the agent.

Continued

Table 10-1. *Continued*

Parameter	NetWare/Windows	*nix	Description
Clear WM:RegisteredWorkstation attributes	`-wm -rd`	`-R -Ad -wm`	ZenWorks has a feature called Workstation Manager. It allows Zen agents to control the desktops. Each workstation candidate creates a value of the attribute type WM:RegisteredWorkstation on the partition root entry. It is possible for there to be thousands of such values. High-valued objects can cause high utilization while synchronizing data. The `-wm` option deletes all WM:RegisteredWorkstation values.
Remove all partitions	`-xk2 -rd`	`-R -Ad -xk2`	Removes all replicas from the server, leaving the server as an external reference server. Warning: Be sure you know what you are doing before you use this switch. If you use this switch, you need to manually clean up the replica ring by using DSREPAIR on the master. Also, if used incorrectly, this switch could cause severe data loss.
Reset all external references	`-xk3 -rd`	`-R -Ad -xk3`	Resets all of the external references on the local server so that they can be overwritten during the Backlink process.
Purge trustees	`-xk6 -rvt -rd`	NA	Prompts you whether or not you want to purge all trustees on the volume. This option is not available on non-NetWare platforms.

Parameter	NetWare/Windows	*nix	Description
Purge the Backlink attribute	`-xk8 -rd`	`-R -Ad -xk8`	Marks the first Backlink attribute nonpresent and purges the rest. This is done *only* on a master replica. Warning: This is a very dangerous switch. The Backlink attributes keep track of all objects that have external reference objects. This information is important for processing obituaries. This switch could break the obituary process if not used correctly.
Remove bindery type 258	`-xki -rd`	`-R -Ad -xki`	Removes SAP type 258 (tree name) from the bindery. This was put in place to solve some tree name corruption issues in prior versions of eDirectory.
Report replica synchronization	NA	`-E`	Reports on the status of replica synchronization via the command line.
Check external references	NA	`-C`	Checks all external references.
Check obituaries	NA	`-C -Ad`	Lists all known obituaries.
Time synchronization	NA	`-T`	Reports on the status of time synchronization.

DSTRACE

Each eDirectory-supported platform contains a command-line DSTRACE utility. Along with this, NDS iMonitor contains a DSTRACE mechanism that is consistent over all the platforms. To understand how DSTRACE works, you need to understand the event system that is built into the eDirectory agent. The event system creates an interactive interface to operations that occur within the eDirectory agent. In order for a process to be notified when a specific event occurs, the process must "register" for that event.

The eDirectory agent defines specific events for DSTRACE operations. For instance, if the agent is processing a connection, a DSTRACE message can be generated regarding this connection. The DSTRACE message is assigned to the event DSE_DB_CONN_TRACE. When the specified code path is executed, DSTRACE displays the specified connection message if DSTRACE has "registered" for the DSE_DB_CONN_TRACE event.

Understanding the Different DSTRACE Modules

The process that you must follow to register DSTRACE to a specified event differs slightly from platform to platform. The detailed procedures for registering events with DSTRACE for each platform are described next.

NetWare DSTRACE.NLM

DSTRACE.NLM is an external program that allows you to monitor operations that occur within the eDirectory agent. To start DSTRACE.NLM, simply load the module. After loading the module, at a server console, type **dstrace**.

A table will be displayed on the console of all the available filters as well as configuration options. To turn on a specific filter ("register" for an event), simply type **dstrace +<*filter*>** (e.g., `dstrace +conn`).

If you used the correct syntax, the filter changes colors, notifying you that the filter is now active. Table 10-2 lists available commands that are associated with DSTRACE.NLM.

Table 10-2. *DSTRACE.NLM Commands*

Command	Description
`dstrace -all`	Turns off all filters
`dstrace +all`	Turns on all filters
`dstrace file off`	Turns off logging to a file
`dstrace file on`	Turns on logging to a file (whose location is SYS:\SYSTEM\DSTRACE.LOG)
`dstrace screen on`	Enables messages to be written to the screen
`dstrace screen off`	Disables messages to be written to the screen

Command	Description
`dstrace +<filter>`	Enables a specific filter
`dstrace -<filter>`	Disables a specific filter
`load dstrace.nlm`	Loads the DSTRACE standalone module
`unload dstrace.nlm`	Unloads the DSTRACE standalone module

■ **Note** A separate screen is generated to show the DSTRACE messages. To view the messages onscreen, press Alt+Esc to list all screens and then select the DSTRACE console screen.

NetWare Internal DSTRACE

Along with the standalone DSTRACE.NLM, NetWare has a built-in DSTRACE mechanism within the eDirectory agent. Before enabling the internal DSTRACE mechanism, NDS must be loaded and initialized. To enable the internal DSTRACE mechanism, type the following at a server console:

```
set dstrace = on
```

The commands used for the internal DSTRACE mechanism are very similar to the DSTRACE.NLM commands with the exception that you must use the word `set` in front of each command. Table 10-3 lists available commands that are associated with the internal DSTRACE mechanism.

Table 10-3. *Internal DSTRACE Commands*

Command	Description
`set dstrace = nodebug`	Turns off all filters
`set dstrace = +all`	Turns on all filters
`set ttf = off`	Turns off logging to a file
`set ttf = on`	Turns on logging to a file (which is stored in DSTRACE.DBG)
`set dstrace = on`	Enables messages to be written to the screen
`set dstrace = off`	Disables messages to be written to the screen
`set dstrace = +<filter>`	Enables a specific filter
`set dstrace = -<filter>`	Disables a specific filter

Continued

Table 10-3. *Continued*

Command	Description
`set dstrace = *<process>`	Starts a process; e.g., `set dstrace=*h` triggers the Skulker process
`set dstrace = !<command>`	Executes a command; e.g., `set dstrace=!d` disables the synchronization process for 24 hours

■ **Note** A separate screen is generated to show the DSTRACE messages. To view the messages onscreen, press Alt+Esc to list all screens and then select the Directory Services screen.

Windows DSTRACE Utility

Windows does not have a command-line DSTRACE utility. The Windows DSTRACE utility is a GUI-based utility. To enable the DSTRACE utility in Windows, perform Task 10-4.

Task 10-4. Starting DSTRACE in Windows

1. Launch NDSCONS by going to %SystemDrive%:\Novell\Nds\NDSCons.exe or by clicking the Novell eDirectory Services icon in the Control Panel.
2. Click dstrace.dlm.
3. Click Start.

Through the Edit ➤ Options menu, you can enable or disable events and configure your screen options.

Linux, Solaris, HP-UX and AIX DSTRACE Utility

In the *nix environments, the DSTRACE mechanism is built into a module called `ndstrace`. The `ndstrace` executable is located under /usr/bin directory. To execute the `ndstrace` utility, from a terminal, type **ndstrace**. A DSTRACE screen appears that allows you to configure the different filters as well as view the messages onscreen.

Note If you cannot see all the options onscreen, exit `ndstrace` by typing **exit**. Make your terminal screen larger and then re-execute `ndstrace`.

Table 10-4 lists the different command syntaxes for `ndstrace`.

Table 10-4. *ndstrace Command Syntaxes*

Command	Description
`set dstrace = nodebug`	Turns off all filters
`set dstrace +all`	Turns on all filters
`set ttf = off`	Turns off logging to a file
`set ttf = on`	Turns on logging to a file (which is stored in /var/nds/dstrace)
`dstrace +`<*filter*>	Enables a specific filter
`dstrace -`<*filter*>	Disables a specific filter
`set dstrace = *`<*process*>	Starts a process; e.g., `set dstrace=*h` triggers the Skulker process
`set dstrace = !`<*command*>	Executes a command; e.g.; `set dstrace=!d` disables the synchronization process for 24 hours
`exit`	Unloads the `ndstrace` module

The `ndstrace` module on the *nix platforms can be used for more than just tracing specific operations. It can be used as an interface into the eDirectory agent. The `ndstrace` module supports a `-c` option, which allows you to pass a command to the eDirectory agent. For instance, to display the current status of all the eDirectory agent threads, type **ndstrace –c threads**.

Table 10-5 lists all the available commands that can be passed to the eDirectory agent through `ndstrace`.

Table 10-5. *ndstrace Commands*

Command	Description
`-c threads`	Shows the status of all threads that are allocated to the NDSD process.
`-c modules`	Displays all modules that are running in the NDSD process space.
`-l > <file>`	Runs `ndstrace` in the background and pipes the results to a file. For instance, `ndstrace -l > /home/user1/ndstrace.log` would run `ndstrace` in the background and pipe the results to a file called ndstrace.log.
`-c "<inline command>"`	Configures `ndstrace` to monitor operations in one command rather than going into the utility and issuing multiple commands. This is very useful when you want to execute a `dstrace` in a script. For example, to trigger the Backlink process and pipe the results to a file, you would execute the `-l` command and then type `ndstrace -c "set ndstrace +blnk; set ndstrace=*b"`.
`-c "load <module>"`	Loads a specified module into the NDSD namespace. For instance, if you want to load NDS iMonitor, you would type `ndstrace -c "load imon"`. The best way to figure out what the module name is would be to run `"ndstrace -c modules"`. This lists all available modules as well as their status.
`-c "unload <module>"`	Unloads a specified module.

NDS iMonitor

NDS iMonitor is a cross-platform tool, which means that it looks the same regardless of the operating system or platform eDirectory is running on. The Trace Configuration page is a good example of this. The command-line utility DSTRACE is available on each platform in which eDirectory runs. The command-line utility will have a different name and different syntax, depending on the platform. In eDirectory environments in which you have multiple platforms, trying to remember which tool does what can get confusing. If you use NDS iMonitor, the DSTRACE configuration looks exactly the same.

The trace that is captured will write to an HTML page. An archive of HTML traces is maintained. The exact location of the HTML files will depend on the platform from which you are running eDirectory. However, regardless of platform, the HTML pages are always located in the relative directory, dstrace. On NetWare, the relative directory is located in SYS:\SYSTEM\NDSIMON. In Windows, it is located in \Novell\Nds\Ndsimon. On Linux, Solaris, HP-UX, and AIX, it is located in /var/nds.

The direct URL is `http://`*<server address>*`:`*<clear-text port>*`/nds/trace` or `https://`*<server address>*`:`*<secure port>*`/nds/trace`.

Monitoring the DSTRACE Operations

DSTRACE must be configured to display a specific operation. Table 10-6 lists all the different commands per DSTRACE utility that you would use to configure DSTRACE to monitor a specific operation. For instance, Table 10-6 states that `+conn` monitors connections with DSTRACE.NLM, so you would type `dstrace +conn` within the DSTRACE utility if you wanted to monitor connection operations.

Tip If you are not sure what operation you should monitor to troubleshoot a specific issue, turn on all the operations in DSTRACE and execute whatever you are trying to troubleshoot. You can search for a particular error or symptom in the trace screen or trace log.

Table 10-6. *DSTRACE Operations*

Operation	DSTRACE.NLM	set dstrace (NetWare)	Windows	*nix	Description
Show Operations	+tags	+tags	Screen tab ➤ Option Tag	+tags	Displays what operation tag generated the message.
Time	+time	+time	Screen tab ➤ Time Stamp	+time	Displays the time the event occurred.
Allocated Memory	+aloc	NA	Allocated Memory	+aloc	Used mostly with debug versions of the eDirectory agent to trace when memory is allocated and deallocated.
Audit	+aumn	+a	Audit	+aumn	Used to see auditing messages.
Audit NCP	+aunc	+an	Audit NCP	+aunc	Monitors the auditing NCP engine.
Audit Skulk	+ausk	NA	Audit Skulk	+ausk	Monitors the auditing synchronization messages.
Authentication	+auth	+authen	Authentication	+auth	Displays messages specific to the authentication routines. Activities such as SEV calculations, accessing rights, etc. are displayed.
Backlinker	+blnk	+blink	Backlinker	+blnk	Monitors the Backlink background process, which maintains external references.

Operation	DSTRACE.NLM	set dstrace (NetWare)	Windows	*nix	Description
Backlinker Detail	`+bldt`	`+bklkdetail`	Backlinker Detail	`+bldt`	This option has limited usage. It is used in one instance to track an internal process that initializes the Backlink process.
Agent Buffers	`+buff`	`+buffers`	Buffers	`+buff`	Produces detailed information about all information that is being processed through the eDirectory agent. An actual packet dump is shown with all information that is going in and out of the agent. Most of the time, this information is too much. However, if you are trying to track down a specific request or reply and feel that the content is suspect, turning on Agent Buffers is your best option.
Change Cache	`+chng`	`+change`	Change Cache	`+chng`	Tracks activities that occur while processing entries in Change Cache.

Continued

Table 10-6. *Continued*

Operation	DSTRACE.NLM	set dstrace (NetWare)	Windows	*nix	Description
Client Buffers	+cbuf	+cbuf	Client Buffers	+cbuf	Similar to Agent Buffers, dumps a packet dump of the request coming from a client, such as dclient.
Collisions	+coll	+collision	Collisions	+coll	Displays a message in the Collisions filter if duplicate requests are made on the same object for the same operation. This is used in the Backlink process, Obituary process, Skulker process, and other processes.
Connection Trace	+conn	+conn	Connection Trace	+conn	Tracks information in the bad address cache as well as other connection processes.
Distributed References	+drlk	+drl	Distributed References	+drlk	Monitors the Distributed Reference Link (DRL) background process, which manages the replication of changes of a specified state of an object. It is similar to the Obituary process in maintaining the state change until all replicas

Operation	DSTRACE.NLM	set dstrace (NetWare)	Windows	*nix	Description
Distributed References *(continued)*					see the change. It was implemented to provide a more scalable way of handling modified objects.
DRL Detail	`+drld`	`+drldetail`	DRL Detail	`+drld`	Monitors the initialization of the DRL process. There is only one message that is displayed in one place in code.
DNS	`+dnsv`	`+dns`	DNS	`+dnsv`	Not currently being used in eDirectory.
Agent Requests	`+areq`	`+dsa`	DS Agent	`+areq`	Used to monitor any request coming from the eDirectory agent.
Emulated Bindery	`+bemu`	`+emu`	Emulated Bindery	`+bemu`	Shows legacy bindery requests.
Fragmented Requests	`+frag`	`+frag`	Fragmented Requests	`+frag`	Generates messages based off of operations that occur in the fragmentation process. Most of the directory requests and replies are too large to fit into one packet, so they are fragmented and defragmented by an internal process within eDirectory.

Continued

Table 10-6. *Continued*

Operation	DSTRACE.NLM	set dstrace (NetWare)	Windows	*nix	Description
Inbound Synchronization	`+sync`	`+in`	Inbound Synchronization	`+sync`	Monitors and displays all inbound object synchronization.
Initialization	`+init`	`+init`	Initialization	`+init`	Tracks agent initialization messages.
Inspector	`+insp`	`+i`	Inspector	`+insp`	Validates the data on an object. It is used during the Backlink process as well as during the Skulker process.
Janitor	`+jntr`	`+j`	Janitor	`+jntr`	Used to purge objects from the tree. Used in the obituary process.
LDAP	`+ldap`	`+ldap`	LDAP	`+ldap`	Reports all LDAP requests, replies, initializations, and LDAP errors.
LDAP Stack	`+lstk`	NA	LDAP Stack	`+lstk`	Not currently being used by eDirectory or the LDAP server.
Limber	`+lmbr`	`+limber`	Limber	`+lmbr`	The Limber background process updates the server network addresses on the NCP server object and in the replica ring attributes on the partition root objects. The Limber option monitors this activity.

Operation	DSTRACE.NLM	set dstrace (NetWare)	Windows	*nix	Description
Locking	+lock	+locks	Locking	+lock	Generates messages whenever the database is locked or unlocked.
Lost Entry	+lost	+lost	Lost Entry	+lost	Used during the obituary process. Most errors during the obituary process are generated through the +lost option. It is also used if errors occur during a delete or add of an object.
Miscellaneous Distributed Operations	+misc	+misc	Misc Distributed Operations	+misc	Used for several background processes. This is a good default option to use when troubleshooting general issues.
Move Object	+move	+move	Move	+move	Used to monitor a Move SubTree operation.
NCP Client	+vcln	+dc	NCP Client	+vcln	Used to monitor connections. It can be used to monitor the creation, deletion, and upgrade of connection contexts. It also monitors incoming NCP verbs.

Continued

Table 10-6. *Continued*

Operation	DSTRACE.NLM	set dstrace (NetWare)	Windows	*nix	Description
NCP Engine	`+ncpe`	NA	NCP Engine	`+ncpe`	Monitors all backend NCP server activities.
Object Producers	`+objp`	`+objproducer`	Object Producers	`+objp`	A programmatic instance of a class in memory is called an object. In this case, the objects are used for several background processes. The `+objp` option monitors the creation of and deletion of these objects.
Obituaries	`+obit`	`+obit`	Obituaries	`+obit`	Prompts the Obituary background process to generate messages.
Outbound Synchronization	`+sklk`	`+s`	Outbound Synchronization	`+sklk`	Prompts all outbound synchronization activities to generate messages.
Outbound Sync Detail	`+sydl`	`+detail`	Outbound Sync Detail	`+sydl`	Generates messages regarding stream values, auxiliary classes, and filtered replica handling.
Partition	`+part`	`+part`	Partition	`+part`	Tracks all partition operations and displays informational and error messages.

Operation	DSTRACE.NLM	set dstrace (NetWare)	Windows	*nix	Description
Purge	+purg	+purge	Purge	+purg	Tracks the purging of objects from the directory as well as modifications of the Purge attribute.
Resolve Name	+rslv	+rn	Resolve Name	+rslv	Tracks the activities of finding a real object. If a real object is requested and that real object does not exist on the local database, the Resolve Name process walks the tree to find a server that contains the real object. The Resolve Name option displays messages about these activities.
SAP	+sadv	+sap	SAP	+sadv	Monitors all server advertisement messages to other name services. The advertisement could be a SAP or SLP message.
Schema	+scma	+schema	Schema	+scma	Monitors the Schema Synchronization process.

Continued

Table 10-6. *Continued*

Operation	DSTRACE.NLM	set dstrace (NetWare)	Windows	*nix	Description
Schema Detail	`+scmd`	`+schemadetail`	Schema Detail	`+scmd`	Displays messages about the backend schema process. Rather than display schema objects that are being synchronized, it shows things like locking of the schema partition, verifying schema version, monitoring global schema operations like schema resets, etc.
Search	`+srch`	`+search`	Search	`+srch`	Monitors DSASearch requests. Information about the iterator, base, and scope are displayed.
Search Detail	`+srdt`	`+searchdetail`	Search Detail	`+srdt`	Monitors search results.
Server Packets	`+spkt`	`+serverpacket`	Server Packets	`+spkt`	Similar to the Buffers option, except that it is used only on Windows and UNIX platforms.
Storage Manager	`+recm`	`+recman`	Storage Manager	`+recm`	Monitors information about the FLAIM database processes, such as search requests, indexes being used, and other database operations.

Operation	DSTRACE.NLM	set dstrace (NetWare)	Windows	*nix	Description
Streams	`+strm`	`+streams`	Streams	`+strm`	Monitors all stream file activities, such as searches, replication, and opening and closing of stream files.
Thread Scheduling	`+thrd`	`+th`	Thread Scheduling	`+thrd`	Displays the time delta between the start of an operation and the completion of that operation. It also monitors the start and stop of background processes.
Time Vectors	`+tvec`	`+tv`	Time Vectors	`+tvec`	Monitors the modification and reading of transitive vectors.

Along with monitoring eDirectory agent processes, DSTRACE also has the ability to monitor external module information. Table 10-7 lists the available modules to monitor.

Table 10-7. *Monitoring External Modules Through DSTRACE*

Module	DSTRACE.NLM	set dstrace (NetWare)	Windows	*nix	Monitors
DirXML	`+dxml`	`+dxml`	DirXML	`+dxml`	DirXML and Identity Manager activities
DirXML Drivers	`+dvrs`	`+dvrs`	DirXML Drivers	`+dvrs`	DirXML Driver activities
HTTP Stack	NA	NA	HTTP Stack	`+http`	eDirectory HTTP stack activities
NDS iMonitor	`+nmon`	`+nmon`	NDS iMonitor	`+nmon`	NDS iMonitor activities
NICI Extensions	`+nici`	NA	NICI Extensions	`+nici`	Calls into NICI
NMAS	`+nmas`	NA	NMAS	`+nmas`	Authentication requests that come through NMAS
PKI	`+pkii`	NA	PKI	`+pkii`	Server certificate processes
PKI API	`+pkia`	NA	PKI API	`+pkia`	Operations that use the PKI APIs
Repair	NA	`+repair`	Repair	NA	DSREPAIR operations
Repair Detail	NA	NA	Repair Detail	NA	Detailed operations like database locking, etc.
Secret Store	`+sstr`	NA	Secret Store	`+sstr`	Secret Store operations
Secure Sockets	`+ssli`	NA	Secure Sockets	`+ssli`	NTLS and SSL information
Wanman	`+wanm`	NA	Wanman	`+wanm`	Wan Traffic Manager operations

DSTRACE can also be used to "trigger" a background process in the eDirectory agent. This is accomplished by proceeding the command with an asterisk (*). For instance, if you want to trigger a Skulker process on NetWare, you could type `set dstrace = *s`. Table 10-8 lists all of the available triggers.

Table 10-8. *Executing Triggers Within DSTRACE*

Trigger	Description
*.	Unloads and reloads eDirectory
*a	Resets bad address cache
*ad	Disables bad address cache
*ae	Enables bad address cache
*b	Forces Backlink process
*c	Displays connection table statistics for outbound connections
*cd	Displays connection table in a comma-delimited format
*ci	Displays idle time statistics for the connection table
*cr	Displays routing table packets for connection table
*ct	Displays connection table in a space-delimited format
*c0	Resets connection table statistics
*d#	Aborts the Send All Objects (*i) operations
*f	Forces the Flat Cleaner and Janitor process
*g	Rebuilds change cache
*h	Forces replica synchronization (heartbeat)
*hr	Clears last send request
*i	Forces a Send All Objects request
*j	Forces the partition Purge process
*l	Forces the Limber process
*lh	Shows lock state holders
*lmb	Shows lock activity
*lme	Don't show lock activity
*ls	Shows lock state
*lw	Shows lock state waiters
*m#	Sets the maximum size of the DSTRACE.DBG file in bytes
*of<EntryID>	Flushes the filtered replica cache for the specified server
*op<EntryID>	Dumps the local servers replica filter to the screen
*od	Disables outbound filtering
*oe	Enables outbound filtering

Continued

Table 10-8. *Continued*

Trigger	Description
`*p`	Displays eDirectory tunable parameters
`*r`	Resets DSTRACE.DBG file
`*s`	Schedules Skulker process
`*sc`	Shows connections
`*sm`	Shows statistics
`*smb`	Begins statistics monitoring
`*sme`	Ends statistics monitoring
`*smr`	Resets statistics monitoring
`*ss`	Forces a schema sync
`*ssa`	Forces a schema sync to all known servers and rebuilds the schema sync list
`*ssd`	Deletes the schema sync list
`*ssl`	Shows the schema sync list
`*st`	Displays status of all background processes
`*stl`	Shows the limber status
`*sto`	Shows the obituary status
`*sts`	Shows the schema status
`*stx`	Shows the external reference status
`*t`	Triggers a transitive vector read
`*u`	Changes the status of all servers to UP
`*ud`	Changes the status of all servers to DOWN
`*umb`	Shows update activity
`*ume`	Disables the display of update activity
`*z`	Shows background process threads

Lastly, DSTRACE can also be used to change the default eDirectory settings. To perform a setting change through DSTRACE, you need to preface the command with an exclamation mark (`!`). For instance, to disable synchronization, you would type `set dstrace=!d`. Table 10-9 lists all of the available settings that can be changed through DSTRACE.

Table 10-9. *DSTRACE Settings*

Command	Setting
`!a#`	Adjusts Time Slice interval to # of minutes (e.g., `set dstrace=!a10`)
`!b#`	Adjusts Backlink interval to # of minutes
`!d#`	Disables Replica Sync for # minutes (also disables priority sync in eDirectory 8.8)
`!di#`	Disables Inbound Replica Sync for # minutes
`!do#`	Disables Outbound Replica Sync for # minutes
`!e`	Enables Replica Sync (also enables priority sync in eDirectory 8.8)
`!ei`	Enables Inbound Replica Sync
`!eo`	Enables Outbound Replica Sync
`!f#`	Sets the Flatcleaner interval to # of minutes
`!g#`	Sets the Request in Progress Give Up Times to # of minutes
`!h#`	Sets the Heartbeat interval to # of minutes
`!i#`	Sets the Heartbeat Base Schema interval to # of minutes
`!j#`	Sets the Janitor interval to # of minutes
`!so#`	Disables All Schema Sync for # minutes
`!sio#`	Disables Inbound Schema Sync for # minutes
`!soO#`	Disables Outbound Schema Sync for # minutes
`!s1`	Enables All Schema Sync
`!si1`	Enables Inbound Schema Sync
`!so1`	Enables Outbound Schema Sync
`!t#`	Sets the server State UP Threshold
`!v#`	Lists DS Version Restrictions
`!w#`	Sets IPX RIP Delay in # of minutes
`!x#`	Sets the IPX retries (default: 3)
`!y#`	Sets the IPX Timeout Scale Factor (default: 2)
`!z#`	Sets the IPX Timeout Shift Factor (default: 4)

■ **Note** Although it is handy to use DSTRACE to manage many of the different aspects of the directory, it is advisable to use NDS iMonitor in most cases. NDS iMonitor gives you an easy-to-use GUI, a listing of all the default settings, and online help menus that describe the settings.

NDSConfig

NDSConfig is a command-line utility that is available only on Linux, Solaris, HP-UX, and AIX. NDSConfig is used to create and configure instances of the database. There are four different operations that allow you to create, remove, or upgrade a particular eDirectory database. To execute one of the operations, type **ndsconfig** ***<operation>*** from a terminal screen. For instance, if you wanted to create a new instance of eDirectory on the local server, from a terminal screen, you would type `ndsconfig new`. Table 10-10 lists the four basic operations that are supported with NDSConfig.

Table 10-10. *NDSConfig Operations*

Operation	Usage
`new/def`	Create a new tree. The `def` option creates a new tree with default settings. This should only be used in a test environment to set up a default tree quickly.
`add`	Add the local server into an existing eDirectory tree. If the partition that contains the local server object contains less than three replicas, a replica of the partition is added to the local server.
`rm`	Remove the instance of the database from the local server. This does not uninstall eDirectory. It does, however, remove the existing server object from the tree and removes all associated links and references to the local server's object.
`upgrade`	Upgrade an existing database to the release version that is equivalent to the version of NDSConfig that is on the local server. To identify the version of NDSConfig, type **ndsconfig --version**.

■ **Note** Refer to the help page for a listing of all the switches that are associated with the operations that are listed in Table 10-10. To access the help pages, type **ndsconfig –h**.

Another powerful use of the NDSConfig utility is to dynamically get and set eDirectory environment variables that are stored in the /etc/nds.conf file. If you type `ndsconfig get`, you get all the parameters that are set in the /etc/nds.conf file.

Tip Not all settings that are displayed through the `ndsconfig get` command are located in the /etc/nds.conf file. If the /etc/nds.conf file does not explicitly define an environment variable, `ndsconfig get` displays the default values.

To change one of the eDirectory environment variables, you would type `ndsconfig` *<variable name>*=*<value>*. For instance, if you want to change the Janitor background process to 5 minutes, you would type `ndsconfig set n4u.nds.janitor-interval=5`. To detect the available variable names, use the `ndsconfig get` command.

LDAPConfig

LDAPConfig is a utility similar to the NDSConfig utility. It is also available on the Linux, Solaris, HP-UX, and AIX platforms. LDAPConfig is used specifically to configure the LDAP server object. There are two major functions available with LDAPConfig:

- `get`: Gets the available LDAP configuration options as well as their values
- `set`: Sets new values to the available LDAP configuration options

Note Unlike the NDSConfig utility, the LDAPConfig utility requires a successful authentication to the directory. If you do not pass the user and password on the command line (e.g., `ldapconfig get -a admin.novell -w adminpassword`), you will be prompted to type in the user and password.

To make a setting change, you type `ldapconfig set` *<variable name>*= *<value>*. For instance, if you wanted to change the LDAP server to accept clear-text connections, you would type `ldapconfig set 'Require TLS for Simple Binds with Password'=yes`.

Note Notice that the preceding example includes single quotes ('). The single quote must be used if there are spaces in the variable name.

When you use the `set` command, the changes are stored on the LDAP server object as persistent changes.

NDSStat

NDSStat is used on the Linux, Solaris, HP-UX, and AIX platforms to check the status and version of eDirectory. The `ndsstat` command reads information from within eDirectory. If the NDSD process is down, an error message is generated stating that the utility "Failed to obtain a Novell eDirectory Server Connection."

If the NDSD process is running, `ndsstat` displays the version of eDirectory as well as the server and tree name. It is important to note that the information displayed is coming from the server object on the local database. Often, it takes a few minutes for this information to be updated. If, for instance, you apply a patch to eDirectory and then immediately type `ndsstat`, you may find that the version does not reflect the patch version. In these cases, give it a few minutes for the version information to be synchronized to the NCP server object.

The following two additional switches can be added to `ndsstat`. To use these switches, append the option to the end of the command (i.e., `ndsstat -`*`<option>`*).

- `-r`: Lists all the replicas known to the local server
- `-s`: Lists all servers known to the database

Note The `-r` and `-s` switches use SLP to gather the information about other servers and replicas. If SLP is not configured, you will receive errors while using these switches.

NDSLogin

NDSLogin is a utility that you can use to troubleshoot eDirectory. If you are having problems logging into eDirectory from an external source, you can eliminate network type issues by using NDSLogin. NDSLogin is a tool that resides on the local server. It is available only on the Linux, Solaris, AIX, and HP-UX platforms.

Note In NetWare, you can perform a similar operation through DSRepair ➤ Advanced Options ➤ Log file and login configuration.

NDSLogin acts like a client and allows you to authenticate to eDirectory. NDSLogin is used to test authentication. There really is not much you can do once you are logged into the directory.

To see the available options with NSDLogin, at a terminal window, type **ndslogin**.

NDSSch

NDSSch is a tool that allows you to process an SCH file. SCH files have schema definitions. When the SCH file is processed, the defined schema in the SCH file is added to eDirectory. NDSSch is a tool that is available on all platforms. On NetWare and Windows, the tool is built into the Install/Configuration utilities.

To access the tool from NetWare, go to nwconfig ➤ Directory Options ➤ Extend Schema. From this menu you can specify a directory in which all schema files reside or you can specify a particular SCH file location and filename.

To access NDSSch from Windows, open NDSCons.exe, located in the main eDirectory directory (the default is c:\novell\Nds), click install.dlm, and then click Start.

To access the tool from the Linux, Solaris, AIX, and HP-UX platforms, at a terminal window, type **ndssch**. You will see command-line options that you can use to authenticate to the directory and specify the SCH filename.

The required syntax used to create an SCH file is mostly undocumented. Typically, the only time you would use an SCH file is if you were installing a Novell product that requires schema extensions into an existing eDirectory tree. By default, the SCH files are kept in the following directories, by platform:

- *NetWare*: SYS:\SYSTEM\SCHEMA
- *Windows*: %SystemDrive%:\Novell\Nds\
- Linux, Solaris, AIX, HP-UX: /usr/lib/nds-schema

EDIRUTIL

EDIRUTIL is a script that launches the eMBox Java application. As with all Java applications, the Java executable needs to be executed and a class path must be specified. The command line is fairly lengthy. Novell has made this process easier by creating EDIRUTIL. The script launches Java, specifies the class path, and runs the eMBox Java application. The script also takes command-line parameters. Typically, the two parameters that are used are the following:

- `-i`: Interactive mode. This switch launches the eMBox client into command-line mode. From within the client, you can execute eMTools. To understand the different syntaxes, just type **help** from within the client.
- `-g`: Graphical mode. This switch launches a graphical display. If you are accessing this tool through a remote session, you need to make sure that the display is exported or you will get an error. From within the graphics client, you can go to the Advanced menu and select Show the command line. This displays all commands and switches that you would need to use to execute the specified operation if you were in interactive mode.

To execute EDIRUTIL from NetWare, Linux, Solaris, AIX or HP-UX, from a console, type: **edirutil –<*option*>** (e.g., `edirutil -g`). To execute EDIRUTIL from Windows, go to %SystemDrive%:\Novell\Nds\ and execute the edirutil.exe file.

ICE

ICE stands for the Novell Import Convert Export Utility. ICE is a powerful LDAP client tool that is available on all eDirectory-supported platforms. ICE allows you to import LDIF files into eDirectory via LDAP or export data from within eDirectory to an LDIF file or a Comma Separated Value (CSV) file. In addition, ICE allows you to convert or better migrate one LDAP directory to another.

ICE can be executed from ConsoleOne, iManager (through the eDirectory Maintenance role), or from the command line. ConsoleOne and iManager contain ICE wizards that ask you for some information and then create the ICE command line for you based on your answers and execute ICE. Running ICE from the command line, however, requires you to formulate your own commands.

ICE has a complex set of options. ICE uses the following command-line syntax:

```
ice <general options> -S <LDIF | LDAP)> <source options> ➥
-D <LDIF | LDAP> <destination options>
```

The `-S` stands for *source*. If you are importing data from an LDIF file, the source would be LDIF. If you are exporting data from eDirectory, the source would be LDAP. The `-D` stands for *destination*. The destination would be LDIF if you are exporting data from eDirectory to an LDIF file or LDAP if you are importing data from an LDIF file. Each component of the command line has different options. To get general help on the options, from a terminal, just type **ice**.

Note ICE is not installed on Windows with eDirectory by default. However, if you install ConsoleOne onto your Windows box, within the ConsoleOne/bin directory, there is an ice.exe file.

If you want specific information about the different handlers, you can type one of the following:

```
ice -h LDAP
ice -h LDIF
ice -h CSV
```

Summary

The command-line options are useful because you can quickly access the directory from within the directory terminal. However, to avoid having to learn a lot of new switches, I recommend that you use iManager and NDS iMonitor to manage eDirectory. With iManager and NDS iMonitor, you get a cross-platform, unified view of the tools. iManager includes plug-ins that make it easy to understand what information the specified tool requires and gives you clear interfaces for providing the required data.

CHAPTER 11

Troubleshooting Common Issues

The following topics are covered in this chapter:

- High processor utilization
  - Detecting the offending process
  - Bindery issues
  - Looping requests on connections
  - Synchronization issues
  - Schema synchronization issues
  - Offending functions
  - Trends
- High memory consumption
  - Identifying the process that is consuming most of the memory
  - Identifying the process within eDirectory that is consuming the memory
  - Identifying memory fragmentation issues
- Slow Logins Using Client 32
  - Eliminating workstation and network issues
  - Troubleshooting eDirectory bottlenecks
  - Troubleshooting tree-walking issues

There are many different issues that may occur in eDirectory. The purpose of this chapter is to outline a few of the biggest issues that you may encounter as you administer eDirectory: high processor utilization, high memory consumption, and slow logins.

High Processor Utilization

All applications, regardless of the platform, require processor time to execute. eDirectory is a multiple-thread application. Each thread requests time from the processor (or processors) to execute the instructions that come through that thread. In certain conditions, hundreds of threads are all fighting for time on the processor. In other scenarios, one thread with a very large request can take over the processor and not release it for other threads to execute. In either of the described conditions, the end result is that almost 100 percent of the processor time is used, not allowing information to process. The fallout from this condition is that the server appears to "hang" and does not process any new requests.

This section discusses how to determine whether eDirectory is the source of high processor utilization and, if it is, how to focus your troubleshooting efforts to find the offending activity that is causing high-utilization conditions within the eDirectory process space.

Detecting the Offending Process

The first step in troubleshooting high utilization is to eliminate variables to determine the offending process. You can easily figure out if eDirectory is directly or indirectly involved in activities that are causing high utilization simply by unloading eDirectory. To unload eDirectory, perform the following, per platform:

- *NetWare*: At a console, type **unload ds.nlm**.
- *Windows*: Through the Services tab (located in Control Panel), stop the NDS Server service (dhost).
- *Linux, Solaris, AIX, HP-UX*: At a console, type **/etc/init.d/ndsd stop**.

After eDirectory is stopped, observe processor utilization. If it immediately drops, eDirectory is directly or indirectly involved in activities that are causing high utilization. eDirectory does not have the ability to monitor the entire server and all of its applications. You need to rely on the platform's native tools to monitor high utilization. Many such tools are available, some of the most common of which are listed here, per platform:

- *NetWare*: MONITOR.NLM
- *Windows*: Task Manager
- *Linux*: `top`
- *Solaris, AIX, HP-UX*: `pstat`

Proving that eDirectory is directly or indirectly causing the high utilization is just the first step. If you determine that eDirectory is causing high utilization, you need to find the offending activity. With the exception of NetWare, all platforms can have multiple applications or modules running within the ndsd/dhost process space. You need to eliminate each module and/or application within the ndsd/dhost process space to determine the offending module or application.

To perform this operation in Windows, simply use the NDSCons utility, which will list each module and application that is running within the dhost service on Windows. Stop each module by highlighting it in NDSCons and clicking Stop.

■ **Note** Some modules are required to run if ds.dlm is running. These cannot be unloaded. Also note that if you stop ds.dlm, all modules will be stopped, which does not help you determine the offending module. Unload all other modules first.

To unload each module from within the Linux, Solaris, AIX, and HP-UX platforms, use the `ndstrace` utility. At a terminal, you would type `ndstrace -c "unload` *`<module>`* `"`. For instance, to unload NDS iMonitor, you would type `ndstrace -c "unload imon"`.

■ **Note** To get a listing of all available modules to unload, at a terminal, type **ndstrace –c modules**.

On NetWare, you simply need to unload each individual module. For instance, to unload the LDAP module, you would type `unload nldap`. The best way to determine which modules are loaded is to refer to the SYS:\SYSTEM\AUTOEXEC.NCF file. Simply remark out all modules and reboot the server (or unload them one at a time from the console).

After you have unloaded all the modules except for the core eDirectory modules, if high utilization is still an issue, you can safely say that the core eDirectory modules are directly or indirectly the cause of high utilization.

■ **Note** If you identified a noncore eDirectory application or module that is causing high utilization, you can use DSTRACE to troubleshoot these modules. For more information about how to use DSTRACE, refer to Chapter 10. For further information, please refer to the documentation for that application or module. There are a lot of TIDs that can help you at `http://support.novell.com`. It is beyond the scope of this book to discuss each module and application individually. Thus, this book discusses only the core eDirectory modules.

Although there are many different issues that can cause high utilization, only a few items typically cause high-utilization conditions within the eDirectory process space. The top issues that you should troubleshoot first are the following:

- Bindery issues
- Looping requests on connections
- Synchronization issues
- Schema synchronization issues

Bindery Issues

Prior to NDS 4.x, the directory was stored in a flat format called "bindery." The need for identity services forced the bindery type format to change into a multilayered, hierarchal tree. However, a lot of hardware vendors and applications that exist in today's market still rely on the flat bindery format. Therefore, even the latest versions of eDirectory support bindery requests.

Because bindery requests are legacy type requests, eDirectory emulates the old bindery format by creating what is called a *bindery context*. The bindery context is a specified container. eDirectory can advertise this container as the top of the tree, and objects directly within that container are considered to be part of the bindery partition. As with the older versions of NDS, eDirectory allocates only one thread to process all bindery requests. If an application or hardware makes thousands of bindery requests, the single thread cannot process all of the requests in an efficient manner. In these conditions, it is possible to cause a condition where high utilization occurs on the server.

To determine whether or not you are experiencing high utilization because of bindery, use DSTRACE to track bindery issues.

■ **Note** If you do not know how to use the DSTRACE utility, refer to Chapter 10 for more information.

You can use the `+emu`, `+bemu`, or Bindery Emulation option (based on which DSTRACE utility you are using; refer to Chapter 10) to track bindery requests. Turn on the Bindery Emulation option in DSTRACE to track all bindery requests that are coming into the server. While monitoring the DSTRACE screen, if bindery messages are scrolling by at a fairly rapid rate, it is very possible that bindery requests are causing the high utilization. The bindery messages should tell you what type of bindery request is coming in and from whom.

Typically, most bindery requests in today's market are bindery printers. It is advisable to convert these bindery printers to NDPS or iPrint printers. Sometimes, however, the old printer hardware will not support NDPS. For such cases, eDirectory now includes a process that will throttle the bindery requests, called the Quality of Service (QoS) mask. The idea with QoS is that as bindery requests are sent into the server, the eDirectory agent will put the requests into a waiting queue and process them on a delayed basis. The end result is that the bindery requests do not create high utilization. The adverse effect is that the request is delayed, which will give the appearance that bindery requests are processed slower than regular requests. Because of this adverse effect, it is advisable to upgrade all bindery-dependent applications or hardware to eDirectory-aware applications and hardware whenever possible.

■ **Note** For more information about QoS masks and how to configure them, refer to Novell's Knowledgebase at `http://support.novell.com`.

Looping Requests on Connections

Another common issue that causes high utilization is created by an errant application or connection that keeps making requests to the directory over and over again. When you unload the eDirectory modules, high utilization goes away. This can give you a false impression that eDirectory is the cause of the high utilization. In the condition where an errant application or connection is causing the high utilization, when you unload eDirectory, that connection is lost and processor utilization goes down.

DSTRACE is a great tool to identify errant applications and connections. To use DSTRACE to find connection problems, use the +dsa, +areq, or Agent Requests option (depending on the DSTRACE utility that you are using). While watching the DSTRACE screen, you will see the same connection number over and over again while the server is experiencing high utilization. The message in DSTRACE will show you the connection number of the connection that is associated to the message, as shown in the example in Figure 11-1.

```
04:41:42 46AF6BB0 Agent: Calling DSAResolveName conn:14 for client .[Public].
04:41:42 46AF6BB0 Agent: Calling DSAGetServerNetAddress conn:14 for client .[Public].
04:41:42 46AF6BB0 Agent: Calling DSAResolveName conn:14 for client .[Public].
04:41:42 46AF6BB0 Agent: Calling DSARead conn:14 for client .[Public].
04:41:42 46AF6BB0 Agent: Calling DSABeginAuthentication conn:14 for client .[Public].
04:41:42 46AF6BB0 Agent: Calling DSAFinishAuthentication conn:14 for client .[Public].
04:41:42 46AF6BB0 Agent: Calling DSAReadObjectInfo conn:14 for client .admin.novell.RKOESVMLINUXTREE.
04:41:42 46AF6BB0 Agent: Calling DSAReadObjectInfo conn:14 for client .admin.novell.RKOESVMLINUXTREE.
04:41:42 46AF6BB0 Agent: Calling DSAResolveName conn:14 for client .admin.novell.RKOESVMLINUXTREE.
04:41:42 46AF6BB0 Agent: Calling DSARead conn:14 for client .admin.novell.RKOESVMLINUXTREE.
04:41:42 46AF6BB0 Agent: DSARead failed, no such attribute (-603).
04:41:42 46AF6BB0 Agent: Calling DSARead conn:14 for client .admin.novell.RKOESVMLINUXTREE.
04:41:42 46AF6BB0 Agent: Calling DSARead conn:14 for client .admin.novell.RKOESVMLINUXTREE.
04:41:42 46AF6BB0 Agent: DSARead failed, no such attribute (-603).
04:41:42 46AF6BB0 Agent: Calling DSARead conn:14 for client .admin.novell.RKOESVMLINUXTREE.
```

Figure 11-1. *DSTRACE connection number*

Using NDS iMonitor, you can get a lot of information about this connection number through the Connections ➤ Inbound Connection page, shown in Figure 11-2.

Inbound Connection

Number	Flags	Signing Level	Entry ID	DN	Address Type	Address Length	Address	Reply Size	Authentication Level	Authentication Time
0	Supervisor, Console Operator, Local	None	00008054	.rkvmoeslinux.novell.RKOESVMLINUXTREE.	Internal	6	000000000000	0	Licensed	05/30/05 03:34:09 AM
1	Supervisor, Remote	None	00008054	.rkvmoeslinux.novell.RKOESVMLINUXTREE.	TCP	6	10.0.0.2:1032	0	Authenticated	05/30/05 03:34:24 AM
2	Supervisor, Remote	None	00008054	.rkvmoeslinux.novell.RKOESVMLINUXTREE.	TCP	6	10.0.0.2:1033	0	Authenticated	05/30/05 03:34:26 AM
3	Supervisor, Remote	None	00008054	.rkvmoeslinux.novell.RKOESVMLINUXTREE.	TCP	6	10.0.0.2:1035	0	Authenticated	05/30/05 03:34:26 AM
4	Supervisor, Remote	None	00008054	.rkvmoeslinux.novell.RKOESVMLINUXTREE.	TCP	6	10.0.0.2:1036	0	Authenticated	05/30/05 03:34:26 AM
5	Supervisor, Remote	None	00008054	.rkvmoeslinux.novell.RKOESVMLINUXTREE.	TCP	6	10.0.0.2:1038	0	Authenticated	05/30/05 03:34:27 AM
6	Supervisor, Remote	None	00008054	.rkvmoeslinux.novell.RKOESVMLINUXTREE.	TCP	6	10.0.0.2:1037	0	Authenticated	05/30/05 03:34:27 AM
7	Remote	None	FF000001		TCP	6	10.0.0.2:1046	0	None	
8	Remote	None	FF000001		TCP	6	10.0.0.2:1041	0	None	
9	Remote	None	FF000001		TCP	6	10.0.0.2:1040	0	None	
10	Supervisor, Remote	None	00008055	.admin.novell.RKOESVMLINUXTREE.	TCP	6	10.0.0.2:1047	0	Authenticated	05/30/05 04:37:58 AM
11	Remote	None	FF000001		TCP	6	10.0.0.2:1080	0	None	
12	Remote	None	FF000001		TCP	6	10.0.0.2:1094	0	None	
13	Supervisor, Console Operator, Local	None	00008055	.admin.novell.RKOESVMLINUXTREE.	TCP	6	10.0.0.1:1139	0	Licensed	05/30/05 04:37:58 AM
14	Supervisor, Remote	None	00008055	.admin.novell.RKOESVMLINUXTREE.	TCP	6	10.0.0.1:1205	0	Licensed	05/30/05 04:41:42 AM
16	Supervisor, Remote	None	00008055	.admin.novell.RKOESVMLINUXTREE.	TCP	6	10.0.0.1:1207	0	Authenticated	05/30/05 04:41:40 AM

Figure 11-2. *Inbound Connection page*

As you can see in Figure 11-2, you can also find the user DN and the network address of the client that is making the connection. Typically, you will trace the network address back to a specific workstation. Regardless of the client, turn the client off or disconnect it from the network. For instance, if the client is a workstation, just unplug the network drop cable from the workstation. Observe processor utilization on the server. If processor utilization immediately drops, you now know who is making the requests. Continue to troubleshoot the client. Your method of troubleshooting from here will depend on what the client is and what type of requests it is making.

Synchronization Issues

If you are adding a replica to a server or have created some other condition that generates a lot of synchronization traffic, it is possible that synchronization is causing the high-utilization issues. The best way to determine if synchronization is causing the high utilization is to disable synchronization. You can disable synchronization traffic through NDS iMonitor. In NDS iMonitor, go to Agent Configuration ➤ Agent Synchronization, as shown in Figure 11-3.

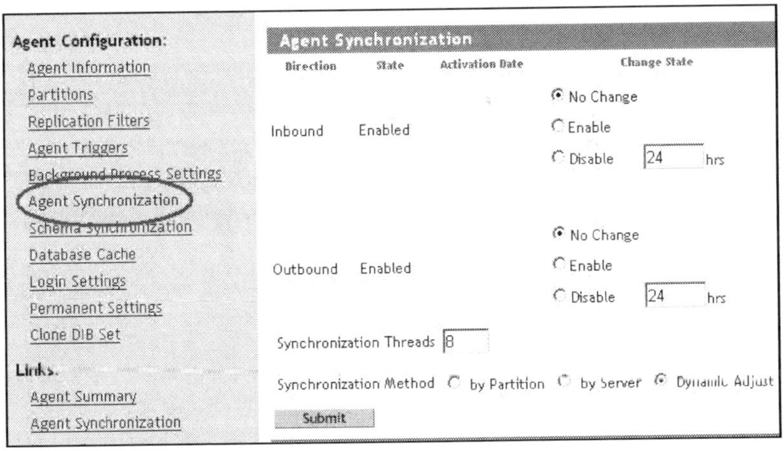

Figure 11-3. *Disabling synchronization*

In the Agent Synchronization frame, disable both the inbound and outbound threads. After disabling the synchronization threads, monitor processor utilization. If utilization immediately drops, synchronization is the cause of the problem. Once you have determined that synchronization is the issue, you can troubleshoot the problem. There are two main causes of high utilization due to synchronization traffic:

- Errors in synchronization
- Synchronization threads

Note Don't forget to re-enable synchronization before troubleshooting synchronization errors.

Errors in Synchronization

Use NDS iMonitor to find errors in synchronization. The first place to go in NDS iMonitor is the Agent Health page, which shows you whether errors exist in the partition/replication operations by displaying a graphical red minus sign in the Results column (see Figure 11-4).

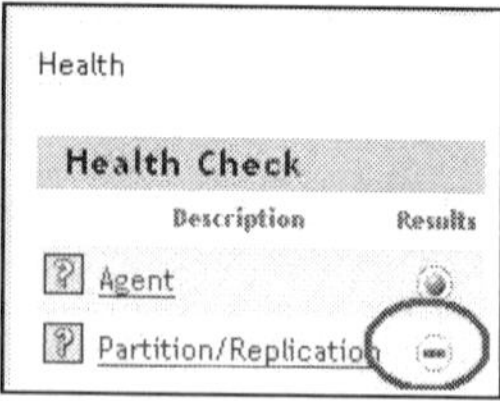

Figure 11-4. *Agent Health screen*

If you see a red minus sign like the one shown in Figure 11-4, you can click the Partition/Replication link to get more detailed information about why the results are in a "warning" state. If you are seeing errors in the replica synchronization screens, you can use DSTRACE to identify the errors in synchronization. In DSTRACE, use the `+s`, `+sklk`, or Outbound Synchronization option (depending on the DSTRACE tool you are using) to identify synchronization errors. It is beyond the scope of this book to discuss how to troubleshoot specific synchronization issues. Refer to the Knowledgebase at `http://support.novell.com` for information about specific synchronization errors and how to remedy them.

Synchronization Threads

eDirectory 8.7.1 and greater allows multiple threads to be used during outbound synchronization. However, eDirectory may get too aggressive with how many threads it allocates to process synchronization traffic, in which case the server may not be able to handle the parallel workload. To alleviate this problem, you can throttle the thread usage.

In NDS iMonitor, go to Agent Configuration ➤ Agent Synchronization. In the Synchronization Threads field, you can manually specify how many threads to use for synchronization (refer to Figure 11-3). Start by changing the value to 1. Monitor processor utilization. If utilization drops, increase the thread count by one. Repeat this process until you determine the maximum number of threads that the server can handle without causing high utilization.

Schema Synchronization Issues

Like object synchronization, schema synchronization errors can also cause high utilization. You can use NDS iMonitor to troubleshoot schema synchronization issues as well. The best place from within NDS iMonitor to view schema synchronization status is in the Agent Process Status page. While viewing the page, look for errors in the Schema Sync Status area (see Figure 11-5).

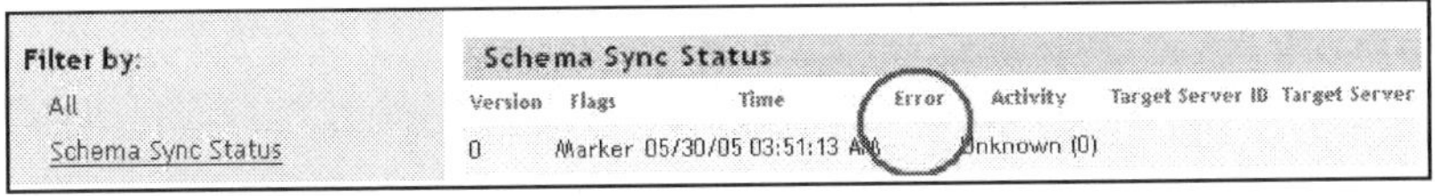

Figure 11-5. *Agent Process Status page*

■ **Note** In Figure 11-5, no errors are present in the Error column, which indicates that the schema synchronization status is healthy.

If errors are reported in the Schema Sync Status Error column, you can use DSTRACE to troubleshoot the errors. Use the `+schema`, `+scma`, or Schema option (depending on the DSTRACE utility that you use) to troubleshoot schema. It is beyond the scope of this book to discuss how to troubleshoot specific schema synchronization issues. Refer to the Knowledgebase at `http://support.novell.com` for information about specific schema synchronization errors and how to remedy them.

Offending Functions

If none of the most common issues described in the preceding sections is causing the high utilization, you need to use NDS iMonitor to try to identify the specific function within eDirectory that is causing the high utilization. The best place to go in NDS iMonitor to determine what eDirectory is doing at any one time is the Agent Activity page, shown in Figure 11-6, which enables you to view the activity of current events and verbs.

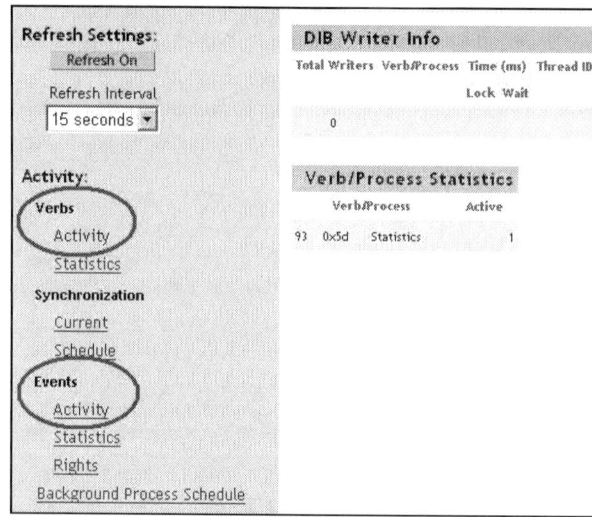

Figure 11-6. *Agent Activity page*

Monitor both the Events ➤ Activity and the Verbs ➤ Activity screens while the server is experiencing high utilization. Look for a verb or event that seems to be in the active queue more than any of the others. The verb name or event name will give you hints regarding what eDirectory is doing at the time that the server is experiencing high utilization. After you have identified the specific verb or event that is causing high utilization, you can refer to the Novell TIDs and documentation regarding offending verbs and events.

■ **Note** Often, the high utilization condition will not allow you to see active refreshes of the Verbs and Events Activity screens. In these cases, you can use the historical data available on the Statistics page from within the Agent Activity page. The Statistics page shows you the high, low, and average values for each event and verb. You can identify the most active verbs and events to give you a hint of where to start troubleshooting the high-utilization issues.

Trends

Your server simply may not have the horse power to handle the operations within eDirectory. If many requests are made against eDirectory, and your server simply cannot process them quickly enough, the processor will continually be working, causing a high-utilization issue. The only way to determine whether this is a problem is to watch the processor utilization statistics over a period of time. If you find that your server seems to spike in the mornings, the login traffic may be too much for the server to handle. If it seems to happen just before quitting time, you can look at what is going on during that time. It may be that a specific eDirectory-aware application is causing the high utilization because it put too much load on the server.

If you find that your server cannot handle the load requested, you need to offload work or increase the horsepower of the server by increasing the amount of processors or the speed of processors, depending on the load that is being put on the server. For more information about operations that affect the processor, see Chapter 12.

High Memory Consumption

Memory conditions are very hard to troubleshoot. To identify memory issues from within eDirectory, you need to perform the following:

1. Identity the application/process that is consuming most of the memory.
2. If eDirectory is consuming the most memory, identify the process that is causing the memory buildup.

Identifying the Process That Is Consuming Most of the Memory

If your server is running out of memory or you are getting memory errors, you can easily determine whether or not the eDirectory process is using the memory. You can do this by using the native tools that are included with each platform. The following sections describe some tools, per platform, to determine whether or not eDirectory is the cause of low-memory conditions.

NetWare

Novell Remote Manager (NRM) is the best tool to determine how much memory is being used by eDirectory. You can access NRM by typing in a browser the IP address or DNS name of the server plus the port (e.g., `http://10.0.0.2:8008`).

■ **Note** NRM runs by default on port 8008 for clear-text connections and 8009 for SSL connections.

From within NRM, choose Health Monitor ➤ Available Memory (see Figure 11-7).

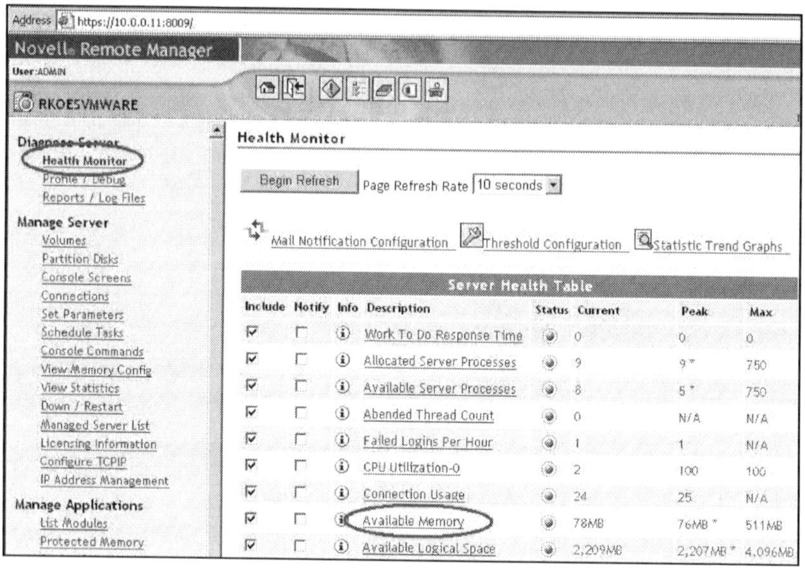

Figure 11-7. *NRM Health Monitor page*

On the Available Memory screen, click NLM Memory. This will list all modules that are loaded on the NetWare server along with how much memory they are consuming. If eDirectory is consuming most of the memory, you can troubleshoot eDirectory to determine why the memory is being taken up, as discussed later in this chapter.

Windows

Task Manager is the best place to determine how much memory each module is taking up in the Windows environment. To access Task Manager, right-click the taskbar and select Task Manager. Click the Mem Usage column under the Processes tab. If dhost.exe is consuming most of the memory, you can troubleshoot eDirectory to determine why the memory is being taken up, as discussed later in this chapter.

Linux

A great utility that ships by default on most Linux distributions is `top`, which allows you to view how much memory each process is taking up. To execute `top`, at a terminal, type **top**. The %Mem column shows you what percentage of memory each process is taking up. If the NDSD process is consuming most of the memory, you can troubleshoot eDirectory to determine why the memory is being taken up, as discussed later in this chapter.

Solaris, HP-UX, AIX

You can use `top` to troubleshoot Solaris, HP-UX, and AIX. However, you need to find the platform-specific tool on the Internet and compile it on your server. For information on native tools to use for Solaris, go to `http://www.sun.com`. For HP-UX, refer to the Hewlett-Packard site at `http://www.hp.com`. For information about AIX tools, refer to the IBM site at `http://www.ibm.com`.

Identifying the Process Within eDirectory That Is Consuming the Memory

Once you have determined that the eDirectory process is causing the memory buildup, you need to determine what within the eDirectory process is causing the issue. With the latest versions of eDirectory, there are no known memory leaks. However, to verify that eDirectory is not leaking memory, you can unload eDirectory. If the available memory goes up, eDirectory is consuming memory but not leaking memory. If the available memory does not go up after unloading eDirectory, you may have a memory leak. In the case of memory leaks, contact Novell Technical Support.

There are a few things that you can look at within the eDirectory process space to figure out what is consuming memory. The following sections discuss some of the biggest memory consumers.

FLAIM Cache

Data loaded in memory can process much faster than data on disk. For this reason, eDirectory tries to load as much of the eDirectory database into memory as it can. This allocated memory is called FLAIM cache. By default, eDirectory allocates as much available memory as it possibly can to FLAIM. In NDS iMonitor, go to Agent Configuration ➤ Database Cache to view how much memory is being taken up by FLAIM. If you find that most of the memory taken up by the eDirectory process is being consumed by FLAIM cache, you can adjust the FLAIM cache settings from within NDS iMonitor. For more information on how to adjust these settings, see Chapter 12.

■ **Note** A common mistake is to think that FLAIM cache is the total amount of memory that is used by the eDirectory process space. The Database Cache statistics shown in NDS iMonitor reflect only the memory consumed by the eDirectory database, not the entire eDirectory process.

Available Threads

eDirectory uses the default Light Weight Process (LWP) threads (or Service Process threads on NetWare) to process all of its requests. Each thread consumes memory. If the server gets behind in processing all of the eDirectory requests, the LWP threads will build up, consuming a lot of memory. To determine how many threads are being consumed by eDirectory, perform Task 11-1, Task 11-2, or Task 11-3, depending on your platform.

Task 11-1. Evaluating Service Process Threads in NetWare

1. At the console, type **monitor**.
2. Look at the Current service processes value.

NetWare protects against thread buildup by setting a Maximum service processes value. If the Current service processes value is equal to the Maximum service processes value, then all subsequent requests from any application will be denied, giving the appearance of a lockup. The danger of increasing the Maximum setting is that if the server gets behind on the requests, the queued requests will consume memory.

Task 11-2. Evaluating dhost Threads in Windows

1. Go to the Administrative Tools.
2. Select Performance Monitor.
3. Click Add a Chart.
4. Select Edit ➤ Add to Chart.
5. Under Object, choose Thread.
6. Under Instance, count the number of dhost threads.

Task 11-3. Evaluating NDSD LWP Threads in *nix

1. At a terminal, type **ndstrace –c threads**.
2. To determine what the maximum value is, at a terminal, type **ndsconfig get | grep n4u.server.max-threads**.

If you find that you are using a large number of threads, which is consuming too much memory, the most likely case is that there is too much traffic on the server. The server cannot keep up with the requests. Consider off-loading some of the requests to another server.

Modules

It is possible that a module or application from within the eDirectory process space is consuming all of the memory. You can unload each application or module one by one and monitor memory consumption. Once you identify which module or application is consuming memory, you can refer to Novell's Knowledgebase at `http://support.novell.com` to try to remedy the issue.

Identifying Memory Fragmentation Issues

Sometimes, you will find that you are getting memory errors on the server console or in the eDirectory logs even though the available memory on the server is sufficient. In this case, you most likely are experiencing memory fragmentation issues. As technology grows, each application vendor is finding it harder to find ways to manage memory. As available physical memory exceeds the operating system's virtual memory space (addressable memory), it is possible to consume memory faster than the operating system's garbage collector can free memory. In these conditions, memory fragmentation is possible.

To minimize memory fragmentation, consider doing the following:

- *Decrease FLAIM cache*: FLAIM does not release memory once it obtains it. If FLAIM has requested memory all throughout the virtual memory space, you may run into a condition in which there are insufficient contiguous blocks of memory to perform the requested operation, the result of which will be an out-of-memory error. You can minimize this from happening by using NDS iMonitor to create a static limit of FLAIM cache. For more information on optimized FLAIM cache settings, see Chapter 12.
- *Minimize NSS cache on NetWare*: There are several different memory algorithms that you can use in NetWare. There are very good TIDs on how to configure NSS as well as how to set different memory management algorithms. See Novell's Knowledgebase at `http://support.novell.com` for more information about the NetWare-specific settings.
- *Upgrade eDirectory*: eDirectory 8.7.3.6 (or greater) has a FLAIM memory manager that enables you to preallocate memory that will be used by FLAIM. The idea is that when the eDirectory process is loaded into memory, a specified amount of memory will be requested from the operating system. Because this is one request, the memory will come in contiguous blocks of memory. FLAIM's built-in memory manager manages the memory that it uses for FLAIM cache. In current implementations, this change in eDirectory has shown to be very useful in solving memory fragmentation issues. For more information about how to configure the preallocated memory, refer to Novell's Knowledgebase at `http://support.novell.com`.

Slow Logins Using Client 32

Slow logins is a hard issue to troubleshoot. Often, eDirectory is not the cause of the slow logins. Many variables are involved in the login and authentication process. Each variable needs to be eliminated to find the root cause. This section discusses how to determine whether or not eDirectory is the root cause of the slow logins. If the cause is not eDirectory, refer to the Knowledgebase at `http://support.novell.com` to troubleshoot the issue.

It is not easy to determine whether or not eDirectory is the root cause of slow logins. The best way to determine this is to monitor the overall health of eDirectory. If eDirectory is experiencing high-utilization or high-memory conditions, requests cannot be processed and thus you will experience slow logins.

The basic steps in troubleshooting slow logins are as follows:

1. Eliminate workstation and network issues.
2. Troubleshoot eDirectory bottlenecks.
3. Troubleshoot tree-walking issues.

Eliminating Workstation and Network Issues

Use the default eDirectory login tools from the server console to log into eDirectory. By using the login tools from the server console, you can eliminate all client- and network-related issues. Tasks 11-4 through 11-6 describe how to use the platform-specific tools.

Task 11-4. Using DSREPAIR on NetWare to Log Into eDirectory

1. At a console, type **dsrepair**.
2. Go to the Advanced options menu.
3. Select Log file and login configuration.
4. Enter a username with full context and password.
5. Press [Enter].

Task 11-5. Using install.dlm on Windows to Log Into eDirectory

1. Launch %SystemDrive%:\Novell\Nds\NDSCons.exe.
2. Select install.dlm and click Start.
3. Click Next.
4. Fill in the Name, Context, and Password fields and click OK.
5. Click Cancel to cancel the schema import operation.

Task 11-6. Using NDSLogin on *nix to Log Into eDirectory

At a terminal, type **ndslogin –s *<username and context>* –p *<password>***.

If you find that the server-based login utility authenticates to eDirectory in a sufficient manner, you can conclude that something is wrong with the workstation or the network. Refer to Novell's Knowledgebase at `http://support.novell.com` to troubleshoot the specific issue. If you find that authenticating to eDirectory using the server-based login utilities is still slow, proceed to the "Troubleshoot eDirectory Bottlenecks" section.

Troubleshooting eDirectory Bottlenecks

Before you can determine the health of eDirectory, you need to identify which eDirectory server is being used for authentication. This is fairly tricky. You can use the connection table information in Client 32 to try to determine this. After a successful login to the directory, right-click the red N in your system tray and select NetWare Connections.

Once you have determined which eDirectory server you are connected to, go into NDS iMonitor on that server. Go to the Agent Health page and click the Agent link. Within this page, you will see a list of statistics that can help you identify eDirectory bottleneck issues. Pay particular attention to the Database Lock fields and the Outstanding Requests field (see Figure 11-8).

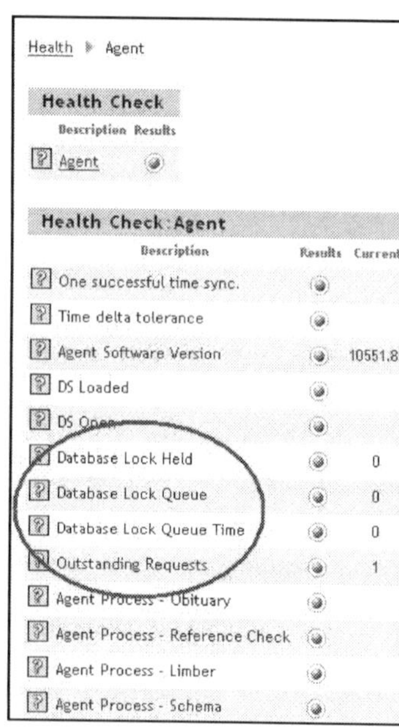

Figure 11-8. *Identifying eDirectory bottleneck issues*

If you find that eDirectory is behind in processing requests, you can troubleshoot the issue. Various problems could cause bottlenecks. The most likely problem is high utilization or low available memory. Refer to the corresponding sections for these specific topics at the beginning of this chapter. If high processor utilization or low available memory is not the cause of the bottleneck, refer to Novell's Knowledgebase at `http://support.novell.com` for more troubleshooting tips that are specific to the condition that you are observing.

Troubleshooting Tree-Walking Issues

If the necessary objects for a successful login do not reside on the server to which you are authenticating, eDirectory will attempt to resolve to another server to obtain the necessary objects. If there are tree-walking issues in your environment because of downed servers, network outages, or nonroutable addresses that are bound to the NIC, you will experience slow logins.

The following is a typical scenario that can cause slow logins:

1. User A authenticates to Server A.
2. Server A does not have User A's object.
3. Server A discovers that Server B does have User A's object.
4. Server A gets a list of address referrals for Server B.

5. Server A attempts to connect to Server B.
6. Server B has two NICs. NIC 1 is reachable by Server A, but NIC 2 is not.
7. Server A attempts to connect to Server B by using the address on NIC 2 (although Server A cannot reach NIC 2, NIC 2 is advertised by Server B so it is written as a valid referral within eDirectory).
8. Server A attempts to connect to Server B on the address of NIC 2 for 58 seconds.
9. After 58 seconds, Server A tries NIC 1 (the order of addresses is determined by how they are written in eDirectory).

During an authentication process, you may need to view ten or more objects. In the case of the preceding scenario, viewing ten objects would create approximately a ten-minute authentication attempt. To prevent such a condition, you need to configure the nonroutable interface to not advertise its address. If other servers are dependent on this advertisement, you should make sure that all required objects are on the server to which you are authenticating, so that it does not need to walk the tree.

Disabling an interface from advertising is platform specific. Tasks 11-7 through 11-9 describe the procedure on a per-platform basis.

Task 11-7. Disabling Interface Advertisement on NetWare

1. From the console, type **monitor.nlm**.
2. Go to Server Parameters.
3. Choose NCP.
4. Enter in the NCP Exclude IP Addresses field the IP addresses of the addresses you want to exclude.
5. Rerun the Limber process (for more information on this process, see Chapter 10).

Task 11-8. Disabling Interface Advertisement on Windows

1. Launch %SystemDrive%:\Novell\Nds\NDSCons.exe.
2. Go to the Transports tab.
3. Expand either NCP, HTTP or HTTPS.
4. Expand Bound Transports.
5. Highlight the address you desire and click Close.
6. Rerun the Limber process (for more information on this process, see Chapter 10).

Task 11-9. Disabling Interface Advertisement on *nix

1. At a terminal, type **ndsconfig get | grep interfaces**.
2. Locate the n4u.server.interfaces line to see the syntax.
3. Include all interfaces you want to advertise by typing the following (note that additional addresses could be added by following the same pattern):

```
ndsconfig set n4u.server.interfaces=<IP address 1>@524, ➥
<IP address 2>@524
```

   The following is an example:

```
ndsconfig set n4u.server.interfaces=10.0.0.1@524,10.0.0.2@524
```

4. Rerun the Limber process (for more information on this process, see Chapter 10).

If the slow login is not caused by nonroutable interfaces, the network connection may be down or something may be wrong with the eDirectory database on the remote servers. Use DSTRACE to find out to which servers the local Directory Agent is trying to connect. Use the `+rn`, `+rslv`, or Resolve Name option (depending on the DSTRACE utility) to see messages that relate to the connection attempts from the local Directory Agent to the remote servers. Based on the errors reported in DSTRACE, you can identify specific TIDs in Novell's Knowledgebase at `http://support.novell.com`.

If all of these options fail, you can always resort to a LAN trace. Many LAN-tracing applications are available. One free, open-source tool that works on all platforms is called Ethereal (`http://www.ethereal.com`). Use the tool of your preference to trace authentication requests from the client to the eDirectory server. It is beyond the scope of this book to go into detail of how to analyze LAN traces. If you need assistance with this, contact Novell Technical Support.

Summary

This chapter discusses different ways that you can troubleshoot eDirectory issues such as high processor utilization, high memory consumption, and slow logins. Each platform utilizes different utilities to locate the source of these problems. Using a combination of these tools and utilities, tracking down the source of the problem can be done quickly and efficiently.

CHAPTER 12

Large-Scale Considerations

The following topics are covered in this chapter:

- Database cache
    - Configuring dynamic cache settings
    - Configuring static cache settings
    - Using NDS iMonitor to fine-tune database settings
- Memory management
- LDAP considerations
    - Indexes
    - Tree design
- Processor considerations
    - Speed of the processor
    - Number of processors
- Disk I/O
    - Disk cache
    - Direct Attached Storage
    - Checkpoint thread
- DIBClone
- DSREPAIR
    - Repairing a single object
    - Disabling reference checks
    - Repairing a replica
- Management utilities
    - NDS iMonitor
    - iManager

As the identity management marketplace grows, the demand for a scalable directory also grows. eDirectory is more scalable both vertically and horizontally than any of the other available directories. However, as you add more and more objects to eDirectory and make more and more requests to the eDirectory agent, you need to make sure that you have sufficient hardware to handle the load. You also need to consider some configuration issues.

Every eDirectory implementation is different. eDirectory is diverse in its implementation options. Because of this, it is impossible to cover every configuration option and hardware consideration in this text. The purpose of this chapter is to discuss in depth some of the most important things that you should consider when scaling your eDirectory implementation, beginning with the database cache.

Database Cache

The database cache, or FLAIM cache, is the cache that is allocated by the eDirectory agent, which can be utilized by the eDirectory database (FLAIM) to enhance performance. Accessing and updating information in memory is much faster than having to go to the disk system to process the data. Performance may increase if you load as much of the database into memory as possible without starving other processes of memory.

The following database configuration considerations are discussed in this section:

- Configuring dynamic cache settings
- Configuring static cache settings
- Using NDS iMonitor to fine-tune cache settings

Configuring Dynamic Cache Settings

The task at hand is to determine the maximum amount of memory to allocate toward eDirectory database cache. For general use, eDirectory has a built-in algorithm that attempts to do this. The dynamic mode cache algorithm attempts to allocate as much memory as it possibly can, leaving a sufficient amount of memory for other processes. Unfortunately, it is very hard to predict how much memory other processes require (the other processes also include the eDirectory application itself, as well as all other modules that run in the eDirectory process space). By default, dynamic mode consumes up to 80 percent of available cache. Often, however, 20 percent is not sufficient memory for all other applications and processes.

You can configure the dynamic mode options in NDS iMonitor. You can change how much memory the eDirectory agent should leave for other processes on the machine. To configure these settings in NDS iMonitor, go to Agent Configuration ➤ Database Cache (see Figure 12-1).

Database Cache Configuration	
Dynamic Adjust	(•)
Cache Adjust Percentage	60 % of Available Memory
Cache Size Constraints	> 0 KB < Total Available Memory - 0 KB

Figure 12-1. *Configuring dynamic cache*

As a general recommendation, if you use dynamic cache, do not set the Cache Adjust Percentage above 60 percent. This will vary, of course, depending on how much memory is on the server as well as what type of eDirectory operations are happening on the server.

Note You should make configuration changes to database cache only if the performance of eDirectory and other applications on the same server is not acceptable and the performance degradation is a result of the lack of memory resources.

Configuring Static Cache Settings

For most large-scale implementations, it is recommended that you use a static cache setting rather than a dynamic cache setting because static cache gives you better control over how much memory is being allocated to FLAIM. Furthermore, even though eDirectory has very efficient methods of doing cache lookups, there are many database background processes used to maintain cache that can impact the overall performance of eDirectory if too much cache is allocated toward FLAIM.

It is a common misconception that more memory is better. Typically, the biggest bottleneck is the file system, so you would logically think that you should load as much of the directory data as you can into memory. However, too much memory allocated toward Novell eDirectory can cause unwanted effects. By default, eDirectory database cache will consume up to 80 percent of available RAM. Often, in large environments, this is too much. Database cache background processes consume resources that can indirectly affect performance. As database cache grows in size, the potential of performance degradation increases.

Each entry in eDirectory could potentially be loaded into cache three or four times. If, for instance, the DIB size is 4GB and the hardware limits memory to 2GB for database cache, it would be unwise to allocate all of the 2GB for database cache. This means that eDirectory would need up to 16GB to cache the entire database. Basic mathematics suggests that eDirectory will be going to disk more than cache to get entries.

Live testing has found that setting the cache between 250MB and 1GB achieves optimal performance in large eDirectory implementations (especially with a lot of LDAP traffic). If a lot of writes (such as bulk-loads) are occurring, testing has found that optimal performance can be achieved by setting the cache limit between 250MB and 500MB, with block cache at 75 percent. Testing has found that setting cache limits below 250MB causes adverse performance. Also, increasing database cache above 1GB shows minimal, if any, performance increase and can result in a significant decrease in performance.

When setting static limits, undesired performance degradation will occur if you allocate too little or too much memory. If you allocate too little memory, eDirectory will not be able to perform even basic functions without going to disk, significantly impacting performance. In larger systems, do not set the static limit lower than 250MB. Similar performance issues can occur indirectly by setting the static limit too high. A good rule of thumb is to not set the static limit over 50 to 75 percent of total physical memory and to never exceed over 1GB of memory allocated to eDirectory database cache.

If you attempt to set the database cache settings higher than the operating system will allow or lower than 16MB, NDS iMonitor will automatically adjust the cache to the maximum and/or minimum allowed. However, if you set the cache setting manually in the ndsdb.ini file, it is possible to specify an amount beyond the limits for the application. In these cases, eDirectory converts the amount to a 32-bit value and uses that value. Depending on the operating system, this could cause adverse effects. For example, if 4.5GB is specified as database cache, after converting the value to a 32-bit value, the database setting actually may be as low as 20MB. With this in mind, it is advisable to use NDS iMonitor to make the settings, to help protect against undesired results.

Using NDS iMonitor to Fine-Tune Database Settings

Four types of cache measurements are shown in NDS iMonitor:

- *Cache hits*: Measures how many times an item in cache is found and used
- *Cache looks*: Measures how many links (more specifically, how many links on the collision chain) are followed through cache until the entry is found

- *Faults*: Indicates how many times an attempt was made to find an entry in cache and the entry was not found in cache
- *Fault looks*: Indicates how many links are followed through cache only to find out that the entry is not in cache, thus generating a fault

The formula *cache looks / cache hits* * 2 gives an average of how long the collision chain is (the collision chain is the number of links that must be gone through to find an object). The factor of 2 is derived from the fact that, on average, a hit would be found halfway down the collision chain.

The formula *fault looks / faults* determines how large the collision chain potential is, because every fault results in as many fault looks as there are collision links.

The primary metric by which you can measure cache performance is by determining the number of faults per request. Each fault results in expensive increases in overhead. Each fault, depending on the operating system, could result in hundreds of CPU instructions.

■ **Note** Although these statistics identify cache performance, they do not identify overall performance. Generally speaking, increasing cache performance increases overall performance. However, increasing cache performance at the cost of starving resources from other processes could create degradation in performance.

Increasing cache hits by adding more memory, thus loading more entries to cache, may realize little, if no, gain if the fault and fault looks are not decreased. The balance comes in trying to limit the collision chain links by decreasing the amount of memory being used without starving available memory so much that cache hits drop too low.

When you have determined that performance is unacceptable, set the static cache settings between 500MB and 600MB. Rerun the performance tests, incrementing cache 50–100MB at a time until performance is optimal.

Memory Management

You need to understand eDirectory application memory when you are configuring eDirectory. Each platform handles the virtual memory space a little bit differently. This section describes how the different platforms handle virtual memory space.

NetWare

NetWare has only one virtual memory space in which all processes run. All associated modules, including DS.NLM, NLDAP.NLM, EMBOX.NLM, etc., share the virtual memory space with all other applications, such as NSS, TCP/IP, GroupWise, IDMgr, etc.

Windows

Microsoft Windows assigns a virtual memory space for each process that runs. If a resource is required to load into memory for a process, the resource must be loaded within the virtual memory space assigned to that process. The maximum amount of virtual memory that can be assigned to each process is 2GB.

■ **Note** By modifying some of the Microsoft Windows files, you can increase this maximum to 3GB.

The 2GB limit also applies to dhost (the main eDirectory process). Any library, thread, module, or cache (such as eDirectory's database cache) that dhost needs to load into memory must reside within the assigned 2GB virtual memory space.

Linux, Solaris, AIX, and HP-UX

Like Windows, Linux and UNIX operating systems also assign virtual memory space to the eDirectory process (NDSD). The Linux and UNIX operating systems assign a 3GB limit for all NDSD processes and necessary resources, including eDirectory's FLAIM cache.

■ **Important** Based on the maximum amount of memory assigned to the eDirectory processes, dhost on Windows and NDSD on the Linux and UNIX platforms cannot exceed maximums imposed by the operating system. Depending on the operations that are being performed when the maximums are met, adverse effects such as nonresponsiveness, sluggishness, application timeouts, and possible shutdown of the eDirectory processes can occur. Novell has attempted to minimize the impact that this has on end users. However, if eDirectory is consistently consuming memory close to the maximum allowed, you should explore configuration options that will decrease the amount of memory being consumed.

LDAP Considerations

eDirectory is frequently used as an LDAP directory for web applications and other LDAP-enabled applications. As with any other protocol, LDAP has a number of uses. This section presents a few key configuration options that you should consider when using LDAP to interface to eDirectory. The following issues are discussed:

- Indexes
- Tree design

Indexes

Indexing is the most important factor in optimizing LDAP searches. An *index* is an ordered list of keys. Novell eDirectory allows you to create an index on any user-defined attribute. The index will contain the EntryID for an object and list the attribute or key that has been defined for that index. When a specific value of an attribute is requested, eDirectory does not need to scan through all values until the correct one is found. Because the index is ordered, eDirectory can do a quick lookup to find the specified value.

Indexing is a valuable tool when dealing with performance. However, you should remember that maintaining indexes in eDirectory requires additional memory, disk, and processor resources. Any time the indexed attribute is modified (from adds, deletes, moves, and so on), performance is affected. The degree to which performance is affected will vary depending on the size of the index and the type of index. The greatest performance hit for indexes will come from partition moves, bulk-load imports, and operations that affect many objects that contain attributes that have been indexed.

eDirectory does not automatically index every user-defined attribute, so you will often need to choose which attributes you want to index. Before creating indexes, you must know how the directory is going to be used. If the directory is fairly static and used mainly for reads, indexing will increase performance with little effect on update performance. In general, you should create an index for the attributes that are used most often.

When deciding whether you want to index, there are three main ways in which you can detect what attributes are used the most:

- Use DSTRACE
- Use Predicate Stats
- Analyze the applications

Using DSTRACE

You can set the +recman, +recm, or Storage Manager option (depending on the DSTRACE tool you are using) to monitor all requests and replies that go through the SMI layer to the FLAIM database. In the trapped messages, you will be able to identify the attribute that is being used and any indexes that are being used when searching for the specified attribute.

A typical search request will look like the following in a DSTRACE screen with the Storage Manager option turned on:

```
Iter #4b01f83c setIndex( 262)
Iter #4b01f83c query partID==4 && Obituary$258A$
Iter #4b01f83c index = Obituary$IX$262
Iter #4b01f83c first( ID_INVALID)
```

In this example, a request to read the Obituary attribute was called and the Obituary index 262 was used.

The idea is that you will be able to identify attributes that are searched for multiple times and where FLAIM does not use an index to search for the attribute. These attributes would be good candidates for you to manually create an index.

Using Predicate Stats

Predicate Stats is an automated procedure that collects information about each attribute that is searched for as well as the index that is being used for the specified attribute. You should keep in mind that Predicate Stats is very processor and memory intensive. You should not collect statistics for a long period of time.

To configure Predicate Stats, perform Task 12-1.

Task 12-1. Configuring Predicate Stats

1. Go to ConsoleOne.
2. Locate the NCP server object that corresponds to the server that you will add an index to.
3. Go to the Properties dialog box of the NCP server object.
4. Click the Predicate Data tab.
5. Select the Predicate Data object through the browser. (If one does not exist, you need to create one manually before continuing.)
6. Click Properties next to the Predicate Data Object DN and then click Advanced.
7. Select Enable and Display Value Text. Deselect Write to Disk.
8. Click OK three times to exit.

The Predicate Stats information is hard to read, because all FLAIM queries are represented in these statistics. You need to be able to identify the queries that are looking specifically for an attribute. As an example, Figure 12-2 shows that the Obituary attribute was searched for nine times.

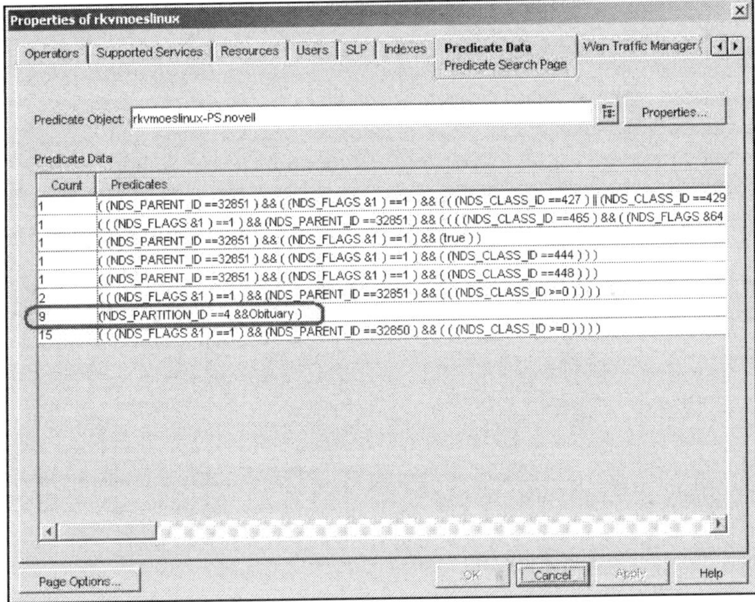

Figure 12-2. *Viewing Predicate Stats information*

Analyzing the Applications

The last method to determine what indexes to select is to understand the application you are running. If you are using an LDAP client, knowing what basic queries are performed will give you the information that you need to decide which indexes to use. If the LDAP client makes the same query over and over, it would be advisable to index the attributes that are contained in the LDAP query.

Creating the Index

Determining which type of index to use is just as important as choosing what to index. Three indexing types are available in eDirectory:

- Value indexes
- Presence indexes
- Substring indexes

Presence indexes and substring indexes should be used sparingly. A *presence index* simply tells Novell eDirectory whether or not an attribute exists on an object; it does not provide any other information. The attribute is stored in the index, but its actual value is not. One major problem with presence indexes is that they do not distinguish between a nonpresent value (a deleted value that has not been purged) and a present value. Because LDAP reads only present values, presence indexes are not typically used by LDAP queries. Presence indexes are only valuable to some internal eDirectory processes, such as the Obituary process, which needs to read both present and nonpresent values. For this reason, eDirectory will use a *value index* rather than a presence index to determine if an attribute exists on an object.

A *substring index* is very costly. It can be up to 100 times larger than a value index. You should be certain you need an index before using a substring index. If an LDAP search asks for a substring, but the first characters on the left are given (for example, cn=bob*), eDirectory will use a value index rather than a substring index. A substring index is used only if the query has wildcards on both sides of the name (for example, cn=*bob or cn=*bob*).

Tree Design

Designing where your objects reside can greatly impact performance, especially when using LDAP. There are two tree design considerations:

- Designing your tree for optimized searches
- Designing your tree for optimized overall performance

Designing Your Tree for Optimized Searches

To effectively design a tree, you need to understand how Novell eDirectory performs LDAP searches. You should be familiar with three key parts of an LDAP search request in relation to the actual database search:

- *Base*: Tells eDirectory where to start the search
- *Scope*: Tells eDirectory how much of the tree to search (base only or the entire subtree, starting at the base)
- *Search filter*: Tells eDirectory what objects to find, based on the values of the attributes on those objects

The key to tree design is understanding the order in which eDirectory evaluates the preceding components in the LDAP search. eDirectory first evaluates the search filter. It looks at each attribute in the search filter and determines if an index or indexes exist on those attributes. If more than one index is available for the attributes listed in the search filter, eDirectory determines the optimal index to use by evaluating the size of the selected indexes.

After eDirectory chooses the index (if there was an index to choose), it evaluates the scope. A default eDirectory index indexes the objects directly underneath each container. If the search is base only, the parent container index is added to the already selected index, making the search much faster because all objects outside of the base can be eliminated immediately. The search is then performed. When an object is found, the Distinguished Name (DN) is evaluated to determine whether or not the object falls within the base parameter that was passed into the query. If it does, the object is added to the results table.

So, for instance, if you wanted to locate 50 objects underneath a specific container in a 20-million-user tree, the LDAP search could take a significant length of time if the scope is set to subtree, because eDirectory will apply the filter first and then evaluate each object to see if the DN falls within the base. In the preceding scenario, it's conceivable that all 20 million objects could be evaluated to find the 50 objects. With eDirectory, this type of search could appear to be slow because, after the query is sent, nothing is displayed on the screen for several minutes. In reality, eDirectory is very fast, searching through millions of objects behind the scenes, even though it seems to be doing nothing. In a case like this, it would be faster to send several base-only LDAP searches to just the containers in question, because the parent index would be applied, eliminating the other 20 million objects.

■ **Note** eDirectory 8.8 changes the LDAP search algorithm. In eDirectory 8.8, each object in the tree contains an attribute called the Ancestor ID. This attribute is indexed. When a search request is made, the eDirectory agent changes the number of ancestors for the specified object versus the number of objects in the filter. If the number of ancestors is smaller, eDirectory will apply the base and scope before applying the filter. In this case, if you had 20 million objects in a tree and you want 10 objects in a specific container (with subcontainers), prior to eDirectory 8.8, the eDirectory agent would have to evaluate all 20 million objects. With eDirectory 8.8, if the base is set to the container with the 10 objects, only the 10 objects will be evaluated.

Designing Your Tree for Optimized Overall Performance

Most LDAP functions assume that a real copy of the object being searched is actually on the LDAP server. Therefore, replica placement should also be considered. For better performance, try to keep on the LDAP server a real copy of all objects required to perform an LDAP search. With the scalability features of Novell eDirectory, millions of objects can exist on the same directory server.

Processor Considerations

If you are trying to decide what type of hardware you need to have to obtain optimal LDAP performance, you should consider both the number of processors and the speed of the processor. eDirectory is very processor intensive, especially with LDAP reads and writes. However, more is not always better.

Speed of the Processor

The good rule of thumb with speed is that the faster the processor, the more transactions per second that can be performed. The rule of thumb is true for any kind of LDAP or non-LDAP operation.

■ **Note** This rule applies only if the processor is the bottleneck. If disk I/O, memory, or something else is pushed to its limits and the processor utilization percentage is still below 90 to 95 percent, increasing the processor speed will not increase the number of transactions per second.

Number of Processors

The number of processors affects how many concurrent connections can reside on a specified server. If you have only one connection making thousands of requests to the eDirectory agent, increasing the number of processors will not help performance. However, if you have thousands of users connected to eDirectory, all making requests, increasing the number of processors will help load-balance the connections, giving you better performance.

As with all other hardware considerations, more is not always better. There is a law of diminishing returns where at some point, the overhead required to swap requests from processor to processor outweighs the advantage of running on multiple processors. At some point, adding more processors will have zero effect.

The number of processors you should implement varies based on the type of requests, the number of concurrent connections, and the activity of the connections. With an average setup, some tests show that going from 1 to 2 processors doubled the efficiency, whereas going from 15 to 16 processors increased efficiency only by 1 percent.

Note Remember that the efficiency ratios are based on the concept that the bottleneck is the number of concurrent connections, not some other factor.

Disk I/O

The disk system is by far the biggest potential for bottlenecks in large eDirectory environments. The reason for this is that it is impossible to load even a portion of the database into database cache. Most of the objects that are read and written will come from the disk. The obvious rule of thumb is that the faster the disk system the better the performance. There are several different parts of the disk system that need to be considered:

- Disk cache
- Direct Attached Storage (DAS)
- Checkpoint thread

Disk Cache

Cache on the disk helps to improve search performance. The more disk cache the better. Although disk cache improves search performance, it does not really help write performance, especially if large numbers of continuous writes are being made to the eDirectory database.

Direct Attached Storage

The faster your Direct Attached Storage (DAS) system, the better performance you will achieve. In most situations, having numerous drives that are small and fast is better than having fewer drives that are bigger and faster. However, time slicing on a SCSI bus introduces a significant amount of overhead as more disks are added to the SCSI bus. There are storage systems other than SCSI that write to multiple drives in parallel, which avoids the time-slicing issues. However, a lot of these solutions are not as reliable as SCSI, which will require you to use a RAID 5 or RAID 1+0 setup to minimize data loss.

Checkpoint Thread

The checkpoint thread is a process that runs in the background that writes dirty blocks from the eDirectory database cache to disk. For performance reasons, if the processor is busy, eDirectory does not write data that has changed in memory (FLAIM block cache) to disk immediately. It leaves the "dirty" blocks in cache until the processor is idle, at which time the checkpoint thread attempts to write the information to disk.

If the amount of time before all current dirty blocks are written to disk exceeds the checkpoint interval (because the processor is too busy to process the dirty blocks), then the eDirectory agent locks the database and writes the changes to disk. During this checkpoint process, it appears that the server has locked. After the data is written to disk, the agent is unlocked and all of the queued requests are processed.

Many LDAP-based applications have a default setting of ten seconds for the LDAP request time out. When eDirectory writes changes from database cache to the file system in large eDirectory environments, the excessive disk I/O can cause eDirectory to take longer than ten seconds to respond to LDAP requests. Because the disk can be very busy writing changes, often times eDirectory can become unresponsive to all requests that require disk access. The end result is that the LDAP-based application times out and aborts the connections.

eDirectory provides several configuration options to avoid this type of a scenario. Before discussing the different configuration options, a few terms need to be clarified:

- *Dirty cache*: Entries in block cache that have been modified and need to be committed to the database
- *Checkpoint interval*: A specified interval that controls when a forced checkpoint is run
- *Forced checkpoint*: Occurs when the checkpoint interval is exceeded
- *Checkpoint thread*: Locks the database until a checkpoint is established
- *Checkpoint*: Achieved when *all* dirty cache blocks are written to disk and the database is in a consistent state on disk

The Checkpoint Process

As previously described, the checkpoint thread is a background thread spawned by eDirectory that continually monitors eDirectory's block cache for dirty cache blocks that need to be written to disk. The checkpoint thread is a very low-priority thread that performs the following process after it determines that information needs to be written to disk:

1. The checkpoint thread makes sure that no eDirectory update transactions are in progress or waiting to start. If update transactions are pending, the checkpoint thread yields until the pending update transactions are completed.
2. When there are no in-progress or pending update transactions, the checkpoint thread starts to write blocks to disk.
3. The checkpoint thread puts a lock on the eDirectory database so that other threads cannot update transactions while the checkpoint thread is flushing blocks to disk.
4. If a new update transaction from a different thread makes a request for the database, the checkpoint thread yields to the new thread.
5. After all blocks are written to disk, the checkpoint process is completed.

Because the checkpoint thread yields to all other threads, it might never get an opportunity to complete a checkpoint on a busy eDirectory server. To prevent the on-disk database from becoming too out of date with the database in cache, predefined conditions have been established in eDirectory that will bump the priority of the checkpoint thread to the highest priority. As a result, the checkpoint thread obtains a lock on the database and does not release it (even to waiting update transactions) until the dirty cache blocks are written to disk.

When the checkpoint thread locks the database, other update transactions are blocked until the checkpoint is completed. The following is a list of problems that could occur when the checkpoint thread is blocking update transactions:

- *Failed logins*: If the Update Login Properties setting is enabled, logins could be delayed or rejected (based on the timeout values).
- *Delayed partition operations*: Updating replicas during replica synchronization and other partition operations are delayed.
- *Other delayed operations*: Any operation that requires updates to the database is delayed.

Identifying Conditions That Force a Checkpoint

There are three scenarios that will cause the checkpoint thread to force a checkpoint:

- *Checkpoint interval is exceeded*: If the checkpoint interval exceeds the last time that a successful checkpoint was completed, a forced checkpoint is initiated. The default checkpoint interval is three minutes.
- *eDirectory agent is shut down*: Any time that the eDirectory agent is shut down, a checkpoint is forced before the agent will close.
- *I/O errors or out-of-disk messages occur on the roll-forward log volume*: The roll-forward log (RFL) volume is the volume that contains the RFL files. By default, the RFL volume is the same volume that contains the other eDirectory database files.

Making Checkpoint Configuration Changes

At certain times, it may be necessary to change the default checkpoint options to ensure the least amount of down time. All checkpoint settings can be changed by modifying the _ndsdb.ini file, which is located in the same directory as the eDirectory database. The following are some of the parameters that you can modify and a description of when the settings should be applied:

- `maxdirtycache=`<*maximum number of bytes of dirty cache*>: When the number of dirty cache blocks is greater than or equal to `maxdirtycache`, regardless of the checkpoint interval, the database is locked and the dirty cache blocks are flushed to disk until the number of dirty cache blocks is less than or equal to the `lowdirtycache` setting.
- `lowdirtycache=`<*minimum number of bytes of dirty cache*>: All dirty cache blocks up to the `lowdirtycache` setting are written to disk. By setting `lowdirtycache=0`, a checkpoint will be achieved whenever `maxdirtycache` is exceeded, because all dirty cache blocks are written to disk.
- `cpinterval=`<*number of seconds*>: This setting allows you to adjust the checkpoint interval time. As explained previously, when the last checkpoint exceeds the `cpinterval`, a forced checkpoint is initiated. This setting should rarely be changed from the default because it is very hard to predict how many update transactions will need to be written to disk in the specified time.

Determining What Checkpoint Settings to Use

Most of the time, you should not change the checkpoint settings. If, however, an application is timing out because of excessive locks on the database, you may need to alter the checkpoint settings.

It is advisable not to alter the `cpinterval`. You have less control over this option; in most cases, it should be left at three minutes.

You need to calculate how many random disk writes per second you can achieve. You can do this by timing a large number of disk writes or through third-party tools. The idea is that you determine what the application time-out value is and make sure that you set the `maxdirtycache` settings low enough that the entire amount of dirty cache can be written to disk before the application time out occurs. For instance, if an LDAP application times out after ten seconds of no response and if your disk system will allow 10 MB/s of random disk writes, you should set your `maxdirtycache` setting no higher than 100MB.

DIBClone

DIBClone is a feature that was first added to eDirectory 8.6.2. It was officially supported by Novell with eDirectory 8.7.1. A problem arose in the eDirectory 8.6.2 time frame in situations where eDirectory administrators were trying to build trees with millions of users. It took several hours and sometimes days to replicate 30 or 40 million objects to several servers to create a fault-tolerant system. Novell developed a feature called DIBClone (aka DSClone) to solve these issues.

DIBClone performs the following:

1. Creates a new NCP server object in the existing eDirectory tree.
2. Modifies the replica rings of all partitions contained in the main server that is being cloned by adding the new NCP server object to the replica rings.
3. Sets the DIB to a special state, preparing it to be cloned.

Once the DIBClone operation is performed, you can simply copy the DIB from the cloned server (source) to the new server (target). You can then open both agents. The target server recognizes that the DIB is in a cloned state. The target server's directory agent opens the DIB, changes the pseudo server ID to itself, and opens the database. The end result is that you have an exact replica of the source server, with all objects, without having to perform a synchronization of the objects across the wire.

To initiate the clone process, use NDS iMonitor. Choose Agent Configuration ➤ Clone DIB Set and configure the settings shown in Figure 12-3.

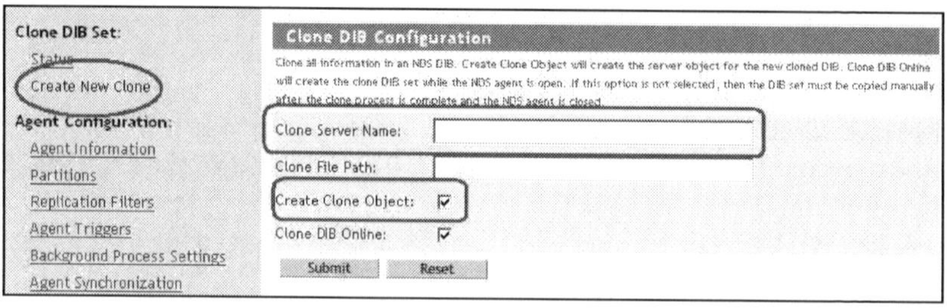

Figure 12-3. *Configuring a clone*

For more information about DIBClone, refer to the *eDirectory Administration Guide* at `http://www.novell.com/documentation`.

DSREPAIR

DSREPAIR has some built-in features specifically built for larger trees. With larger trees, you should use NDS iMonitor health checks for your proactive monitoring of the database. DSREPAIR should only be used to reactively fix an identified issue. If you attempt to run a local repair on a multimillion-user tree that extensively uses references (large groups, etc.), it may be hours or days before the repair finishes. This is not something that you would want to do on a regular basis. There are three things that you should be familiar with when using DSREPAIR in large environments:

- Repairing a single object
- Disabling reference checks
- Repairing a replica

Chapter 10 discusses at length the different command-line options to perform these types of operations. If you wish to use the command line, please refer to Chapter 10. This chapter describes how to perform these operations through iManager. To access the DSREPAIR tool through NDS iManager, go to the eDirectory Maintenance role.

Repairing a Single Object

Single object repair allows you to repair just one object in the tree. If you use NDS iMonitor correctly to diagnose the problem, you should be able to narrow the problem down to one object. Perform Task 12-2 to repair a single object in iManager.

Note Many of the Advanced Options in NDS iMonitor allow you to verify and repair a selected object when viewing the object from the Entry Information screen.

Task 12-2. Repairing a Single Object Through iManager

1. In the eDirectory Maintenance role, select the Repair eDirectory task.
2. Select the local server object and click Next.
3. Fill in the Username, Context, and Password and click Next.
4. Choose Single Object Repair and click Next.
5. Browse for the object in the tree and then click Start.

Disabling Reference Checks

When running a local repair, it is wise to turn off reference checking in large environments unless keeping it on is absolutely necessary. The reason for this is that a reference check must scan the entire database, looking for objects that reference the object being repaired. Sometimes, this is necessary. However, if it is not, you should turn this option off. By default, reference checking is enabled. To turn it off, perform Task 12-3.

Task 12-3. Disabling Reference Checks Through iManager

1. In the eDirectory Maintenance Role, select the Repair eDirectory task.
2. Select the local server object and click Next.
3. Fill in the Username, Context, and Password and click Next.
4. Select Local Database Repair and click Next.
5. Uncheck the Check Local Reference box.
6. Click Start.

Repairing a Replica

eDirectory DSREPAIR allows you to repair just one replica instead of all the replicas that are contained on a server. This significantly cuts down on the amount of time it takes to perform a local repair if there are a lot of replicas on the specified server. To repair a selected replica, perform Task 12-4.

Task 12-4. Repairing a Replica Through iManager

1. In the eDirectory Maintenance Role, select the Replica Repair task.
2. Select the local server object and click Next.
3. Fill in the Username, Context, and Password and click Next.
4. Select Repair Selected Replica and click Next.
5. Browse to the container that is the partition root entry for the desired partition.
6. Click Start.

Management Utilities

Using iManager and NDS iMonitor in a large-scale environment can be more difficult than in smaller environments. Both web-based utilities must load into memory the objects that you are going to view before they can display them. As long as you are aware of this issue, both tools are very effective in large-scale environments. This section discusses both tools and some of the caveats that you may experience.

NDS iMonitor

When you are browsing a container that contains millions of objects in NDS iMonitor, it could take a while to build the entire list. There are three things to be aware of that will help you in these situations:

- *Use the Esc key*: When you click a container to browse its child objects, you can press the Esc key at any time and NDS iMonitor will stop building the list of objects. NDS iMonitor will show you all the objects that it has gathered into memory thus far.
- *Use the URL*: NDS iMonitor is just a bunch of hyperlinked HTML pages. You can modify the URL to find the exact object you need. For instance, if you are currently viewing the Entry Information on a user called admin, your URL may look something like this: `https://10.0.0.11:8009/nds/object?dn=/CN'=admin,O'=Novell,OES-TREE`. To quickly change your view so that you are in the container ou=Users and viewing information about a user called user1, you can change the URL to look like this: `https://10.0.0.11:8009/nds/object?dn=/CN'=user1,OU'=Users,O'=Novell,OES-TREE`. If OU=Users has ten million users in it, modifying the URL would be much faster than building the entire list of users and clicking user1.

- *View Subordinate Count in top-right corner of screen*: If you are not sure how many objects are in a container, you can use the Subordinate Count on the screen when viewing the container (see Figure 12-4). This value can be used to quickly check all replicas to make sure all data has been synchronized.

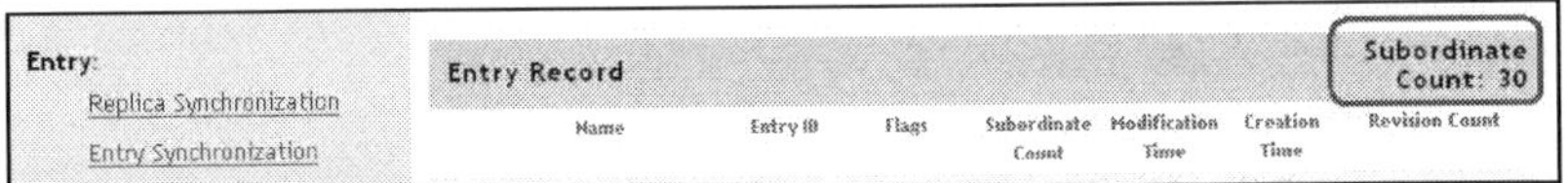

Figure 12-4. *Viewing the Subordinate Count value*

iManager

The biggest issue that you will run into when using iManager in a large environment is that the browse capabilities are more cumbersome, because the more objects that are in the database, the longer it takes for pages to come up, meaning that it takes longer for you to find the object that you are looking for. It could take a very long time to load the objects in a large container while browsing, so iManager helps to prevent this by limiting to 2000 the number of objects that will display. To get around this issue, use the Simple Selection or the Advanced Selection options whenever possible (see Figure 12-5).

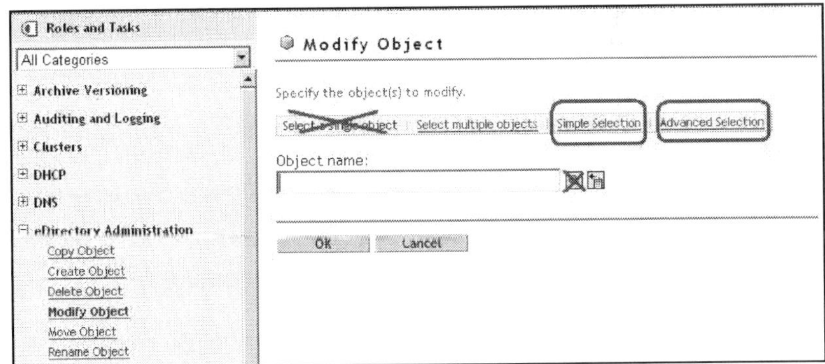

Figure 12-5. *Choosing the Simple Selection or Advanced Selection options*

Summary

eDirectory is a very scalable identity management system. It has a lot of built-in features to handle most scaling needs. However, in very large environments, it is important that you understand the different ways to configure and administer eDirectory for optimal performance.

CHAPTER 13

Troubleshooting Security

The following topics are covered in this chapter:

- Troubleshooting NICI
    - Deleting corrupt NICI files
    - Creating new NICI keys
- Troubleshooting server certificates
- Troubleshooting user certificates
- Troubleshooting the CA
- Troubleshooting the tree key

Chapter 2 went into great detail about the eDirectory security infrastructure and all of its associated objects. This chapter will not repeat that information. Instead, this chapter focuses on different troubleshooting techniques for the key security components. These security components are part of eDirectory's own built-in security infrastructure and enable you to do the following in eDirectory:

- Create server-specific keys
- Generate tree keys
- Encrypt and decrypt data with the generated keys
- Create and sign certificates for servers and users
- Configure applications to use SSL communication

This chapter is designed to help you troubleshoot problems that you may encounter while performing these activities.

Troubleshooting NICI

NICI is the core of eDirectory security. All keys and certificates are based on the server NICI keys. Each server has a unique set of keys. The NICI keys are created for the server when NICI is installed for the first time. The NICI keys are not stored within eDirectory. They are stored on the file system of the local server.

It is critical to ensure that all NICI keys are protected and backed up on a regular basis. The most critical server is the server that is the certificate authority (CA). If this server loses its NICI keys, the entire security infrastructure will have to be re-created.

■ **Note** NICI keys are not re-created when NICI is upgraded or reinstalled. When eDirectory is removed from a server, the NICI keys still remain. The only way to remove the NICI keys is to manually delete them from the file system.

When NICI first loads, it looks for the NICI server keys. If the keys are present, it uses the keys to initialize the main NICI engine. If the keys are valid, NICI will successfully initialize. If there is something wrong with the keys, NICI may load but it will not initialize. Both NDS and PKI require NICI to be initialized before they can initialize. A fast way to determine whether NICI initialized correctly is to look for NICI (14xx) errors when the PKI and NDS modules load. You will find the errors by taking the following action, per platform:

- *NetWare*: Load and unload PKI.NLM and DS.NLM and look for errors on the Logger screen.
- *Windows*: Launch the %SystemDrive%:\Novell\Nds\NDSCons.exe file. Stop and start ds.dlm. You will see NICI errors on the console screen.
- *Linux, Solaris, HP-UX, and AIX (*nix)*: Look in the /var/nds/ndsd.log file and look for NICI errors on the NDSD *and* PKI processes.

If NICI errors occur when the DS and PKI modules load, there are three possible issues:

- The NICI files are missing
- The NICI files are corrupt

■ **Note** On the *nix platforms, it is possible for eDirectory to load and for the database to initialize even if NICI does not initialize. In these cases, any time you try to create certificates or use existing certificates, you will get NICI errors. For instance, if you have a valid server certificate and you configure LDAP to use the certificate, when you load LDAP, the secure port will not open and you will see a NICI error in the ndsd.log file.

Deleting Corrupt NICI Files

If the NICI files are corrupt, you must delete them before you can create new ones. Important: Be sure that they are corrupt! Remember that once they are deleted, *all* data that was encrypted using these keys will be lost. You will have to re-create the data.

The following are the file locations for the NICI files, per platform:

- *NetWare*: SYS:\SYSTEM\NICI
- *Windows*: %SystemDrive%:\%WindowsDir%\System32\Novell\Nici
- **nix*: /var/novell/nici/0

In the preceding directories, you should see files that start with an x. Delete all such files.

■ **Note** In Windows, you may need to boot in Safe Mode before you can delete the files. On all platforms, you must unload DS and PKI and shut down the eDirectory process before deleting the files.

Creating New NICI Keys

To establish a secure environment, you need to create new NICI keys for the server. Each platform has a slightly different way to create these files. Tasks 13-1 to 13-3 describe the different procedures per platform.

Task 13-1. Creating NICI Files on NetWare

1. Find the NetWare license file (the filename that ends .nfk).
2. Rename the *.nfk file **nicifk**, with no file extension.
3. Copy the file to the SYS:\SYSTEM\NICI directory.
4. Reboot the server.

Task 13-2. Creating NICI Files on Windows

1. Boot up in Safe Mode.
2. Go to Add/Remove Programs.
3. Remove NICI.
4. Boot up in Normal Mode.
5. Obtain the license file (the filename that ends .nfk).
6. Rename the *.nfk file **nicifk**, with no file extension.
7. Copy the file to %SystemDrive%:\%WindowsDir%\System32\Novell\Nici.
8. Reinstall NICI.
9. Reboot the server.

Task 13-3. Creating NICI Files on *nix

1. Obtain the license file (the filename that ends .nfk).
2. Rename the *.nfk file **nicifk**, with no file extension.
3. Copy the file to the /var/novell/nici/0 directory.
4. At a terminal, type **/var/novell/nici/primenici**.
5. Restart the NDSD process by typing **/etc/init.d/ndsd restart**.

After the NICI keys are re-created, you need to regenerate any and all data that used those keys, such as the following:

- Server certificates
- Tree keys on the local server
- CA objects (if the server is the CA)
- User certificates (if the server is the CA)

Troubleshooting Server Certificates

Server certificates are used to create SSL connections. The LDAP server, the HTTP stack, and Apache Web Server are a few products that can use the server certificates for secure authentication. If the certificates become invalid for any reason, you have to re-create them. Some typical reasons for a corrupt certificate are the following:

- The certificate expired
- The DNS name or the IP address of the server changed
- The server crashed and corrupted the certificate

When you re-create the certificates, it is advisable that you keep the default names. Also, before re-creating the certificates, make sure that they are Novell signed certificates. If they are third-party certificates, you need to get them reissued from the third-party CA, which can be quite expensive.

To re-create the server certificates, perform the following, per platform:

- *NetWare*: Type **pkidiag** at the server console and follow the prompts.
- *Windows*: Use iManager or ConsoleOne and manually create new server certificates. Refer to the *eDirectory Administration Guide* at `http://www.novell.com/documentation` for more information on how to do this.
- **nix*: Delete the bad certificate objects in eDirectory (see Chapter 2 for specific object names) and then, at a terminal, type **ndsconfig add –m SAS**.

Note eDirectory 8.8 has introduced new functionality in the PKI server on all platforms. When PKI loads, it verifies that the certificates are valid. If they are not valid, for any reason, PKI generates new certificates in the background. The end result is that there are always valid server certificates with default names.

Troubleshooting User Certificates

There is not a good way to rebuild user certificates. If the certificate is bad because the CA is corrupt, the NICI files are corrupt, the certificate expired, or for any other reason, the only thing you can do is generate new certificates through iManager or ConsoleOne. You can find the procedure for generating new certificates in the *Novell Certificate Server Administration Guide*, available at `http://www.novell.com/documentation`.

Troubleshooting the CA

If you are getting NICI errors while trying to generate new server certificates or while trying to perform any operation on the CA through iManager or ConsoleOne, the most likely reason is that the NICI files are missing, corrupt, or have been replaced with new ones. In all of these cases, you need to re-create a new CA object.

Perform the following tasks, per platform, to re-create the CA object:

- *NetWare*: Delete the existing CA object in iManager or ConsoleOne and run **pkidiag** from a server console.
- *Windows*: Delete the existing CA object in iManager or ConsoleOne and then re-create a new one manually in iManager or ConsoleOne.
- **nix*: Delete the existing CA object in iManager or ConsoleOne and then, from a terminal, type **ndsconfig add –m SAS**.

Once you have created a new CA, you must perform the following:

1. Re-create the server certificate objects and SAS objects for the local server.
2. Re-create the server certificate objects and SAS objects for all other servers in the tree. (This is optional. The certificates are technically invalid but will still work until they expire.)
3. Re-create all user certificates.
4. Re-export the trusted root certificate to the file system. NetWare has a default certificate in the SYS:\PUBLIC directory called RootCert.der. If you have exported other certificates, you need to re-export them.
5. Re-create any trusted root containers that you may have created.
6. Fix any keystore files that may have the trusted root certificate (IE Tomcat and iManager use a keystore for SSL certificates). Refer to the application documentation for instructions on how to do this.

As you can see, having to re-create the CA can be painful. Therefore, it is recommended that you export your trusted root certificate and private key for the CA and save them somewhere safe. If you have the private key, you can create a new CA and import the private key, and the CA will be restored. No other objects will have to be re-created. For more information on how to export the private key, refer to Novell's Knowledgebase at `http://support.novell.com`.

Troubleshooting the Tree Key

The tree key was created when the Security Domain Infrastructure (SDI) was created. The purpose of the tree key is to have a consistent key that all servers in the SDI can use to encrypt and decrypt secrets. NMAS uses the tree key to encrypt and decrypt users' secrets. The most common secret that is encrypted by NMAS is the Universal Password. If the tree key is lost or corrupted, it usually is not a big deal because it can be resynchronized by another server. If thc only copy of the tree key is lost, all data that used that key is also lost.

The tree key is located on the file system of the server. The default locations are as follows:

- *NetWare*: SYS:\SYSTEM\NICI
- *Windows*: %SystemDrive%:\%WindowsDir%\System32\Novell\Nici
- **nix*: /var/novell/nici/0

The tree key name is nicisdi.key. The file itself is encrypted with the server-specific key. If the server-specific key is corrupt or replaced, you need to delete the nicisdi.key file and resynchronize it from another SDI domain server. The nicisdi.key file can actually contain multiple tree keys (this feature appears in NICI 2.4.2 or greater).

The SDI contains two types of objects: domain servers and login servers. Domain servers can synchronize with each other and can send their keys down to the login servers. The domain servers are defined through the Security.KAP.W0 object. There is an attribute on the W0 object called NDSPKI:SD Key Server DN. If a server is listed in this attribute, it is considered a domain server.

The SDI synchronization process works as follows:

1. A server boots up or the eDirectory process loads on Windows or *nix.
2. NICISDI is loaded.
3. NICISDI resolves to the Security.KAP.W0 object to see if the local server is a domain server.
4. NICISDI checks to see if it has a nicisdi.key file.
5. If it does have a nicisdi.key file and it is a domain server, NICISDI does nothing more.
6. If it is not a domain server, NICISDI contacts a domain server and asks for its tree keys.
7. The domain server sends the keys.
8. NICISDI merges the domain tree keys with its own tree keys.

Most of the time, the preceding process keeps all tree keys synchronized with all servers. However, there are certain occasions in which all of the tree keys are not synchronized to all servers. Consider the following scenario:

1. A new tree called treeA is created on serverA.
2. A new tree key with the value of abcd is created and placed on serverA.
3. A new tree called treeB is created on serverB.

4. A new tree key with the value of wxyz is created and placed on serverB.
5. The DIB instance is removed from serverB.
6. serverB is added into treeA.
7. serverB gets serverA's tree key when serverB is added to the tree.
8. Because serverB is not a domain server in treeA, serverB does not send its tree key to serverA.
9. The end result is that serverA has tree key abcd and serverB has the tree keys abcd and wxyz.
10. A user changes its Universal Password on serverB using tree key wxyz.
11. The same user tries to authenticate to serverA using the new password.
12. An NMAS error is returned because serverA does not have the correct tree key to decrypt the password.

The only way that the NMAS error can be resolved in the preceding scenario is to make serverB a domain server in treeA and then synchronize the tree keys between the two servers. Novell provides a tool called SDIDiag to accomplish this type of procedure. The SDIDiag utility comes as an NLM or as an EXE file. You can run the sdidiag.exe file from a Windows box and pass command-line parameters to log into any server in the SDI, regardless of platform. SDIDiag allows you to synchronize keys from domain server to domain server or synchronize keys from the domain server down to all other servers.

Another powerful feature of SDIDiag is the ability to revoke keys. In the preceding scenario, you could revoke one of the keys. By doing this, the revoked keys can be used to decrypt data that was encrypted with the specified key, but all new encryption would be done with a nonrevoked key.

For more information on the command-line switches available with SDIDiag as well as a link to download SDIDiag, see Novell's Knowledgebase at `http://support.novell.com`.

Note eDirectory 8.8 provides a feature called *multiple instance.* On the *nix platforms, you can create more than one instance of the directory. If you use the same IP address for both instances, you have to change the NCP port from the default 524 to some other port. By default, SDIDiag uses port 524 to authenticate and synchronize. When specifying the IP address in the `sdidiag` command-line utility, you can specify the port as well (e.g., 10.0.0.2:1524).

Summary

If problems arise with the server security infrastructure, you need to know how to troubleshoot the different security components that eDirectory uses. You may need to repair NICI files or even generate new server certificates. Tree keys provide a way for all servers in the environment to use the same set of keys to encrypt and decrypt data. SDIDiag can be used to diagnose and fix tree key issues.

APPENDIX

Comparison of eDirectory Versions

There have been many different versions of eDirectory over the past several years. From its early existence, eDirectory has progressed from NDS 5.x, NDS 6.x, NDS 7.x, and NDS 8.x, to eDirectory 8.5.x, eDirectory 8.6.x, eDirectory 8.7.x, and now eDirectory 8.8. Between NDS 7.x and NDS 8.x, the database structure was changed from a RecMan, linked-list database to a FLAIM, tagged database. FLAIM is much more scalable and robust.

After NDS 8 shipped, Novell started porting the directory to other platforms. There were variations of NDS 8 that shipped on Windows and Linux. However, the name was changed from NDS to eDirectory with eDirectory 8.5, which was really the first full cross-platform identity management directory. The different versions of eDirectory have stabilized the back end, made the directory more secure and more scalable, and opened up several new interfaces to the directory, which made it more adaptable as well.

The purpose of this appendix is to provide a very high-level feature comparison between eDirectory 8.6.x, eDirectory 8.7.x, and eDirectory 8.8. This information will be valuable to you as you move forward with Novell in implementing the latest and greatest in the identity management space.

Although each new version of eDirectory may contain new features, some of these features are very subtle. It is beyond the scope of this appendix to list all the features. Thus, this appendix discusses only the major feature set changes.

Changes in eDirectory 8.6.x

The main focus of eDirectory 8.6.x was synchronization. The internal versions of eDirectory 8.6.x range from version 10110.xx to version 10350.xx. The main features introduced in eDirectory 8.6.x are as follows:

Note eDirectory 8.6.x is currently discontinued. It is no longer shipped, maintained, or supported by Novell.

- *Faster replica synchronization*: Several replication enhancements were added to eDirectory 8.6.x, some of which are listed here:
  - *Multithreaded outbound synchronization*: Multiple threads can be used to complete an outbound synchronization. You can specify whether the threads are allocated by partition or by server. In the past, synchronization was one threaded. Multithreading not only increases performance but also is more fault tolerant. In the past, if the one thread was tied up talking to a slow-responding server, no other servers in the replica rings could get updates. Now, only the slow-responding server misses the updates, because other threads can service all the other servers in the replica ring.
  - *Synchronization points*: Synchronization points track the synchronization process. If an error occurs, the entire synchronization is not started over. The synchronization can continue where it left off.
  - *Greatest Value Time Stamp (GVTS)*: A new vector called GVTS was introduced. This enabled the eDirectory agent to scan only the GVTS to find updates, instead of scanning every value within an entry. This feature greatly enhanced performance with the synchronization process.
- *Dynamic groups*: Dynamic groups offer a lot of advantages when dealing with group memberships. Unlike static groups, dynamic groups do not have static memberships. They have what is called a `memberQuery` filter, an LDAP query string that defines which members may be in the group. If a particular object meets the criteria specified, it is automatically deemed a member of the group and receives all the rights that the dynamic group contains. This alleviates the need for very large, multi-valued membership lists that require a lot of memory and processor power when synchronized. Dynamic groups also speed up login times because they are not used to calculate the original Security Equivalence Vector (SEV).

- *Improved transitive vector synchronization*: The packet structure for synchronization traffic is more defined and more efficient. Fewer packets are required to finish a synchronization and merge transitive vectors.
- *Improved obituary process*: In the past, the obituary process used the purge vector to determine whether or not an obituary needed to be processed. Unfortunately, the purge vector is updated by the synchronization process. There were certain scenarios in which the purge vector would be updated before all of the obituaries were processed. The end result was that obituaries would be orphaned. To remedy the issue, eDirectory 8.6.2 introduced the obituary vector. This vector is stored in memory and provides a better way to track whether or not obituaries have been seen by all servers. The end result is that if the master of the partition is eDirectory 8.6.2 or greater, you will rarely see a stuck obituary.
- *Improved auxiliary class support*: Novell started development of auxiliary classes with NDS 8.x. As time has passed, defects have been fixed and issues have been resolved so that auxiliary classes are backward compatible and work as they were intended.

Changes in eDirectory 8.7.0

The main focus of eDirectory 8.7.0 was improvement of the security and management interfaces. The internal versions of eDirectory 8.7.0 range from version 10410.90 to version 10411.xx.

Note eDirectory 8.7.0 is discontinued. It is no longer shipped, maintained, or supported by Novell. At the time of this writing, eDirectory 8.7.3 is the currently supported version of eDirectory 8.7.x. For current information about the product lifecycle, see `http://support.novell.com`.

The main features introduced in eDirectory 8.7.0 are as follows:

- *Enhanced backup and restore capabilities*: eDirectory 8.7 introduced a new focus for backup and restore, called hot continuous backup. Hot continuous backup was introduced using the Backup eMTool. The backup provides online backup with a restore that supports transactional replay to bring the data right back up to the state it was in when the server went down.

- *Transport Layer Security (TLS)*: Support for TLS/SSL services based on the OpenSSL source code was introduced. This is all provided through the NTLS modules.
- *Enhanced dynamic groups*: The ability to convert existing static groups to dynamic groups was added.
- *SASL support for eDirectory and LDAP logins*: Support was added for Simple Authentication and Security Layer (SASL), an authentication negotiation framework that allows the use of various other authentication methods.
- *eDirectory event monitoring*: The event system was exposed on all platforms, allowing for cross-platform event monitoring.
- *Extensible match LDAP search filters*: Provides partial support for extensible match (defined in LDAPv3, RFC 2251) for matching on DN attributes. This allows inclusion of DN elements in the search criteria. At the time of this writing, it does not yet support matching rules in the extensible match filter, and it ignores matching rules specified in the extensible match filter.
- *Simple Network Management Protocol (SNMP) monitoring*: Provides an SNMP subagent that has precompiled the eDirectory MIB.
- *iManager 1.5.2*: Provided a web-based, cross-platform management tool that allowed you to administer your eDirectory system from a web browser.
- *iMonitor 2.0*: Provided detailed information about the directory over a secure port. You could monitor events, verbs, and other internal messages as well as view the raw data that was stored in the eDirectory database.
- *eGuide 2.1*: Provided a web-based corporate address book and self-administration tool. eGuide allowed users to get information about other users in the directory and modify their own information. It contained all the people, places, and things you needed to know in a single location.

Changes in eDirectory 8.7.1

The main focus of eDirectory 8.7.1 was on new platform support and enhanced administration. The internal versions of eDirectory 8.7.1 range from version 10510.38 to version 10550.97.

Note eDirectory 8.7.1 is discontinued. It is no longer shipped, maintained, or supported by Novell. At the time of this writing, eDirectory 8.7.3 is the currently supported version of eDirectory 8.7.x. For current information about the product lifecycle, see `http://support.novell.com`.

The main features introduced in eDirectory 8.7.1 are as follows:

- *New platform support*: Support was added for the following additional platforms: Red Hat Linux 8.0, SuSE Linux Enterprise Server 8, Solaris 9, and HP-UX 11.11.
- *Improved indexing*: Indexing was improved by increasing the size of keys that are supported.
- *Universal Password*: Universal Password provides strong, policy-based passwords that can be synchronized to disparate systems. It also uses the common UTF-8 encoding to support a universal character set.
- *CloneDIB set*: You can literally clone another server with all of its partitions and objects. The new server is added to the tree as if it were added through regular mechanisms.
- *Clientless install*: The ability to install eDirectory on a Windows NT or 2000 server without the Novell Client was added. OpenSLP is installed on a clientless machine.
- *Enhanced dynamic groups*: The interface to configure dynamic groups was improved in iManager. Also, several bugs dealing with dynamic groups were resolved.
- *iManager 2.0.1*: Provided a single web-based management console for the administration of Novell products on NetWare 6.5, Windows, Linux, Solaris, AIX, and HP-UX.
- *iMonitor 2.1*: New Advanced options were added and localization support was added.
- *eGuide 2.1.1*: New provisioning enhancements were added.

Changes in eDirectory 8.7.3

The main focus of eDirectory 8.7.3 was on bug fixes. The internal versions of eDirectory 8.7.3 range from version 10550.98 to version 1055x.xx.

Note eDirectory 8.7.3 has had several Interim Releases (IRs). These are bug fixes only. Open Enterprise Server (OES) shipped with eDirectory 8.7.3 IR5. OES SP1 shipped with eDirectory 8.7.3 SP7.

The new features introduced in eDirectory 8.7.3 are as follows:

- *Support for Microsoft Windows Server 2003*: Was added to allow for the installation of eDirectory on a Windows Server 2003 machine.
- *UNIX package-based installation*: Package installation for all eDirectory server components for Linux, Solaris, and AIX was added.
- *New memory manager*: The open-source memory manager called HOARD was added to Windows to allow for higher scalability during heavy loads. An updated Geodesic memory manager was added to the Linux and UNIX builds to resolve memory leaks and dumping of cores. (The latest IR releases of 8.7.3 removed Geodesic completely, using the Solaris native memory managers).
- *Faster writes*: Writing improvements were made, allowing two to three times more efficient writes.
- *Default port change*: The default port was changed from 80 and 443 to 8008 and 8010 for the HTTP stack for Windows, Linux, and UNIX.
- *eGuide 2.1.2*: Provides support for Role-Based Services (RBS) used in iManager 2.0.
- *Certificate Server 2.7*: New features included OCSP over SSL and directory name CRL support.
- *iManager 2.0.2*: The installation for iManager was improved as was support for multivalue user-defined attribute administration.
- *NMAS 2.3*: New features in NMAS included advanced password policy enforcement, NMAS Web Server Agent, challenge/response login method, challenge response API, and Kerberos method.

Changes in eDirectory 8.8

The new features of eDirectory 8.8 focus on scalability and encryption enhancements. The internal versions of eDirectory 8.8 start with 201xx.xx.

The main features introduced in eDirectory 8.6.x are as follows:

- *Security container caching*: With Universal Password becoming more popular, an issue arose with scalability. Universal Password requires that each authentication request walks to the security container at the top of the tree. This can cause a slowdown in login attempts. eDirectory 8.8 can cache the required information on the local server, which eliminates the need to walk the tree.
- *Data import improvements*: New switches are added to ICE to allow the throttling of the convergence of objects that are bulk-loaded into the tree. This prevents all servers from trying to synchronize data all at once after a large bulk load.
- *Priority sync*: A new synchronization method was added that allows you to specify specific attributes that you want sent immediately to all replicas. This will bypass change cache or the regular synchronization interval.
- *Multiple instance support*: The Linux and UNIX platforms now support multiple instances of the same tree or a different tree on the same server.
- *Non-root installation*: The Linux and UNIX platforms now support the installation and running of the eDirectory process as a non-root user.
- *Encrypted attributes*: eDirectory 8.8 provides the ability to define what attributes are encrypted on disk. In past versions of eDirectory, the attributes that were encrypted were hard-coded and could not be changed.
- *Encrypted synchronization*: All platforms except NetWare will allow you to send synchronization data over a secure NCP channel.
- *Backup/restore enhancements*: Single-object backup and restore is now available through LDAP.
- *Optimized LDAP searches*: A new Ancestry ID is added to each object in the tree when eDirectory 8.8 is installed. This new attribute is indexed, which enables the directory to now determine whether it will apply the base and scope first or the filter first. This will improve many LDAP search requests when the base and scope are limited.
- *Case-sensitive passwords*: eDirectory 8.8 enables you to enforce case sensitivity with passwords with a non-NMAS client.

Index

Numbers

Symbols

A

D

F

G

H

I

M

N

O

P

Q

R

S

X

Y

Z

Breinigsville, PA USA
13 September 2009

223955BV00009B/1/P